LUCY PARSONS

American Revolutionary

by Carolyn Ashbaugh

1976 Chicago
CHARLES H. KERR PUBLISHING COMPANY
Published for the Illinois Labor History Society

478

Acknowledgments

The Harold A. Fletcher Award from Grinnell College, the Ralph Korngold Fellowship from the Newberry Library, and a Youthgrant from the National Endowment for the Humanities have supported my research. I owe special thanks to Lawrence W. Towner, Director of The Newberry Library and to Richard Brown and James Wells, the Associate Directors of the Library, and to Mrs. Piri Korngold who furnished the Ralph Korngold Fellowship. My good friend Jane Marcus has encouraged and assisted my work on Lucy Parsons since its beginning, when I was a student and she a teacher at the Associated Colleges of the Midwest and Newberry Library Seminar in the Humanities the fall of 1972.

Special thanks to my friends Leslie Orear, President of the Illinois Labor History Society, who first suggested I write a book about Lucy Parsons, and to Professor William Adelman of the University of Illinois Institute of Labor and Industrial Relations and author of *Touring Pullman* and *Haymarket Revisited,* who has shared his extensive research and the excitement of each new discovery about Lucy Parsons with me.

Joseph Giganti, Fred Thompson, and Irving Abrams, board members of the Charles H. Kerr Pub. Co. have shared their recollections of Lucy Parsons with me. Joe and Fred have offered valuable suggestions for improving the manuscript. Irwin St. John Tucker recounted the 1915 Hunger Demonstration for me. Stella Nowicki, Eugene Jasinski, Mario Manzardo, Francis Heisler, Henry Rosemont, Clarence Stoecker, Vera Buch Weisbord, Albert Weisbord, Sid Harris, George Winthers, Abe Feinglass, Sam Dolgoff, Lucy Haessler, Arthur Weinberg, and the late James P. Cannon have all shared their knowledge of Lucy Parsons with me and enriched my knowledge of the history of the labor and radical movements. The late Boris Yelensky shared his impressions through lengthy correspondence.

A special thanks to Mrs. Lucie C. Price of Austin, Texas, who researched the Texas careers of William and Albert Parsons at the Archives of the University of Texas and the State Historical Library of Texas.

I owe a debt of appreciation to William D. Parsons and to Katharine Parsons Russell for discussing with me the effect of the Haymarket Affair on the Parsons family and to William Parsons for the picture of his great-grandfather, General William Henry Parsons.

My friends Sandra Bartky, Laura X, Sara Heslep, Anne Walter, Mrs. Mae Coy Ball, Tom DuBois, Marcus Cohen and many others have inspired and encouraged me. Thanks to the members of the history department at Grinnell College—Don Smith, Alan Jones, Joseph Wall, David Jordan, Philip Kintner and Greg Guroff—who have offered suggestions and stimulated my work and to Florence Chanock Cohen for her critical comments and editorial suggestions on my manuscript.

Thanks to Hartmut Keil and Theodore Waldinger for translations from the German. Thanks to Barbara Morgan and Martin Ptacek for photography. Thanks to Jamie Fogle for art work and to Sara Heslep for proofreading.

Dione Miles of the Wayne State Labor Archives; Dorothy Swanson of the Tamiment Institute, New York University; Edward Weber of the Labadie Collection at the University of Michigan Library; Mary Lynn Ritzenthaler and Mary Ann Bamberger of the Manuscript Collection, University of Illinois at Chicago Circle; Charles P. LeWarne; Judge William J. Wimbiscus of the State of Illinois Thirteenth Judicial Circuit; Irene Moran and Diane Clardy of the Bancroft Library; Dr. Josephine L. Harper and Miss Katherine S. Thompson of the State Historical Society of Wisconsin; Archie Motley, Linda Evans, Neal Ney, Larry Viskochil, John Tris, Julia Westerberg and Miriam Blazowski of the Chicago Historical Society; the staff of Newberry Library; and staff members of other libraries too numerous to mention have assisted my research.

My thanks to the following for permission to use unpublished material: the Illinois Labor History Society for permission to quote from Lucy Parsons; Kathleen S. Spaulding for permission to quote from George Schilling; University of Illinois at Urbana for permission to quote from the Thomas J. Morgan Papers; Houghton Library, Harvard for permission to quote from letters by Dyer D. Lum, Carl Nold and Robert Steiner in the Joseph

Ishill Collection; the Bancroft Library for permission to quote from the Thomas Mooney Papers; the Manuscript Collection, University of Illinois at Chicago Circle for permission to quote from the Ben L. Reitman Papers; the Washington State Historical Society, Tacoma, Washington for permission to quote from Thomas Bogard; Labadie Collection at the University of Michigan Library for permission to quote from Agnes Inglis; and the State Historical Society of Wisconsin for permission to quote from the Albert R. Parsons Papers and the Knights of Labor Collection.

The cover picture and the picture on page 12 are from the 1903 edition of *The Life of Albert R. Parsons,* courtesy of the Chicago Historical Society.

July, 1976   Carolyn Ashbaugh

Preface

Lucy Parsons was black, a woman, and working class—three reasons people are often excluded from history. Lucy herself pointed out the class bias of history in 1905 when she criticized historians who had written about "the course of wars, the outcome of battles, political changes, the rise and fall of dynasties and other similar movements, leaving the lives of those whose labor has built the world. . . in contemptuous silence." The problem of piecing together Lucy Parsons' life (1853-1942) from fragmentary evidence was more difficult than the usual problem of writing about a working class rebel, because the forces of "law and order" seized her personal papers at the time of her death.

Even among histories by and about socialists, the work of women has been largely ignored. On the left, the view of Lucy Parsons as the "devoted assistant" of her martyred husband Albert Richard Parsons is prevalent. Feminists who have forgotten the radical working class roots of the feminist movement have also overlooked Lucy Parsons. Editors of the Radcliffe *Notable American Women* three volume work consigned Lucy Parsons to their discard file on the grounds that she was "largely propelled by husband's fate" and was "a pathetic figure, living in the past and crying injustice" after the Haymarket Police Riot.

However, Lucy Parsons, a black woman, was a recognized leader of the predominately white male working class movement in Chicago long before the 1886 police riot. Even *Labor's Untold Story,* which offers a sympathetic although sentimental account of Lucy, states that she became involved in the radical movement only after her husband was sentenced to death and then primarily to save his life. Lucy Parsons was not interested in saving Albert Parsons' life. She was interested in emancipating the working class from wage slavery. Lucy and Albert were prepared—even eager—to sacrifice his life, believing his death as a martyr would advance the cause. Lucy was eager to offer her own life as well in the struggle for economic emancipation. Only Howard Fast in *The American,* his fictionalized biography of John Peter Altgeld, has thus far captured the strength, character and determination of Lucy Parsons.

The impression that Lucy Parsons devoted her life to clearing her husband's name of the charge of murder is erroneous, generated by the fact that when reporters heard her lecture they stressed her connection to Albert Parsons and emphasized the comparisons she made between the contemporary situation in the labor movement and the events of 1886-1887. If Lucy spoke for an hour and a half on the Sacco and Vanzetti case or the Tom Mooney case, then alluded to the Haymarket case for 15 minutes, the newspapers reported that she had denounced the police for murdering her husband in 1887. However, Lucy Parsons was one of many labor radicals, liberals, and reformers who connected each frame-up case with the legal precedent for political conspiracy trials, the trial of the Haymarket "anarchists" in 1886.

On May 1, 1886, the city of Chicago had been shut down in a general strike for the eight hour working day—the first May Day. On May 4, the police broke up a meeting in Haymarket Square that had been called to protest police brutality. Someone threw a bomb, and the police began shooting wildly, fatally wounding at least seven demonstrators. Most of the police casualties resulted from their own guns. Eight radical leaders, including Albert Parsons, were brought to trial for the bombing. All the prosecution had to prove was that the men on trial were the same men who had been making speeches on the lakefront and publishing the radical workers' papers the *Alarm* and *Arbeiter-Zeitung.* The court ruled that although the defendants neither threw the bomb nor knew who threw the bomb, their speeches and writings prior to the bombing might have inspired some unknown person to throw it and held them "accessories before the fact" in the murder of policeman Mathias Degan. All eight were convicted, and on November 11, 1887, Albert Parsons, August Spies, Adolph Fischer, and George Engel were hanged.

Lucy Parsons remained active in the radical labor movement for another 55 years. She published newspapers, pamphlets, and books, traveled and lectured extensively, and led many demonstrations. She concentrated her work with the poorest, most downtrodden people, the unemployed and the foreign born. She was a member of the Social Democracy in 1897, a founding member of the Industrial Workers of the World in 1905, and was elected to the National Committee of the International Labor Defense in 1927.

Lucy Parsons was a colorful figure whose style was to capture headlines. She had a commanding appearance—tall, dark, and beautiful, a beauty which turned to a mellow, peaceful expression as she aged—and a tremendous speaking voice which captivated audiences with its low musical resonance. Lucy was a firebrand who spoke with terrifying intensity when the occasion demanded it.

Lucy's struggle with the Chicago police for free speech lasted for decades. Police broke up meetings only because the speaker was Lucy Parsons; they dealt with her in an aggressive and unlawful manner, systematically violating her right to free speech and assembly. Although Lucy was hated by the police, Chicago liberals often came to her assistance. In about 1898 Graham Taylor of the Chicago Commons Settlement House arranged for her to speak at the settlement's Free Floor Forum without police harrassment. When Lucy was arrested while leading a Hunger Demonstration in 1915 Jane Addams of Hull House arranged her bail. Deputy Police Chief Schuettler denounced Addams and linked the two women: "If Miss Addams thinks it is all right for an avowed and dangerous anarchist like Lucy Parsons to parade with a black flag and a band of bad characters, I suggest that she go ahead and preach the doctrine outright."

By portraying Lucy Parsons as a criminal, the police and newspapers tried to direct public attention away from the real issues which Lucy was trying to raise: unemployment and hunger. Irwin St. John Tucker, the young Episcopalian minister and socialist who was arrested with Lucy in 1915, recently recalled, "Lucy Parsons wasn't a hell-raiser; she was only trying to raise the obvious issues about human life. She was not a riot-inciter, though she was accused of it. She was of a religious nature." "Friar Tuck" found Lucy a likeable and compelling person.

Lucy Parsons' life energy was directed toward freeing the

working class from capitalism. She attributed the inferior position of women and minority racial groups in American society to class inequalities and argued, as Eugene Debs later did, that blacks were oppressed because they were poor, not because they were black. Lucy favored the availability of birth control information and contraceptive devices. She believed that under socialism women would have the right to divorce and remarry without economic, political and religious constraints; that women would have the right to limit the number of children they would have; and that women would have the right to prevent "legalized" rape in marriage.

Lucy Parsons' life expressed the anger of the unemployed, workers, women and minorities against oppression and is exemplary of radicals' efforts to organize the working class for social change.

Lucy Parsons, guest of honor at the November, 1927
International Labor Defense convention.

CONTENTS

Illustrations follow page 142

Lucy E. Parsons

Good-By Ku Klux Klan

In 1872 Lucy Gathings and Albert Parsons left Waco, Texas together. Albert had been a Confederate scout during the Civil War, but he had become a Radical Republican and an advocate of civil rights for black people after the war. Lucy was of mixed blood, and she had been living with the former black slave Oliver Gathings. Lucy and Albert were hated as miscegenationists by fellow Texans and when the Reconstruction government came to an end in 1873, they knew they would have to leave Texas.[1]

Albert's older brother William, who had raised him, had gone from a Confederate General to a Republican state senator. From William, Albert had learned the skills of oratory and journalism. Albert had edited a Radical Republican paper, the *Spectator,* in Waco in 1867-1868 and had then been given a job in the District Clerk's office by the Republicans. He had become involved in many violent and potentially violent situations. Albert was shot in the leg, thrown downstairs, and threatened with lynching for his attempts to register black voters. In 1870 he had gone to Austin to be secretary to the Senate of which his brother was a member, and he had later become a Federal revenue collector. By the time Albert and Lucy left Texas, Albert was hated as a scalawag, a miscegenationist and a Revenue man.[2]

Before the war William Parsons had put out a militant secessionist and white supremacist newspaper, the *Southwest,* which advocated reopening the slave trade. He had planned to write a book, *Negro Slavery, Its Past, Present and Future,* and in the announcement for the book had written, "Shall political power remain exclusively in the hands of the dominant white race, or shall we submit to the degradation of the *mongrel results* which have so universally attended emancipation, and the fraternization of the races throughout the Spanish Republics of the two American Continents?" For William Parsons the important issue had been "the purity of blood and supremacy as a distinct race of the Anglo-American upon this continent."[3]

Unless he underwent a very basic change of consciousness, William Parsons must have had great difficulty watching his brother contribute to the "mongrel results" of the race. However, William Parsons—and Albert and Lucy—dealt with the issue by insisting that Lucy was Indian and Spanish, not black. Little is known of Lucy's origins. She provided a variety of maiden names on different documents and eventually claimed that her maiden name was Gonzales in an attempt to verify a Mexican ancestry.[4]

It is doubtful that Lucy and Albert were ever formally married. Laws against miscegenation would have prevented that. Although they claimed to have been married in Austin, Texas, their dates of marriage did not coincide, and no record of the marriage could be found. The question of her marriage and her race were to plague Lucy for most of her life. Her denial of her black heritage is a terrible indictment of the racist society which made her feel compelled to do so.[5]

Waco had been the scene of intense racial brutality in the years following the war. As the Ku Klux Klan gained power, the atrocities committed against black people in Waco were multiplied across the South.

Many years later Lucy wrote that she had seen the atrocities of the Ku Klux Klan in the South. Among the crimes committed by the Klan in or near Waco were the castration of a black boy in January, 1867; the murder of an eight year old black girl by rape in July, 1867; and the murder of a black man in the Waco Public Square in February, 1868.

White vigilantes and the Ku Klux Klan grew bolder as the ineffectiveness of the Republican Reconstruction became apparent. In April, 1868, the Klan mass murdered 13 blacks near Waco. In August they killed the father, mother and brothers of a black woman, Martha Smith. The woman was nearly witless with fright when interviewed by officers of the Bureau. When the Freedmen's Bureau officer and the District Court Judge of the 5th Military District attempted to hold court in the case, the mob brought rope to hang them.

On the night of September 26, 1868, the Ku Klux Klan severely beat 20 black women; they stole the clothing of ten, burned the clothing of six. They robbed one man of 25¢, another of 60¢, a 75 year old woman of 75¢, $9 from another man, $20 from two more each, $24 from another and $40 from another man. They mass raped the freedwomen, and they attempted to rape a seven year old girl. They did all this with impunity, knowing the judges would be "lenient." The Waco Freedman's Bureau Officer asked for a military trial, because he knew that the civil authorities "might possibly fine the perpetrators one dollar each, providing they could not avoid it," but that they would do nothing else.[6]

Perhaps Lucy had seen one of these raids. Perhaps she had been raped. Perhaps friends or members of her family had been victims. She never recounted the details of what she had seen, but she always denounced crimes against black people with passionate anger.

Lucy and Albert were incredibly happy together. Lucy was stunningly beautiful. Her dark skin and vibrant personality radiated with the Texas sun. She was passionate in her loves and in her hatreds. There was nothing lukewarm about Lucy. Her skin was golden brown, that of a mulatto or quadroon. One might believe that her piercing black eyes shot sparks when she was angry. She had soft sensuous lips, a broad nose, curly black hair, and the high cheekbones of her Indian ancestors.

The summer of 1873 was Albert and Lucy's last summer in Texas; they never returned. Albert was elected to the Radical Republican convention in Travis County that summer and after the convention, he accepted a free train tour from the Missouri, Kansas and Texas Railway, as a journalist. Lucy joined him in Philadelphia and together they came to Chicago the winter of 1873-74.[7]

The Confederate adventure which Albert had plunged into at age 16 had taken him into Radical Republicanism. His charm and good looks and his brother's political connections had made him welcome in the state's high society, but he had given that up for a life-long commitment to advance the poor and downtrodden. He had become a believer in racial equality and his marriage to Lucy forever identified him with the oppressed.

In Chicago Lucy would no longer have to fear rape by the Klan at every moment. She would have the room to develop her own potential as a crusader for human rights.

Chicago: Relief and Aid
Relieves the Rich

Two years after the Great Fire of 1871, Chicago was again the industrial center of the Midwest. In fact, the devastation of the fire provided the wealthy with a new opportunity for capital investment.

But the boom was short-lived. The collapse of the Jay Cooke banking house, the leading financial establishment in the country, in September, 1873, sent the nation into a great depression. The word "tramp" was coined to describe the thousands of men "tramping" the roads in search of work.

Lucy and Albert Parsons arrived in Chicago amidst great unrest. On December 21, 1873, 10,000 workers and unemployed assembled in front of City Hall to protest the practices of the Relief and Aid Society. For weeks after, demonstrators gathered outside the offices of the Relief and Aid Society. The Society, which had been entrusted with several million dollars after the fire for the relief of the people of Chicago, had become the focus of protest, because Board members George Pullman, Marshall Field, Rufus King, and others had invested the relief money in their own companies at bargain interest rates rather than using it for relief. Finally, some relief for the poor was won, but the Relief and Aid Society made it necessary for a poor person to obtain the endorsement of a rich person to be eligible.

The Chicago ward with the highest population density also had the highest infant mortality; half the children born there died before they were five. Lucy and Albert Parsons lived in these poorest working class neighborhoods. From 1877 until 1882 they lived in a number of flats in the vicinity of Larrabee St. and North Ave.,[1] an area of basement sweatshops, German beer gardens and community gathering places, and refugees from Bismarck's anti-socialist laws.

Albert Parsons worked as a printer and joined Typographical Union No. 16. In March, 1876, he went to hear a lecturer from the Social Democratic Party of North America. He joined the

Party and soon became its leading English language spokesperson. On July 4, 1876, while in Indianapolis lecturing for the Social Democrats, he joined the Knights of Labor. With fellow Social Democrats Thomas J. Morgan and George A. Schilling, he founded the first Knights of Labor Assembly in Chicago. Tommy Morgan was a short, barrelchested English machinist. He was an outspoken and divisive figure in the Chicago movement. George Schilling was a softspoken carpenter who built boxes and barrels in the packinghouses. He might seem quiet and gentle on first encounter, but he was a militant and effective organizer. Tens of thousands of workers trusted George Schilling. He and Albert Parsons became devoted friends.

Through the Social Democratic Party Albert and Lucy Parsons came in contact with the works of Karl Marx and Ferdinand LaSalle. The European socialist traditions were to become a big part of their lives. In the summer of 1876 Albert Parsons was a delegate to the convention in New Jersey which formally dissolved the First International.[2] The Social Democratic Party was dissolved as well, but its members coalesced with several other organizations to form the Workingmen's Party of the United States.

The Chicago English group of the Workingmen's Party met on Monday evenings to discuss their program, politics and strategy; they often met in Lucy and Albert's apartment on Larrabee Street. Here in her own home, Lucy became intimately acquainted with socialist politics. In 1877 Albert Parsons was organizer and T. J. Morgan was corresponding secretary of the small Chicago section. George Schilling later recalled that they often had to contribute their last nickel to renting a hall for a meeting, then walk home instead of ride the streetcar.[3]

Although the neighbors had been apprehensive at first about a white man and a black woman moving into their neighborhood, the German community more easily accepted Lucy's dark skin than white society in Texas or native born Americans in general. She soon found a socialist community which accepted her as a sister and never questioned her racial background.

In the spring of 1877 the party decided to run Albert Parsons as candidate for Alderman in the 15th ward where he and Lucy lived. Socialists from all over the city came to the ward to help in the campaign; they were accused of being "carpetbaggers and imported foreigners," but they drew 400 votes for the party.

From the small group which followed the socialists that spring, thousands had heard of them by mid summer. The Depression of 1873 dragged on; in 1877 employers were still cutting wages and throwing people out of work.

From an estimated 300,000 trade union members in 1872, membership had dropped to only 50,000 members in 1878 due to unemployment, wage cuts, union busting, and hard times.

In the summer of 1877 workers responded to the economic depression with one of the greatest mass strikes in U.S. history. Strikes in textiles and coal mining, where the depression hit hardest, preceeded the greatest strike—on the railroads. Railroad workers were summarily blacklisted if they joined the railroad brotherhoods and orders. The railroads had introduced speed-up and stretch-out in the form of "doubleheaders," trains with twice the usual number of cars and no extra workers.

Railroad speculators, on the other hand, were doing quite well. They had voted themselves huge land grants through their friends and payees in Congress. The rate and magnitude of industrial expansion in the U.S. was unprecedented in world history. The practices of the industrial bosses, the tremendous immigration to the U.S., and the displacement of artisans, farmers, and small shop owners all combined to create an explosive situation. Yet despite the tremendous changes on the urban scene, the majority of the American workforce was still engaged in agriculture.

The industrial capitalists were a new class of men who had overcome the claim to political and economic power of the slaveholders of the South. Their power was undisputed; the millions of immigrants to the United States found themselves at the mercy of capital. Refugees from the war-torn South who came north to seek work in the industrialized cities fared no better. The few blacks who sought work in the North were prevented from getting jobs in many industries by the tightly knit skilled trades unions. No one had organized unskilled workers into an industrial union, and the trades unions did not meet the needs of workers who were no longer skilled artisans, but cogs in a giant industrial machine.

Lucy and Albert Parsons were two of the displaced persons

from Reconstruction; they were political refugees from the Ku Klux Klan and the renascent Democratic party in the South.

Of the 28.5 million immigrants who came to the United States in the 50 years after the beginning of the Civil War, the majority of them took jobs in such industries as railroad and canal building, mining, textiles, iron and steel, and other manufacturing industries.

As capital concentrated, it seized the means of production from the hands of the artisans, forcing them into factories and shops owned and run by capitalists. The great majority—whose numbers were constantly swelled by the daily arrival of boatloads of immigrants—were separated from the means of production and left with only their labor power to sell. Thus they became utterly dependent upon the capitalist for a livelihood; they had to sell their labor from day to day to make a living.

The products of labor belonged entirely to the employer. In the past, the products of labor made it possible for the worker to survive. Under the new mode of production, the product of labor threatened the ability of a person to sell his or her labor power. If there were too many goods (products of labor) for the market, labor power could no longer be sold. If labor power could not be sold or brought a price insufficient to secure the necessities of life, a worker could not survive.

Six years after the Paris Commune, visions of the communards holding Paris gave U.S. industrialists bad nightmares. In 1877, they envisioned the poor seizing American cities. Both rich and poor believed that revolution might be just around the corner. Unrest was widespread, but American capitalism had tremendous energy and potential for expansion. Neither the industrialists nor the socialists who wished to overthrow them could have envisioned the resilience which growing capital possessed.

On July 16, 1877, workers in Martinsburg, West Virginia, responded to an attempt of the Baltimore and Ohio Railroad to cut wages another ten per cent, the second cut in eight months. They refused to take a cattle train out that evening; other trainmen refused to replace the strikers. A crowd gathered, and train crews uncoupled the engines and put them back in the roundhouse. This was the beginning of a popular insurrection which involved hundreds of thousands; it spread like wildfire.

By July 21, strikers from the east had taken trains west to spread the strike to Chicago. Lucy Parsons avidly watched the events. The 1877 strikes had a profound effect on her, as they did on two other future labor leaders, Mother Jones and Eugene Victor Debs. Mary Harris Jones had lost her family to yellow fever in Tennessee and then lost her dress shop to the Chicago Fire in 1871. After the fire she saw its victims and noticed how the poor suffered far more than the rich, and she became interested in the labor movement. During the 1877 strikes she was called to Pittsburgh to help the strikers. Thus, at age 47, she began her second life, that of a labor organizer. Eugene Debs, the young national officer of the Brotherhood of Locomotive Firemen, was shocked at the violence which met the workers' struggle against wage cuts. The workers' resistance in 1877 inspired his leadership of the railway workers.[4]

In Chicago, forty switchmen on the Michigan Central Railroad went on strike; with a crowd of 500, including the strikers who had come from the East, they spread the word. They called out stockyards and packinghouse workers. Five hundred planing mill workers came out and marched down Canal Street and Blue Island Avenue closing factories as they went. They shut down public transportation and declared a holiday. They turned a switch and derailed an engine and baggage cars at 16th and Clark streets.

The leaders of the Workingmen's Party were far behind the militance of the masses in July, 1877. In speeches on July 22, Albert Parsons and Philip Van Patten counseled law and order and voting as solutions; they tried to prevent violence. Van Patten introduced resolutions demanding the gradual acquisition of railway and telephone lines by the government. He urged workers to join unions, to lobby for favorable legislation and to reduce the hours of labor. Albert Parsons charged that the press was controlled by monopolists and tyrants; he attacked the machines which were driving self-respecting craftsmen into factories, depriving them of the tools of their trades. He said it was a lie to think that the proprietor and the worker have equal liberty. "If the proprietor has a right to fix the wages then we are bound hand and foot—slaves—and we should be perfectly happy, content with a bowl of rice and a rat a week apiece! " The crowd shouted, "No! No!" He urged workers to join the Workingmen's Party and vote in the next election, and he announced a mass rally sponsored by the Workingmen's Party for the following night, July, 23, in Market Square.

By this time all the railroad workers in Chicago were out on strike. The news that the "commune was about to rise" precipitated a panic in business. The Board of Trade was paralyzed with fear. Speculators stopped speculating. Banks transported their valuables to safe places and refused to make new loans on grain going into storage. Cash wheat dropped seven or eight cents a bushel.

On Wednesday, thousands of people gathered in the lumber and manufacturing district around 22nd St. and along Canal St. Five thousand businessmen met in the Moody and Sankey Tabernacle to discuss measures for putting down what Mayor Heath termed "the ragged commune wretches." The military and civil officials decided to call up the military, but to let the police try to handle the situation. There were 250 police on active duty and 2000 Illinois National Guardsmen available. The Guard had been created the year before in response to fear of social unrest.

On July 23, 25,000 people gathered at Market and Madison Sts. to hear Albert Parsons, George Schilling and Philip Van Patten. The socialists were suddenly the recognized "leaders" of the rebellion if only because they were visible. However, the mass explosion had been predicted by neither the ruling class nor the radicals.

When Albert Parsons got up to speak, the crowd cheered wildly. The people trusted him. He again urged everyone to remain peaceable and work for legislative solutions. The inflammatory *Chicago Tribune* conceded, "Parsons advocated an obedience to law and order, but a peaceful yet determined maintenance of their rights. He counseled them . . . never to attack anyone until they were attacked." The Party issued a manifesto to "Workingmen of Chicago" denouncing the law which authorized the arrest without warrant "of any workingman out of employment who may wander in search of work" and the law which made it a criminal offense for workingmen to combine to secure higher wages, although "the right of the employers to combine in reducing our wages, and bringing starvation to our homes is protected by all the police and soldiers in the country."

The fury of the strike can only be explained by the anger of Civil War veterans and the families of victims who felt that they had made tremendous sacrifices for a "government of the people, by the people, and for the people." Instead they found themselves the victims of war profiteers and monopolists, who had lowered wages and begun employing large numbers of women and children during and since the war. "Women's wages" had become the standard in many factories.

A crippled Civil War veteran who received $6 a week as a disability payment was one of the most vocal activists in the Chicago uprising.

The day after his speech, Albert Parsons went to his job at the *Times;* he found his name crossed off the list of employees. He had been discharged and blacklisted.

He went to the offices of the *Arbeiter-Zeitung* and *Vorbote,* the radical German papers, and there two men found him conducting strike activities. They said that Mayor Heath wanted to talk with him and took him to city hall. They ushered him into a room filled with police, where Police Chief Hickey was waiting. The police scowled at him; a few minutes later he was taken to the mayor's office. Thirty or so representatives of the business community filed in. Parsons was hoarse from his speech and had caught a cold; he was exhausted and had just found out he'd lost his job.

The chief began to question him. "Who are you? Where did you come from? Are you married? Do you have a family?" Parsons answered the questions. Chief Hickey blamed the strike on him and finally asked, "Don't you know any better than to come up here from Texas and incite the working people to insurrection?" The members of the Citizens' Association snapped "Hang him!" "Lynch him!" "Lock him up!"

Parsons attempted to explain that he as an individual could not have caused all this trouble; he reminded them that he had told the people not to strike, but to go to the polls and vote instead. But the elected officials, police authorities and businessmen wanted an obvious explanation; other explanations might have been obvious, but they could not concede that poor conditions result in strikes. They decided not to arrest Parsons, fearing his arrest would cause additional violence. But they threatened to arrest both Van Patten and Parsons if they appeared in public in the next 24 hours. Hickey warned them that the citizens of Chicago (i.e., the Board of Trade men) would not tolerate "Commune leaders" and that "capitalists would offer any sum to see the leaders of such a mob strung up to a telegraph pole."

The afternoon papers announced his arrest, but he had been released after questioning. About 8:00 P.M. he went to the *Tribune* office hoping to get a night's work and to talk with fellow printers about the strike. Suddenly someone grabbed him from behind and jerked him around. "Is your name Parsons?" Two strangers started to drag him out the door. "I came in here as a gentleman, and I don't want to be dragged out like a dog," he said. They cursed him and yanked him downstairs; one put a pistol to his head and threatened to blow his brains out. The other said, "Shut up or we'll dash you out the windows upon the pavement below." At the bottom of five stories they shoved him out the door saying he'd be arrested if he ever came near the *Tribune* again.

Stunned at the brutality, he walked down Dearborn St. to Lake, then west on Lake to Fifth Ave. (Wells). The Illinois National Guard was loitering around, but they didn't recognize him. He wanted nothing more than a cup of hot soup, a warm bed, a good night's sleep, and to see Lucy. The police had successfully intimidated Parsons and Van Patten, and the two did not take a prominent role in the strike afterwards.

Without leadership and coordination, the strike waned. By this time the police were well organized. The business community realized that it had panicked in the face of an unorganized mass uprising which it could defeat relatively easily. The ruling class was slightly embarrassed that it had taken the situation so seriously. The *Tribune* joked that a 12 year old lad had stopped all traffic on Clybourn Ave. "until the police, by a brave and vigorous charge, dispersed him."

On Wednesday night the Workingmen's Party called a meeting at Aurora Turner Hall to which they invited representatives of the strikers. A strike committee was selected, but it was already too late. The Party issued a directive to all strikers: "Fellow Workers . . . Under any circumstances keep quiet until we have given the present crisis a due consideration," and continued "Let every honest workingman help us to preserve order." It was a far cry from the "Red War" which the *Tribune* had proclaimed.

The papers accused the Workingmen's Party of inciting people to violence, then somewhere in the middle of an article would mention that the W.P. had encouraged people to return to their jobs and vote in the next election. The papers admitted that the rallies called by the party were orderly. But the paper called the crowds "bad elements, soreheads and thieves, communistic-loafers, dirty, howling scoundrels, half-grown lads, small boys, rioters, a crowd of loafers, dead-beats, tramps, and scum generally, sneak thieves in training and the off-scourings of the streets."

On Thursday morning, the 26th, the military was ready for action. It placed one of the city's two cannon at the east end of the 12th St. bridge and the other at the corner of West 12th and Halsted St. Guardsmen were stationed along 12th and along Halsted. There was sporadic fighting during the day and a serious fight at the Halsted St. viaduct that night. The following day casualties of 18 dead and 32 wounded were reported—all on the side of the people. The police barred the printers, iron molders and other unions from holding meetings at all. They broke into the Furniture Workers' meeting in West 12th St. Turner Hall, violently beating and clubbing those present and shooting and killing one person in a completely unprovoked attack.

The *Tribune* praised this attack. "A dozen or two heads were cracked and the Communistic rabble dispersed. The police force are entitled to all praise for their action." The paper attempted to incite the guarantors of private property to further violence. It suggested that every enterprise with a boiler should have a hose attachment made for it. The hose should then be used to direct a stream of boiling water or steam at the crowds. "A rioter has a wholesome distrust of water in any shape, and there is not a mobster on the earth who would quietly stand and be parboiled in the defense of any principle or the protection of any supposed right."

The *Tribune* suggested extermination for all communists. "Least of all does the world owe a living to the dead-beats, vagrants, drunkards, thieves, guttersnipes, Communists, and vicious loafers who came to the front and demanded it in the recent riots. The world owes these classes rather extermination than a livelihood."

On Friday people began going back to work, and the Board of Trade reopened. On Saturday nearly everyone except a few railroad workers were back at work. Between 20 and 35 persons had been killed, 200 seriously wounded. The city had spent $20,000 on special police and arms. For the rulers of Chicago the lessons of 1877 were that the police should be equipped with the rapid-firing Gatling Gun which could mow down hundreds at a time; the following year the Citizens' Association purchased a Gatling Gun and made a present of it to the City. Armories were established in major cities to house soldiers for putting down insurrection, and legislatures passed conspiracy laws aimed directly at workers. The press portrayed working people, especially strikers, as inherently criminal—an image which persists.

Although the role of the Workingmen's Party in the strike was uneven, it brought the ideas of socialism before the people. In the next election Albert Parsons polled nearly 8000 votes and ran 400 ahead of the rest of the Workingmen's ticket. The party was a force to be reckoned with. The railroad strike had taught Albert and Lucy that the bosses would stop at nothing. Hundreds of workers had died. More would die in future struggles. The events of 1877 showed Lucy and Albert that leaders cannot stem mass risings, no matter how well-meaning their programs might be. At the next opportunity they would lead the movement, not follow it.

Albert Parsons learned some hard lessons from the railroad strike, and Lucy learned that she would have to support her family, since the newspapers which said society did not owe communists a livelihood took away Albert Parsons' livelihood, his work as a printer. She opened a dress and suit shop, and Albert took orders for the shop.

The 1877 strikes and the violent response of the Chicago police set a pattern of conflict for a century of labor and radical struggles.

People flocked to the Workingmen's Party after the railroad strikes. The socialists had been visible and workers saw them as a viable alternative to the daily exploitation in the factories and in the mines.

When the Workingmen's delegates met in Newark, New Jersey, in December, 1877, they congratulated themselves on the successful organizing that had been done in July and August and looked to the future with optimism. But instead of conceiving a program to win the masses to socialism, they remained trapped in their organizational difficulties. The Party changed its name to the Socialistic Labor Party and dealt in resolutions and newspapers, rather than in plans for organizing the hundreds of thousands who had joined the strikes only six months before.[5]

The Party considered race and sex questions at the convention. Chinese labor was a major issue throughout the country. At the end of the 1877 railroad strikes in San Francisco, anti-Chinese demonstrators went on a rampage through Chinatown. The Workingmen's Party of California led the anti-Chinese movement, and eastern workers supported a Chinese exclusion act after Chinese strikebreakers were brought to Massachusetts in 1870. Racism against Chinese people was widespread in the labor movement.

The S.L.P. passed a resolution against the importation of contract coolie labor which also called for the freedom of Chinese people already in the U.S. from such contracts. It did not call for the prohibition of all Chinese immigration. There is no evidence to suggest that Lucy or Albert Parsons ever endorsed racist immigration acts, although they were members of organizations in which feelings against Chinese workers ran high. In 1882 Congress passed the Chinese Exclusion Act which prohibited Chinese immigration for 10 years; it was extended in 1892 and made permanent in 1902.

The S.L.P.'s position on sexual equality was more clear-cut than its position on racial equality; the party called for "the perfect equality of rights of both sexes."

One of the biggest debates of the convention was over the party press. The *Labor Standard* had been nearly broke since September, 1876, and had been financed by the party since May, 1877. Then its editors stopped issuing it as a Workingmen's Party paper and put it out on their own. The *Vorbote* in Chicago was badly in debt. The *Socialist* in Detroit was a semi-official paper. The trade unionists, including Albert Parsons, wanted the *Labor Standard* as the party paper. Those who favored political action preferred the *Socialist*. Each faction wanted the English language press located where its greatest strength was. Albert Parsons suggested Chicago, but Cincinnati won. Parsons had his wish within a year, however.

A second controversy was brewing over collaboration with the Greenback or other reform parties. Several members were expelled for collaboration, and the delegates laughed when someone suggested the solution to social problems was to adopt the Greenback platform.

The future looked rosy for the socialists in 1878. In Chicago the work was going well. Albert Parsons founded the Trades and Labor Assembly of Chicago and was elected its first president in 1878. The Lehr und Vehr Verein, the armed German workers, were growing, a consequence of the violence of the police in putting down the strikes the previous summer. But a large armed parade in Chicago in 1878 was enough to get the terrified Illinois legislature to pass an act in 1879 banning workers from forming armed groups.

The question of armed struggle vs. electoral activity was about to split the organization, but the party remained a reform, not a revolutionary organization. In March, 1878, the Chicago socialists met to ratify the convention documents and to commemorate the Paris Commune. Albert Parsons read the party principles which included health and sanitation measures, public baths, public work to be done by the day rather than by contract, eight hours for city employees, a fixed salary for all city officials, city to be run on a "cash and carry" basis, no city property to be sold or exchanged or to be leased for more than 15 years, schools for all, city to take over gas and street car monopolies, full employment, and ward boundaries to depend on population.

"It Is Spreading" read the article in the May 11, 1878, *Socialist*. And indeed "it" was. Benjamin Sibley, John McAuliffe, Paul Grottkau, A. R. Parsons and George Schilling had all been out speaking on Sunday, and the *Tribune* had just interviewed Parsons, whom it had to take seriously since he had just polled nearly 8000 votes in the race for County Clerk.

The first question of a badly frightened ruling class was, "Are the workers arming? Do they intend to achieve power by force?" The *Tribune* was eager for more fuel to feed the fires of anti-communism it had fanned during the railroad strikes and was especially eager to get Parsons to commit himself on the question of force. "Must this social revolution you refer to come about by a resort to arms?"

"Not necessarily," he replied, "although it may take that turn. But the ballot-box is our first remedy." He explained that working men were arming to test their constitutional right to bear arms and to defend themselves against the kind of police attacks which occurred in 1877.

He tried to explain how socialism differed from communism. "The essence of socialism" was "Production belongs to the producer; tools to the toiler." He called strikes and mobs "gut revolutions," which, through intelligent socialism could be directed to choosing socialism at the polls. Only the "capitalistic press" said that communism meant an equal division of property. "The only immediate means of relief, I think, lies in the recovery of the public lands from the railroads and the speculators, and the transfer of all monopolies into the hands of the Government, whereby they may become the property of the people," he said. Government ownership of public utilities and monopolies was considered a panacea for social ills by many reform groups of the 1870's.

He insisted that the socialists would achieve their goals by voting, but that if capitalists kept them away from the polls, they would resort to other means. He believed that wage workers were slaves. "The private ownership of the means of production is the cause of this unnatural and inhuman power . . . to tyrannize over and dictate to the great masses dependent upon the use of the means of production for a livelihood."

In the late 1870's Parsons was committed to legislative solutions. In his second race for Alderman from the 15th Ward, the evidence suggests that he won, but was "counted out." His interest in electoral politics began to decline. Chicago history might have been different had Albert Parsons received his seat.

In early May, 1878, the *National Socialist* suspended publication in Detroit; it had had 3000 subscribers. In August, the Chicago section decided to publish its own paper with $3,000 raised at a picnic and festival. The *National Socialist* was $800 in debt and the Party owed another $500; the National Executive Committee realized that competition from Chicago would break the paper completely; Philip Van Patten made several trips to Chicago and arranged for the Chicago group to buy the subscription list for $400 and publish the paper as a party organ. The N.E.C. hoped to play a role in selecting the editor.

The Chicago group named Frank Hirth, a German cigar-maker, editor at $12 a week and Albert Parsons assistant editor at $8 a week. Lucy provided the rest of the couple's income through her dressmaking shop.

The Chicago movement was at its peak in 1879. In March, the socialists held a tremendous Paris Commune rally in the Exposition Building, despite the opposition of the Stock Exchange and the Board of Trade. Thirty thousand people got inside, while thousands more were turned away. Women and children were admitted free; 17,000 tickets had been sold before the doors even opened. George Schilling introduced Ernst Schmidt, an old friend of Karl Marx and the Party's candidate for mayor, who addressed the crowd in German. Albert Parsons was to have given the English speech, but the building was so crowded the arrangements committee couldn't find him. The socialist military companies, about 385 men, were there in uniform. The *Tribune* had its usual prejudicial remarks about the nature and origin of the crowd," this motley mixture of humanity."

> Drain the Bohemian Socialistic slums of the Sixth and Seventh Wards; scour the Scandinavian dives of the Tenth and Fourteenth wards; cull the choicest thieves from Halsted, Desplaines, Pacific Avenue, and Clark Street; pick out from Fourth avenue, Jackson Street, Clark Street, State Street, and other noted haunts, the worst specimens of feminine depravity; scatter in all the red-headed, cross-eyed, and frowsy servant girls in the three divisions of the city. . . . In short, it was such a gathering as only a Socialistic community could bring out or would tolerate.

The estimated $5,000 proceeds from the festival made the *Arbeiter-Zeitung* a daily paper. A week later Dr. Schmidt received nearly 12,000 votes for mayor and the Socialistic Labor Party elected another three aldermen.

It was during this peak period of success that Lucy Parsons' first known writings appeared in the *Socialist*. Her first literary effort was a poem based on Lord Byron's work which she called "A Parody." Five long years of economic depression—her first five years in Chicago—went into the poem.

"I had a dream, which was not all a dream." . . . .
And men did wander up and down the cheerless earth,
Aimless, homeless, hopeless. . . .
As, by fits, the realization of their impoverished condition
    passed like a vision before them.
Some laid down and hid their eyes and wept
As the cries of their hungry children
And prayers of their despairing wives fell like curses
    upon them;
And some did rest their chins upon their clenched hands
And swear to help abolish the infamous system that could
    produce such abject misery. . . .
And some did gnash their teeth and howl, swearing dire
    vengeance against *all* tyrants.
And War—which for a moment was no more—did glut
    himself again;
A meal was bought with blood (tramps' blood),
And each sat sullenly apart, gorging himself in gloom.
No love was left;
All earth, to the masses, was but one thought—and that was:
    —Work! Wages! Wages!
The pangs of hunger fed upon their vitals.
Men, in a land of plenty, died of *want*—absolute—
And their bones were laid in the Potter's Field.

Her poem expressed bitterness, anger, and despair. She showed the rebellion of the working class which she had seen in 1877, and she suggested the extreme isolation of each worker, who was forced to feed his family at the expense of the unemployed: "a meal was bought with blood (tramps' blood)."

The 1877 strikes and the violence of the police and militia against the strikers shaped Lucy Parsons' consciousness of the contradictions between capital and labor for decades to come. She had reached the conclusion that the interests of labor and capital were hopelessly irreconcilable, and she was developing and interpreting the theories of class conflict, surplus value, and socialist revolution.

In another article, Lucy cited the example of glass-pressers who had been locked out in Chicago and argued that a strike is inherently inconsistent with the concept of harmony between capital and labor, because a strike "means resistance on the part of the oppresssed toward the oppressor." She lamented the fact that "so many apparently honest persons among the wage class . . . still hold to this absurd doctrine. . . .," and she incorporated the labor theory of value into her discussion:

> What harmony 'twixt the oppressor and the oppressed, 'twixt robber and robbed? . . . When will the masses learn that property is his and his *only* who has produced it— *earned* it? and that the thieves who prate about "managing their own factories after their own notions," never *earned* one millionth of what they now hold and claim as theirs? that is the unpaid labor of those very thirteen hundred men that they themselves have locked out to starve, under the plea of the laws which they themselves have made.

Lucy suggested how to resolve the problem. "These so-called laws would not be worth the paper they are written on, twenty-four hours after the producers of all wealth had willed it otherwise."

She exhibited an utter disregard for "property rights." On the other hand, she saw human rights violated all around her. The *Socialist* often printed accounts of widowed mothers who died of tuberculosis, the result of poverty, overwork, malnutrition, and society's refusal to provide medical attention to those unable to pay for it; of starving children; of tramps frozen to death because they were out of work and had been evicted from their homes or tenements; and of people who took their own lives to end the cycle of poverty, disease, and pain.

Lucy Parsons had supreme contempt for the war profiteers who stayed home during the Civil War; every day these war profiteers turned away penniless, homeless veterans from City Hall and sent them to try their luck at the private charities. Lucy remembered the ragged and crippled veteran who had spoken out during the recent railroad strikes. She could compare him to the editor of the *Times* who called the protesting veterans "Relics from the Late Carnage." She charged that the editor had "stayed at home, fared sumptuously, and waxed fat on the spoils of a cruel, cruel war. . . ." She described him as a member of a "usurping, parasitic capitalist class" which had sent the working class to die in its own economic interests. "And so it was," she wrote, "that thousands, yet, tens of thousands workingmen left their all and bravely hastened forward to the defense of what they believed to be *their* country, leaving the slimy cowards at home to furnish pastebottom boots." Twelve years after the war the veterans "are denied by a bloated aristocracy, a cruel monied-ocracy, the commonest right that should be accorded the yellow cur that runs the streets—*the right to live!* and find themselves alluded to in the columns of a hireling, venal press as 'mendicants,' and 'relics from the late carnage,' 'unfortunates,' etc."

With the slaveholding class defeated, the monopolists and robber barons divided the spoils of victory and built their empires of industrial wealth unimpeded. The great trusts and monoplies were consolidated in the 25 years after the Civil War: oil, steel, chemicals, railroads, meatpacking. Lucy Parsons joined the cry of thousands of angry veterans and reformers who found themselves helpless pawns in this mad race for wealth.

As early as 1879 Lucy Parsons stated that the life of the reformer is totally insignificant. She practiced this principle and consistently maintained that her own personal life was inconsequential; she refused to talk about herself.

Her conception of history was movement oriented, not individual oriented. She attacked individuals who used the movement for personal glorification. "There has with every popular wave which swept through the affairs of men having for its object Reformation, been borne to the surface a great many so-called reformers, who having unbounded confidence in themselves, have risen to dizzy heights in their own estimation." According to Lucy Parsons the true reformer must overcome "his own dear self," "the first, nearest, hardest, most contemptible of enemies."

She argued that it was unimportant who made the reform; only the reform itself was important. She argued that the Republican Party had been used by the real reformers, the Abolitionists, "in striking the shackles from the black slave." To her it was not important who freed the slaves; it was important that they were free.

Lucy Parsons, like many other late nineteenth century reformers, saw in the rising American capitalist class a parallel to the European aristocracy. In fact, the highest ambition of some of the new American millionaires was to see their daughters married off to the sons of European "nobility." Lucy took a long excerpt from *Scribner's Magazine* describing the lavish reception of the old aristocracy in the New World and commented, "For all the treasonable schemers are at work to overthrow this— the *people's*—government, and erect on its ruins an aristocracy more hateful, if such a thing were possible, than that which exists in old despotic Europe to-day." In 1879 she believed that the republican form of government was superior to European despotism and monarchy and that the U.S. retained some elements of "people's" government.

She reviewed the history of the French people who had thrown off the monarch only to hand power to an emperor, Napoleon. She feared that without a plan of action the American people might fight a revolution against capital only to end up with a despot like Napoleon.

She contributed an article on women servants. *Scribner's Magazine* had published advice to wealthy women about how to choose a servant girl, how much to pay her, and even prescribed the amount of tea and sugar the girl should be allowed a week. The girl should get a week's notice of dismissal, except in cases of "misconduct." Lucy retorted, "Of course, there is never any 'misconduct' on the part of the mistress, and, any claim on the part of the servant . . . would be considered the height of impertinence, that could only be appeased by peremptory dismissal, without 'recommendation.' "[6]

In early 1879, Albert Parsons was busy editing the *Socialist* with Frank Hirth. He had also been elected Secretary of the Chicago Eight Hour League. He was a member of the committee from the Trades Council which investigated unfit working conditions and testified before the Illinois Legislative Committee about its findings; among the demands was pure air for coal miners. Lucy was busy writing for the *Socialist,* speaking for the Working Women's Union, and she was pregnant with her first child.

Secondary literature gives little information about the Chicago Working Women's Union. It is nearly lost from "herstory." The union was formed in the mid 1870's by housewives and other wageless women. The March 1, 1879, *Socialist* reported a crowded meeting of the Workingwomen's Union. The women said that schools should teach children to honor labor; they demanded a suffrage plank in the S.L.P. platform; they argued that equal pay for equal work was in the interest of both women and men. John McAuliffe offered a separatist solution to the women and attacked the party for not including the suffrage platform; he said women should refuse to help any party, including the S.L.P., until suffrage was included and that they should boycott men in other ways—such as refusing to dance with them—until their demands were met. T. J. Morgan and George Schilling took part in the discussion, but the *Socialist* reported, "Mrs. Parsons made by far the best argument of the evening couched in choice language, and delivered with spirit and animation."

Many leaders of the Chicago Working Women's Union, like Lucy Parsons, were socialists; and in April, 1879, Mrs. Stevens, its president, announced that she had become a socialist. Lucy Parsons was well on her way to becoming a leader in the socialist movement; her commanding figure would soon be well known on the lakefront where the socialists held their mass meetings.

Women were admitted to labor unions only through struggle and over the opposition of many men. Women had acted as strikebreakers, because that was the only way they could get jobs in trades such as printing. Some organizations adopted the principle "equal pay for equal work," because they saw that low wages for women in certain trades meant unemployment for men and lower wages for everyone.

In September, 1879, the Knights of Labor passed a resolution to admit women; but it took two years to get the machinery ready to admit women! In 1880 the Knights appointed a committee to develop a separate initiation ritual for women. In September, 1881, the Knights dropped the idea of a separate admission ceremony and admitted women on the same basis as men. Lucy Parsons, Mother Jones, and many other women joined as soon as they could.

The Chicago Working Women's Union went out of existence in the early 1880's as women began organizing women's assemblies of the Knights of Labor.[7]

As early as 1879 there was controversy within the Chicago movement over how socialists should relate to the eight hour movement. The demand for a shorter work day had been raised during the 10 hour movement of the 1840's and 1850's; the supporters of the shorter work day believed that it would make work for more people and would spread the work out over the year. Many workers were lucky if they had work half the year; during the half they had jobs they worked up to 16 hours a day and got barely enough to live on.

If work could be spread out and wages maintained, workers could enjoy life, have some leisure time and be able to purchase the products of their labor. Ira Steward, a Boston machinist, had worked continually for the eight hour day since the 1860's. His wife Mary composed a jingle which summed up the meaning of eight hours: "Whether you work by the piece or work by the day, decreasing the hours increases the pay."

As an activist in the Chicago Eight Hour League in 1880, Albert Parsons strongly believed that the eight hour day was the starting point from which to improve the quality of life in working class communities. His fellow members of the Socialistic Labor Party, George Schilling and Tommy Morgan, disagreed vehemently; they argued that eight hours was an insufficient demand. Parsons debated Morgan and Schilling in Seaman's Hall on the question a few days before the Eight Hour League's great Fourth of July celebration. Morgan later recorded that he had "discredited" Parsons in the debate.[8]

Albert Parsons invited Ira Steward to Chicago for the Chicago Eight Hour League's three day 4th of July Festival. The festival was a stunning success. The Furniture Union—whose meeting had been shot up by the police during the railroad strikes—had a large wagon drawn by six white horses called the Eight-Hour Car. A hidden bell pealed out 1, 2, 3, 4, 5, 6, 7, 8. On the back were the words: IT WILL STOP OVERPRODUCTION—IT WILL TAKE AWAY TRAMPS—IT WILL GIVE THE IDLE BROTHERS WORK.

The Working Women's Union had a float decked in pink fabric and ribbons, with the banner: IN A UNION OF STRENGTH WE SEEK THE STRENGTH OF UNION on one side and WHEN WOMAN IS ADMITTED INTO THE COUNCIL OF NATIONS WAR WILL COME TO AN END, FOR WOMAN MORE THAN MAN, KNOWS THE VALUE OF LIFE on the other.

The Printers' Union float carried an operating press which was turning out copies of the *Eight Hour Agitator*. Ira Steward was the honored guest and George Schilling the master of ceromonies at the rally in Ogden's Grove following the parade.

In July the Congressional Committee to Investigate the Cause of the Depression took testimony in Chicago. T. J. Morgan, Benjamin Sibley, Albert Parsons, John McAuliffe, George Schilling and Frank Streator testified for the socialists. Schilling, Parsons, McAuliffe, and Morgan testified for the Trades and Labor Council. In 1879 the leaders of the Chicago labor movement were socialists!

The seeming successes of the socialists concealed internal divisions; in the fall, the socialist vote was 7000 less than it had been in the spring. In August, 1879, the controversial *Socialist,* edited by Hirth and Parsons ceased publication; operating on a $50 a week deficit, it had run through its entire $2,600 starting capital in a year. A struggle over the papers was shaping up within the Socialistic Labor Party.

A month after the *Socialist* folded, Lucy gave birth to her son, Albert Richard Parsons, on September 14, 1879. His birth was registered "Negro."9

With the Illinois Legislature's passage of a law forbidding workers to arm and the Illinois Supreme Court upholding that act, the conflict within the S.L.P. over armed struggle came to a head. The central issue was the authority of the Board of Supervision and the National Executive Committee in relation to the autonomy of the locals. Three important issues hinged on the authority of the N.E.C. and the B.O.S.: 1) N.E.C. control of party newspapers, 2) arming and the Lehr und Wehr Verein, and 3) support of the Greenback presidential nominee in 1880.

The Party convention at Allegheny, Pennsylvania, the last week of 1879, resulted in the airing, but not the resolution, of the issues.10 George Schilling sided with Van Patten, the National Secretary, but most of the Chicago German section took a strong stand against him. Van Patten had lost control of the

Cincinnati section—where he lived and where the N.E.C. was headquartered. Albert Parsons and William Jeffers were selected the Chicago delegates, and they strongly opposed Van Patten.

The issue of armed struggle was closely linked to the controversy over the Party papers. The N.E.C. had advised S.L.P. members not to join armed groups. When the N.E.C. had heard that the Chicago sections planned to march with the Lehr und Vehr Verein in a parade the summer of 1879, it issued a warning against the parade. The Chicago sections received the advice with contempt. Frank Hirth ridiculed the N.E.C. in the *Vorbote,* which he edited. Paul Grottkau, the editor of the *Arbeiter-Zeitung,* condemned the N.E.C. in the paper and had several thousand extra copies printed and distributed at the parade.

The actions of the Chicago section were endorsed by the convention, which censured the N.E.C. Albert Parsons led the attack on Van Patten and the authority of the N.E.C. "The question is, shall the Executive Committee be censured for meddling with other people's business," he declared. "The convention must disapprove of the entire course of the National Executive Committee."

The N.E.C. recommended that the S.L.P. not nominate a presidential candidate for the 1880 campaign, but should wait and see if they could combine with the Workingmen's Party of California, the Liberal Party and/or the Greenback Labor Party. The convention did agree to send representatives to the Greenback Labor conference to be held in Washington, D.C. a week after their own convention ended, and they selected Albert Parsons as one of the delegates.

It was then moved that the S.L.P. send delegates to the July 4 Greenback convention in Chicago which would nominate the presidential candidate. Parsons suggested that the socialist delegates could withdraw from the convention if it refused to adopt their platform, but others opposed the suggestion, because delegates from outside Chicago would have Chicago proxies and the Chicago section would control the entire Party's decision. The convention then named a candidate, but Parsons' moved to reconsider the decision and to submit the names of three nominees to the party membership at large. His motion carried, and the issue rested.

In January Albert Parsons went to Washington to attend the Greenback conference and to lobby for the eight-hour day on behalf of the Eight Hour League of Chicago. Lucy was at home with her four month old baby and her dress shop.

The S.L.P. began 1880 in fragments. On January 26 the Board of Supervision suspended the National Executive Committee and the recalcitrant Cincinnati section. Of the three cities which had formed paramilitary organizations the previous summer, San Francisco was already out of the party, Cincinnati was suspended, and Chicago was at loggerheads with the Party officers. On April 20, the B.O.S. followed up the suspension of Cincinnati with an expulsion order.

The Chicago section had not paid dues in eight months, and the N.E.C. decided it could break its power by suspending the section for nonpayment, which it did on April 7, 1880.

In the spring elections of 1880, Frank Stauber was the only socialist who was re-elected, and he had to contest the election. It was months before he got his seat back, and even when the election fraud was proven, the judge ruled that the election officials hadn't "intended" to change the votes and absolved them from culpability.

With the party in disarray, members of both sides attended the Greenback convention in Chicago. Van Patten was there and so was Justus Schwab from New York.[11] Lucy and Albert Parsons were both delegates. Although the previous convention had determined that the party would remain independent, Van Patten's people intended to enter a coalition with the Greenbackers. When the Parsons, the Chicago Germans, and others withdrew from the Greenback convention and nominated their own candidates, it should not have been a great surprise to Van Patten. But with the party splitting up, Van Patten felt the only way to avoid isolation was to work with the Greenbackers. The anti-compromisers nominated Albert Parsons for the legislature from the sixth district opposing Christian Meier, the regular socialist candidate, who was supported by Morgan and Schilling. The regular socialists supported James B. Weaver for president, the Greenback-Labor Party's nominee.

Paul Grottkau and Peter Peterson, editor of the Scandinavian weekly, were summarily expelled from the S.L.P., for their opposition to the compromise. In response, the German section and their friends set up their own party structure. Thomas Morgan, the organizer of the regular party section drafted a letter to the N.E.C. about the situation; he wrote privately to Van Patten, "Speiss cannot be trusted."[12]

An account of "The Chicago Muddle" in the *Labor Review* attacked Grottkau and Peterson, saying that the *Arbeiter-Zeitung* had previously endorsed coalition, then turned on the party leaders as "compromisers," "conspirators," and "Greenback agents." The *Labor Review* admitted that the two expulsions had been "abrupt and without process of trial," and that the nature of the expulsions created a lot of sympathy for Grottkau and Peterson. The Germans took over the next meeting of the section, rescinded the expulsions, and made Peterson and other members of the opposition the section officers. The English Branch, under Morgan, protested, and the dispute went to the Board of Supervision. Chicago, which had been the scene of the party's greatest achievements, was now the scene of its greatest disaster.

On August 2, Van Patten wrote to Schilling demanding to know where the Chicago vote on the coalition with Weaver was. "Let the majority be so large as to utterly crush Grottkau and Co." He had brought charges against the German papers and their editors before the Board and assured Schilling that the trial would be properly conducted this time. He criticized the Chicago section for not giving them a trial in the first place. Morgan had "proven himself a good bulldozer but a poor manager." "He needs to be checked however, and the trouble is that he will not *be* checked," wrote Van Patten.

While Van Patten was attempting to trounce the dissension, Albert Parsons and Paul Grottkau were actively participating in the festivities of the armed sections in Chicago. Lucy Parsons, who was more militant than her husband, applauded the developments. On August 1, they held a "Great Excursion of the Armed Organizations of Chicago and Milwaukee" and featured Paul Grottkau and Albert Parsons as the speakers. In September, the Lehr und Wehr Verein announced shooting practice in South Chicago; they were serious about defending themselves from the next police attack. A decision was made for the two sides to meet in October to elect Main Section officers; all actions taken by either faction since July 1 were nullified.

Van Patten thought the Germans could be defeated if Christian Meier sided against the *Vorbote* and *Arbeiter-Zeitung*. He believed the key to party stability was Chicago, but he was determined to crush his opposition. "When Chicago is harmonized," he wrote, "the balance of the Party will easily be pacified." He knew he would have to work with the Germans again, because they would remain socialists whether or not they remained in the party. He thought they'd be more easily controlled within the organization than outside it. But Morgan would have to stay out of the situation for awhile, since "his appearance is like waving a red rag to a bull and he cannot possibly regain leadership at present."

Van Patten criticized Schilling for attending the dissenters' convention and pledging to support some of their nominees, then attempting to work with the Greenbackers too, and then threatening to unite with the Germans and repudiate the Greenback state and presidential tickets.[13]

In the end, the two factions remained unreconciled, and two tickets ran: the Greenback-S.L.P. ticket and the Trades Assembly-S.L.P. "kickers" ticket, which had nominated Parsons for the legislature. Just before the election, Elizabeth Morgan wrote to Van Patten about Christian Meier's campaign. She was furious with Albert Parsons. "Some of our women mean to go out and peddle tickets for Christian Meier, we all feel like doing anything to beat that D. of *Parsons*. We are all death on that man and he knows it." She complained that "the Grottkau lot are trying all kinds of things to put a stop to the mass meeting we are going to have on Sunday."[14]

Ten members were expelled in October for not recognizing the N.E.C. Among them were Paul Grottkau, Oscar Neebe, Peter Peterson, and August Spies. Paul Grottkau, the editor of the *Arbeiter-Zeitung*, was one of the most prominent and best educated German socialists in America. August Spies was the handsome young German who became the paper's business manager in 1880 and resolved its financial difficulties; he would succeed Grottkau as editor in 1884. He was a brilliant speaker and organizer in both German and English, and he inspired confidence by his friendly, witty, and forthright manner. He had striking blue eyes, fair skin, and a blondish mustache and hair.

He had arrived in Chicago about the same time as Lucy and Albert Parsons, began to study socialism, joined the Lehr und Wehr Verein and was quickly recognized as a leader. Oscar Neebe was a strong, determined socialist organizer, who ran his own small delivery business. The leadership of the next stage of the radical movement was beginning to come together.

Philip Van Patten may have established the authority of the National Executive Committee, but in the process, he lost half the party. By November 15, the New York section had left. The Chicago "kickers" would formally be out within a few months. Tommy Morgan would never forgive Albert or Lucy Parsons.

The roots of Lucy Parsons' political development lie in the factional struggles of 1879-1881. She quickly became a spokesperson for the most militant faction. The establishment press noticed her and thought she "preached the social revolution with more vehemence" than her husband.

During this brief period, Lucy gave birth to her two children; her second child, Lulu Eda, who was born April 20, 1881. The baby girl was denoted "nigger" on her birth certificate.[15] In the meanwhile Lucy's dressmaking shop was doing well, and she bore the financial burden for the support of the family.

Lucy Parsons: Friend to Tramps

By early 1881, splits had occurred in Boston, Philadelphia, Cincinnati, Chicago, St. Louis, and New York. A new paper, the *An-archist* had just appeared in Boston, "a wild revolutionary magazine," said the S.L.P.'s *Bulletin of the Social Labor Movement* "filled with rules for the construction of barricades and other nonsense."[1]

The Socialist Revolutionary Clubs, which Lucy and Albert Parsons joined, advocated "military organization and the study of revolutionary tactics, and opposed political action," so the N.E.C. ruled that an S.L.P. member could not join both. Van Patten charged that the Socialist Revolutionary Clubs were the work of agents provocateur. "As the Socialist movement becomes a power, the capitalistic enemies. . . cunningly adopt the plan of sending their tools among us to shout revolution and clamor for blood. There is every evidence to prove that such a scheme is now being systematically carried out." Van Patten did not offer his evidence, and the extent to which agents provocateur penetrated the movement in the early 1880's has never been fully established.

The *Vorbote* accused the English section of what was left of the S.L.P. of being "hostile to Trade Unions and the struggle for economic emancipation." The trade unionists and the political activists had not been able to work together. For the first time a discussion of anarchism appeared in S.L.P. documents. They charged that "anarchists" were entirely individualistic and opposed to any social regulation. The *An-archist* said the first priority was the overthrow of capitalism; it would discuss concrete programs after the revolution.

Johann Most was one of the collaborators on the magazine; his influence would soon be profoundly felt in the American movement. The paper called attention to the conference European anarchists held in Belgium in Sept., 1880, and to the coming International Congress of Revolutionary Socialists to be held in London in 1881. For the first time "anarchism" found its way into the American vocabulary in a major way; within a few years the word "anarchist" would come to stand for almost any radical.

The Boston group passed several resolutions forming a Revolutionary Alliance of the American Continent consisting of autonomous socialist groups; its fund was to be used for "active revolutionary measures" only. It was specifically not to be used for "any election purposes, the pay of any officers, propaganda of purely *theoretical* literature." Because of the failures they had experienced trying to achieve change through legislative measures, the Parsons decided that other means would be needed, especially direct action at the place of work, strikes, boycotts, union organization, and revolutionary activity.

The London conference in June, 1881, revived the international anarchist movement. In the fall of 1881, the left-wing American socialists met in Chicago and formed the Revolutionary Socialistic Party. In 1882 a central committee led by radical labor organizations was established in Chicago to coordinate activities.

In 1882 the Trades Assembly put up its own ticket; the Socialistic Labor Party cooperated with the Anti-Monopoly Party. The Trades Assembly nominated Albert Parsons, and the Anti-Monopolists nominated George Schilling. Both withdrew from the campaign before the election; it was Albert Parsons' last electoral campaign.

In December 1882 Johann Most arrived in the United States; Johann Most had aspired as a child to be an actor, but a long illness and operations on his face disfigured him for life. Instead of an actor, he became a tremendous radical orator.

Justus Schwab had arranged the tour for Most, who had recently been released from prison in England for cheering the assassination of the Russian Tzar, Alexander II. Most had been a Reichstag member in Germany, but had since rejected parliamentary measures. He was expelled from Germany under the 1878 anti-socialist laws. In 1882 he was advocating "propaganda by the deed," the use of dynamite and other "revolutionary" measures. Most visited Chicago in March, 1883, and there met Albert and Lucy Parsons for the first time. Albert Parsons wrote the account of Most's visit to Chicago for *Truth,* the San Francisco radical paper.

On October 14, 1883, the Revolutionary Socialists convened

in Pittsburgh. There they drafted the Pittsburgh Manifesto and
formed the International Working People's Association. They
believed this congress would be the "Continental Congress" of
labor and would initiate the final conflict between labor and
capital—socialist revolution. Johann Most, Albert Parsons and
August Spies were members of the committee which drafted the
manifesto. The manifesto began with a Jeffersonian justification
of force and a few lines from the Declaration of Independence,
then discussed Karl Marx's labor theory of value. The system
which results in mass unemployment and starvation "is unjust,
insane, and murderous." "It is therefore necessary to totally
destroy it with and by all means." "All laws are directed against
the working people." Education furnishes "the offspring of the
wealthy with those qualities necessary to uphold their class
domination. No ruling class has ever laid down its privileges
without a struggle. It becomes, therefore, self-evident that the
struggle of the proletariat with the bourgeoisie will be of a
violent revolutionary character." "There remains but one recourse—FORCE!" The manifesto became Lucy Parsons' ideological basis; it had six points:

First—Destruction of the existing class rule, by all means,
i.e., by energetic, relentless, revolutionary and international
action.

Second—Establishment of a free society based upon cooperative organization of production.

Third—Free exchange of equivalent products by and between
the productive organizations without commerce and profit-
mongery.

Fourth—Organization of education on a secular, scientific and
equal basis for both sexes.

Fifth—Equal rights for all without distinction to sex or race.

Sixth—Regulation of all public affairs by free contracts between autonomous (independent) communes and associations,
resting on a federalistic basis.

The Revolutionary Socialists were far ahead of their society in
calling for racial and sexual equality and secular education. The
automous federated groups which constituted the organization
were to voluntarily contribute money to the Information Bureau,
and a majority of the groups could agree to call another congress.

After the Manifesto was adopted, the delegates accepted

August Spies' resolution which said that the trade unions "form the advance guard of the coming revolution." The Chicago unionists wanted to be sure that the revolutionaries did not forget that radical unions which opposed wage labor were to be the building blocks of the future social order. Outside Chicago trade union work was not emphasized, and the resolution was easily ignored. The Chicago leaders, as early as 1883, were syndicalists; they had given up political work for work in the unions which they believed would provide the social organization of the future.

Because of their autonomous organizational pattern, their anti-authoritarianism, the reputation of Johann Most, and their identification with the Anarchist International, members of the International Working People's Association were labeled anarchists. Because the European movement had split into Marxian "socialists" and Bakuninist "anarchists," it was easy to assume that divisions in the American movement would follow the same lines. In Europe, the term "anarchist" was one of derision coming from the marxists; Socialistic Labor Party members quickly learned to use the term with the same connotations in the U.S. Thus Lucy Parsons became an "anarchist."

Johann Most was not interested in trade union work—except insofar as it would recruit to the revolutionary movement. He was not interested in the immediate demands for shorter hours, higher wages, and better working conditions. Achieving limited goals would only delay the revolution, in Most's opinion. The Chicago section hedged on the question, but eventually reached the conclusion that socialists had to work for limited (and popular) demands of working people if they weren't to become totally isolated from the working class.

Johann Most shaped the directions of the movement in New York City; but in Chicago, the unionists led the movement.

Lucy and Albert Parsons had little to say about their personal lives; their lives as revolutionaries took precedence. Friends and neighbors all agreed on how remarkable were their love and devotion for each other. A young woman who grew up near Lincoln Park recalled that a German couple who lived in the neighborhood and owned a large two-story house, rented the upstairs flat to Lucy and Albert Parsons. The peaceful neighborhood was scandalized by the news that their German neighbor had rented the apartment to a white man and a black woman. "His immediate neighbors were somewhat shocked and indignant, and the gossips were kept busy for several days." But things settled down, the new tenants were "quiet and unobtrusive," and even the "horrified gossips" became accustomed to them. The young woman recalled, "Lucy was so well-bred and dignified that she commanded the respect of all with whom she came in contact." She put a neat sign over her door: "Mrs. A. R. Parsons, Fashionable Dressmaking."

Lucy played the role of "lady," perhaps emulating the wives of Southern planters she had seen in childhood. She wanted to be a "lady" in all the word meant in the nineteenth century; being a "lady" had been denied her by her color and class, and she did not want to be like the dark women she had seen in Texas who worked the fields and bore children annually. The burden of her sex, race, class and political beliefs made it imperative to "act like a lady" to overcome the many prejudices which could lead to eviction and other forms of discrimination.

As it was, Lucy and Albert moved at least once a year between 1875 and 1886, and sometimes even more frequently. The racial question may have plagued them wherever they went —or it may have been their socialist beliefs or their creditors.

Their schoolgirl neighbor in Lincoln Park saw how they lived. A wooden walk leading to an outside stairway in the back of the Parsons' place went right under her window. As she lay in bed each night, she would hear the footsteps of many people walking quietly to the back of the house and up the Parsons' stairs, where they would stay for several hours. It was a mystery who these men were or why they came. There was an air of intrigue around the place, and when her mother sent the curious girl to Lucy's dressmaking shop on an errand, she looked around eagerly. The apartment was "well-furnished and beautifully neat." A Chicago paper would later refer to the Parsons' flat as "elegant." The doors to two back rooms were open; in these rooms were rows of benches, made by placing long planks on a couple of chairs. The girl had to know what those benches were for, and she asked Lucy, who was absorbed in her sewing.

Lucy was annoyed and disturbed by the question; as she

stepped to the door and closed it, she replied, "My husband gives foreigners instruction in English." It seemed a likely enough answer, but many months later, the neighbors discovered that the Parsons' house was a socialist meeting place. But until that was discovered, Lucy and Albert were delightful neighbors.[2]

Between 1865 and 1880, 41,000 miles of railroad track had been laid, bringing rural artisans into direct competition with factory goods. Hundreds of thousands of rural Americans had lost their farms in the crash of 1873 and moved to the cities looking for work. Eight million European immigrants came to the United States between 1870 and 1890, 5.25 million of them between 1880 and 1890. Another depression in 1883 ended the economic upswing which had started in 1879. Unemployment was less severe, but general wage cuts were more severe than in the previous depression.

As the number of people employed in manufacturing increased, the conditions under which they lived and worked worsened. Conditions in the ghettoes were so bad by 1883 that the Citizens' Association of Chicago sponsored an investigation the winter of 1883-84 which condemned living conditions in the working class neighborhoods. Joseph Gruenhut, the socialist whom Mayor Harrison had appointed Factory and Tenement Inspector, headed the committee. Paul Grottkau went with the investigators the first day. Although Grottkau was reputed to be a cynic, he returned sick to his stomach from what he had seen. He said he couldn't possibly go again, and Michael Schwab covered the investigation for the *Arbeiter-Zeitung*.

Schwab, a tall, scholarly German socialist and former book binder, was shocked by what he saw. The investigators found single rooms housing three or four families. The beds were used in shifts and were never cold. The health officer permitted only part of the inspectors and reporters to go to the second floor of dwellings, afraid that the ceilings would collapse under the weight of all of them. There were rooms lighted only by cracks in the wall, water closets full of excrement, entire families sick, children slowly starving to death, ice cold rooms with no fire in the stove. All the Chicago papers covered the commission and its findings. The official report referred to

the wretched condition of the tenements into which thousands of workingmen are huddled, the wholesale violation of

all rules for drainage, plumbing, light, ventilation and safety
in case of fire or accident, the neglect of all laws of health,
the horrible condition of sewers and outhouses, the filthy
dingy rooms into which they are crowded, the unwholesome
character of their food, and the equally filthy nature of the
neighboring streets, alleys and back lots filled with decaying
matter and stagnant pools.

Notwithstanding the report, the Citizens' Association would
crush any organizing attempts which threatened the profits of
its members.[3]

In the 1880's the working people of Chicago had every reason to be angry about living and working conditions. In 1886
wages in Illinois were lower than they had been in 1882. In
Illinois, the average daily wage of men was nearly $2, for
women it was $1.11, and for children it was 70¢. Statistics
covering 85,000 Illinois industrial workers in 1885-1886
showed they had jobs an average of 37.1 weeks a year.

Fining was common, especially in factories which employed
women and children. Such infractions as singing, talking, coming in late, and looking cross-eyed at the boss were punished
by fines, often without the employee ever knowing why part
of her wages were deducted. The Bureau of Labor Statistics of
Illinois condemned fining in 1886, but that didn't mean it
stopped. A *Chicago Times* investigation in 1888 showed that
working women lost a large percentage of their $3-$4 weekly
wage in fines.

The iron-clad contract (yellow-dog contract) and the black
list were effective means to prevent union organization. Workers were forced to sign an agreement that they were not and
never would become members of a union in order to get a job.
If they joined, they were summarily fired. Those who tried to
organize found themselves fired and blacklisted, as Albert
Parsons had—whether or not they had ever signed an agreement.

Despite the odds against successful unionization, the 1880's
were characterized by strikes and increased union activity—by
both the trades unions and the Knights of Labor. In Chicago,
the brickmakers, tanners, and curriers went on strike in 1882;
the telegraph workers struck the folowing year. Between 1880
and 1883 union membership increased in absolute numbers as
well as in the percentage of foreign born members.

In 1882, Joseph Buchanan, a Knights of Labor and an International Workingmen's Association organizer, began to publish the *Denver Labor Enquirer*.[4] The *Labor Enquirer* became the medium of exchange for English speaking revolutionaries, and Lucy Parsons contributed frequent articles. Although she was a member of the Knights of Labor she felt that some members did not understand the class basis she believed the organization should have. "What are they organized for?" she asked those who encouraged a working person to "rise out of his class."

> Was it for the purpose of making it a laudable act for men to escape from honest labor, or was it organized to devise means by which they may be remunerated sufficiently while employed to insure them against the possibility of want or dying in the poor house? . . . . Then if the Knights of Labor are not organized for the purpose of making it possible for its members to obtain their labor product, what are they organized for? Is it for the purpose of showing their members how to make their "way out of labor circles," and thus become "oppressors" and "enemies?"

Lucy Parsons believed in a class basis for revolution.

Lucy's criticisms of the Knights came from a class and trade union point of view. The Knights were a broadly based reform organization which admitted anyone who was not a lawyer, doctor, banker, or liquor dealer. Women houseworkers, part of the wageless population, were welcomed into membership after 1881.

The Knights' social theory was not based on class struggle; the foundation of Lucy Parsons' world view was class struggle. To her the Knights' leadership exemplified the "croakers about harmony between labor and capital."

In their preamble the Knights stated that wealth had become so aggressive that unless checked it would lead to "the pauperization and hopeless degradation of the toiling masses." The ultimate aim of the order was the establishment of cooperative institutions of production and distribution, after which labor and capital could live in harmony. The Knights' official position did not make the wage system and workplace organizing central issues. Instead, the Knights emphasized the formation of producer and consumer cooperatives.

The Knights missed the very nature of capitalism in this

analysis of the social structure. In many ways the Knights were a "catch-all" organization and never a labor union. Many people who were members of other unions also joined the Knights. Some unionists within the Knights organized on a trade union basis, over the objections of the national leadership.

Within the organization there were similar conflicts as those in the socialist movement between advocates of political activity and advocates of economic activity. In fact many of the same people participated in both conflicts. When Terence Powderly became Grand Master Workman of the Knights of Labor in 1879, he repeatedly attempted to direct the organization toward political activity and away from strike activity. The rank and file did not want to wait for legislative reform; it wanted to win its demands through strikes. It was the strike wave of 1884-1886 which brought hundreds of thousands of new members to the Knights, not the organization of producers or consumers cooperatives.

In general, the Knights advocated working within the system to establish alternative institutions. In dealing with capitalists, they favored arbitration over strikes, legislative lobbying over direct action on the job.

Another woman who shared Lucy Parsons' convictions about class and revolution became her close friend and comrade. Lizzie M. Swank was a widow and a music teacher.[5] She was nearing 40, small and unassuming. In addition to giving piano lessons, she became interested in the "economic question." In March, 1881—about the time Lucy and Albert left the S.L.P.—she was a member of the party and served on a committee with T.J. Morgan; by September, she was the party secretary. She lectured frequently, on such topics as "The History and Philosophy of Music," suggesting that if there weren't music and cushioned pews in church, people wouldn't go.

She became a sewing woman to supplement her income and to get firsthand information on working conditions for women. She was discharged from one job, because she joined the Working Women's Union, and she helped to organize what she thought was the first strike of Chicago sewing girls. Because most of the women did not want to tell anyone how much money they made, they were isolated from each other. Swank reported on the conditions for working women in the radical press, but it took her a long time to get the facts on wages.

The women worked in a long room with dirty walls; cobwebs covered the windows. In shops where steam provided the power, the machines were attached to long tables which seated about 50 girls. Stacks of unfinished cloaks occupied every available space, and ravelings littered the floor. Piles of dust and grease filled the corners. In these fire traps, the women were further insulted by signs reading "Twenty-five cents fine for coming in late." "No talking and laughing." "Extra trimmings must be paid for." "Injured goods will be charged to employees." "No cloaks checked until returned from the presser."

A few women could make a living sewing, but the majority earned between $1.50 and $10.00 a week. A cloak which retailed for $12 or $15 was made for 75¢ to $1 in the shops. Even the women with the best jobs received nowhere near what the products of their labor would cost the consumer. Swank recalled a silk cloak, lined with quilted satin and trimmed with beaver, made for $3; it took a skilled woman more than four days to finish it. A "fashionable dressmaker" would charge $20 for the same cloak.

Lucy Parsons probably charged about $20 for the cloaks she made. Lucy never worked in a commercial sewing shop; perhaps her dark skin made it impossible to get a job outside her home and own small shop. But her neighborhood was filled with basement sweatshops with the worst working conditions in the city, and she could see the women going to work each morning, stooped under the huge bundles she had seen them carrying home at dusk.

The women who carried home huge brown bundles made women's underwear for 75¢ and $1 a dozen, low quality cloaks and wraps at $1.50 a dozen, overalls at $1 a dozen, coarse shirts at 40 or 60¢ a dozen, and trimmed and ruffled calico wrappers at $1.25 a dozen. These women had to work 16 hours a day just to eat, pay rent, buy coal and clothing. They had no time for anything else "and only take as much time to eat and sleep as a good machinist would consume in oiling and cleaning his machine," wrote Lizzie Swank. The sentimental philanthropists could complain about poor housekeeping and dirty children, but what woman who worked 16 hours a day to survive could put energy into housekeeping?

Swank was working at S----- & Co.'s cloak and suit business; as the company prospered, it cut prices paid for piecework. Then the proprietors made a new rule that work could not be credited to an employee's books until it returned from the buttonhole maker and presser. They made no provision for the changeover, and the workers went without any income from two to four weeks. In the meantime they couldn't pay their board, and they complained bitterly when the owners were out of earshot.

Swank suggested they write down their grievances, sign them, and present the petition to the boss. The key was that everyone had to agree to quit if anyone was fired. Swank wrote the paper, and all but four workers signed it. Then one woman took it to the boss; half an hour later he came storming up the stairs and ordered the steam stopped.

He called them ingrates and swore that he always had their interests at heart. He asked why they hadn't come to him privately; he assured them he would have given them an advance when they couldn't pay their board.

"There are only three or four girls in the shop capable of putting you up to such work, and they must leave today!" he shouted. "Miss D——— who presented the paper; and her sister, who is always grumbling; and Mrs. S——— and her sister, for both of them are mischievous disturbers, and would get up a row in any shop." He ordered the four to go finish their books and the rest to go back to work. Not one of the 48 women who signed the petition defended their discharged sisters.

Swank heard later that he'd become "miraculously kind and granted them many privileges." The women gave him the credit and thought they had been foolish to try to organize. But undoubtedly it was the threat of organization and a strike which compelled him to change his behavior.

As the Chicago Revolutionary Socialists and the trade union activists grew in power, the Socialistic Labor Party declined. George Schilling left the party in 1882 after withdrawing as its candidate. In 1882 Tommy Morgan gave it up and retired to Woodlawn park where he built a house, "raised flowers, potatoes and cabbages while Parsons and his associates raised h." Morgan had been defeated, but he refused to admit it; instead he wrote,

"I refused to participate with Parsons and Spies in physical force agitation."[6]

In 1883 Philip Van Patten disappeared leaving a suicide note. This further demoralized the S.L.P. Van Patten later reappeared and explained that he really had intended to commit suicide. At the last minute his sister notified him that their father had been injured in Mexico, and he went to Mexico to bring his father home. In the meantime he decided life might be worth living after all.[7]

After the S.L.P. English section in Chicago folded and after the 1883 Pittsburgh convention, the American section of the International Working People's Association was the primary organization of English-speaking radicals. Lizzie Swank joined the section. William Holmes got to know Albert Parsons in 1884 and left the Socialistic Labor Party, of which he had been a member since 1880, for the American section of the International Working People's Association. Holmes was born in England and came to the U.S. when he was five. He had been in Chicago since 1866. His father was an invalid, and William had to leave school to work as an unskilled laborer in planing mills and box factories. He had had his experiences with company scrip, 12 hour work days, and tramping. He studied shorthand on his own before he got a job as a stenographer at $7 a week.

Lucy Parsons and Lizzie Swank were among the most militant in the movement. To the slogan "The land for the landless; the tools to the toilers; and the product to the producers," Lucy added, "For without this right to the free use of these things, the pursuit of happiness, the enjoyment of liberty and life itself are hollow mockeries. Hence the employment of any and all means are justifiable in obtaining them, even to a forceable violent revolution." She said that anarchists criticize the wage slave system and offer "the advantages of a free society based upon the voluntary association of cooperative industry" in its place. She favored arming workers. "Thus being in a position to argue (?) his case, the final compact might possibly be achieved by very little violence." The two women did not retreat from talking about violent revolution. They did not seem to fear physical danger in a violent confrontation with the ruling class, and they even seemed to look forward to an opportunity to die fighting capitalism.

Lizzie lived near Lucy and Albert on the near West Side of the city, and they took walks together at least once a week. Sometimes another friend or two would join them. Albert would mimic capitalists and politicians and keep his friends in stitches.

The two women defended each other against attacks in the press. A New York critic asked Swank "how much capital it requires to produce a bushel of wheat?" Lucy Parsons replied for her that it might make some difference where the experiment were conducted—in the far north, on the banks of the Amazon or in the wheat belt of North America. She added, "But if Mr. Boyd means by capital, how many *dollars* it will require to raise a bushel of wheat, why, it would seem that the most feasible plan of finding that out would be for him to cover a certain amount of land—say the amount that it would require for labor to produce a bushel of wheat—with dollars and see how long it would take to grow it." It was obvious that dollars would never produce any wheat at all! Thus she demonstrated the labor theory of value. "There is an idea prevalent with some reforms that capital can produce anything. What nonsense! Labor, and labor only can produce wealth."[8]

In May of 1884, Paul Grottkau publicly debated Johann Most in Chicago on "Communism or Anarchism" and stated that he had never acknowledged the Pittsburgh manifesto. He resigned as editor of the *Arbeiter-Zeitung* and left the I.W.P.A. on September 18, 1884. August Spies became editor of the *Arbeiter-Zeitung*. Grottkau went on an extensive speaking tour before settling in Milwaukee to edit the Milwaukee *Arbeiter-Zeitung*. He soon rejoined the Socialistic Labor Party. Frank Hirth had preceeded Grottkau to Milwaukee in 1881 and had attempted to establish a cooperative cigar factory there.[9]

When the International Working People's Association decided to publish an English language paper in 1884, it named Albert Parsons editor and Lizzie Swank assistant editor. The first issue of the *Alarm* went to press with Lucy's "To Tramps" on the front page. "To Tramps" was reprinted by the I.W.P.A. and distributed as a leaflet. The winter of 1883-1884 had been one of the coldest, most bitter in Chicago's history. A biting wind blew off Lake Michigan. The economic depression had found many unemployed Chicagoans without overcoats. The lucky ones left their cold flats each morning, poorly clothed and hungry, in search of work. The unlucky ones built fires in empty lots at night, trying to keep warm in their thin and torn jackets. Exhausted by a night of moving around the fire all night to keep from freezing to death, they went off in the endless—and hopeless—task of finding work each morning. Some of the homeless ones had left their families without food or fuel and had come to Chicago to look for work. Lucy Parsons was angry with the society which had permitted many homeless persons to die of hunger and exposure the previous winter; she expected the winter of 1884-1885 to be as bad or worse.

Many bodies had been found floating in the lake the previous winter—the last remains of people who decided it was best to die quickly rather than by slow starvation. Lucy told the tramp who was on the verge of killing himself that he should not act out his misery alone; he should learn the use of explosives and take a few rich people with him. Part of "To Tramps" has frequently been used out of context to do a disservice to her and her cause: "Send forth your petition and let them read it by the red glare of destruction. . . . You need no organization when you make up your mind to present this kind of petition . . . but each of you hungry tramps who read these lines, avail yourselves of those little methods of warfare which Science has placed in the hands of the poor man. . . . *Learn the Use of Explosives!*" Lucy was more vigorous in her support of propaganda by the deed than was Albert; he tended to be a prophet of social revolution, while all the oppression which Lucy suffered for her dark skin and her womanhood went into the anger with which she encouraged the use of dynamite.

They both believed that the wage slaves of 1884 were no better off than the chattel slaves of 1860, and they believed that wage slavery would be defeated in the same way chattel slavery had been defeated. This time, however, a new force was introduced into the configuration: dynamite.

In the spring of 1884, under the leadership of the Progressive Cigar Makers Union No. 15, a number of left-wing unions left the Trades and Labor Assembly and founded the Central Labor Union, which was closely connected to the I.W.P.A. Other tradesmen joined the Central Labor Union: butchers, metal workers, painters, printers, cabinet makers, and others. The C.L.U represented 22 unions, including the 11 largest in the city, had 12,000 members and was larger than the Trades and Labor Assembly. The metal workers formed an armed section after clashes with Pinkertons and other strike breakers in April, 1885, during a successful strike at McCormick Reaper.

The American group of the I.W.P.A. met every Wednesday evening to discuss the coming social revolution, their union activities, their newspaper, and other organizing work. In 1884 they decided to hold a counter-Thanksgiving Day march. Three thousand persons gathered at the *Alarm* and *Arbeiter-Zeitung* offices; they stood in the mud and slush and listened to speeches, then marched through the Loop, then to the Near North Side and back to the newspaper offices. The *Alarm* reported that at a fashionable club on the corner of Washington and Dearborn, "the demonstrators groaned, hissed and hooted at the old and young sprigs of aristocracy who filled the windows and were beholding their future executioners." Although the rhetoric is strong, the demonstrators were simply showing their contempt for the rich; they neither planned nor did anything violent.

The establishment newspapers also saw the "anarchists" as executioners; they used such expressions as "Cutthroats of Society" in their headlines and made fun of the parade saying "Anarchists Complain That Their Thanksgiving Fowl is Too Lean."

Lucy Parsons was heavily influenced by Johann Most's call to "propaganda by the deed," acts of individual terrorism. Her plea "To Tramps" relied on propaganda by the deed. In the spring of 1885 she wrote "Dynamite! The Only Voice the Oppressors of the People Can Understand" for the *Denver Labor Enquirer*. Lizzie Swank wrote a similar article entitled simply "Dynamite." Lucy argued that a dynamite bomb set off in Westminster Abbey would be "a shot fired in the center of civilization, whose echoes are heard around the world, and the idea of dynamite as a weapon of defense against tyranny is put forward half a century. Thus the 'terror' becomes a great educator and agitator. Who but oppressors need tremble at its advent?" She believed a tramp would be justified in blowing up some of the overproduction so that he could get work producing more. The tramp might reason, "They tell us our class must now perish of hunger because we have produced too much to eat, and go naked because there is too much clothing in the world. I will do my part in destroying the 'over-production.' "

She defended violence in class struggle and added "if some tyrants must be put out of the way, it should be looked upon as a blessing, inasmuch as the more oppressors dead, and the fewer alive, the freer will be the world." Anarchists rejoiced that the working class had access to dynamite, she said. Dynamite could defy armies and overturn thrones. "The voice of dynamite is the voice of force, the only voice which tyranny has ever been able to understand. It takes no great rummage through musty pages of history to demonstrate this fact." To her critics she said, "Don't raise your hands in 'holy' horror and exclaim: 'do you Anarchists endorse such guerilla warfare as this?' We 'endorse' nothing, but take the chances for everything, in attempting to abolish the wage-system."

The rhetoric of violence on the part of the ruling class and the Citizens' Association of Chicago was equally threatening; the events of 1877 had proven that guns backed up the threats.

"Give them the rifle diet." Tom Scott, President of Pennsylvania Railroad.

"Hand grenades should be thrown among these union sailors, who are striving to obtain higher wages and less hours. By such treatment they would be taught a valuable lesson, and other strikers could take warning from their fate." *Chicago Times.*

"It is very well to relieve real distress wherever it exists, whether in the city or in the country, but the best meal that can be given a ragged tramp is a leaden one, and it should be supplied in sufficient quantities to satisfy the most voracious appetite." *New York Herald.*

"When a tramp asks you for bread, put strychnine or arsenic on it and he will not trouble you any more, and others will keep out of the neighborhood." *Chicago Tribune.*

When the ruling class advocated arsenic, Lucy advocated arson. When the ruling class said destroy the human being, Lucy said destroy their property.

The ideological position of the Chicago movement was still undefined in 1885, and there were significant differences of opinion between prominent leaders as to whether the movement was Marxist or Bakuninist. William Holmes described the 1883 Pittsburgh Convention as Bakuninist and said that Albert Parsons and August Spies were conscious of this fact. Holmes described Bakunin's ideology as "collectivist," rejecting both authoritarian Marxism or state socialism and the extreme individualism of Proudhon and Warren. He said that the doctrine of "anarchist-communism" was accepted by the Pittsburgh convention and that the Pittsburgh Manifesto reaffirmed Bakunin and the European anarchists' position.

Albert Parsons made it clear that he considered the I.W.P.A. a Marxist, not a Bakuninist organization.

> The I.W.P.A. was not founded by Bakounine. In 1883 delegates from socialistic societies in the United States, Canada and Mexico, assembled in Pittsburgh, Pa., and revived the I.W.P.A. as a part of the original International, founded by the World's Labor Congress, held in London, England, in 1864. The distinctive feature of the manifesto of the Pittsburgh Labor Congress, was opposition to centralized power, abolition of authoritative, compulsory or force government in any form. This is why we were, and are, designated anarchists. . . .

> The I.W.P.A. is *not* in opposition to Marx. So far from it that one "group" in this city as elsewhere, is called by his name. The first publication ever issued by the I.W.P.A. was written by Marx and Engels in English-German.[10]

Bakunin's theories were oriented to "mass" rather than to "class," and the Chicago revolutionaries were oriented to class and trade unions. By 1885 Lucy Parsons held a position which could be called syndicalist. She rejected the need for a state or political authority, but felt that "economic" authority would fall under the jurisdiction of the trade unions. She believed "natural law" would be the underlying principle of a future society. Lucy did not separate "anarchist" from socialist thinkers. She referred to Kropotkin, Bakunin, Proudhon, Marx, Fourier and others as "renowned anarchists."[11]

She believed that no one needed a government to tell him when he was hungry, or a politician to decide when sewers, houses, railroads, canals, or steamboat lines were needed. The people could call meetings and canvass the population to decide when and where improvements were needed. Her theory of a free society was based upon the natural cooperativeness, rather than the competitiveness, of human beings. She argued that under anarchism 85% of criminal offenses would be eliminated, that is, crimes against "private property." "Anarchists have faith enough in the good judgment of the people, in a 'free society' to take care of the rest, and do it, too, without any intermingling of centralized authority, or political mongering." To get rid of the politician "is worth a good sized revolution any time."

On April 28, 1885, Lucy Parsons and Lizzie Swank, carrying the red and black flags, led the I.W.P.A. march on the new Board of Trade building. Inside, the rich dined at $20 a plate. The flyer for the occasion read, "Workmen Bow to Your Gods." Good music was promised and the leaflet continued, "After the ceremonies and sermons the participants will move in a body to the grand temple of *Usury, Gambling* and *Cutthroatism,* where they will serenade the priests and officers of King Mammon and pay honor and respect to the benevolent institute." Lucy Parsons usually referred to the Board of Trade as the Board of Thieves. Lucy and Lizzie became increasingly obnoxious to the authorities, who always recalled that these were the same two women who led the march on the Board of Trade.

As they came around the corner at the Board, the police drove them back. Someone yelled, "Break through!" but the demonstrators retreated to the *Alarm* and *Arbeiter-Zeitung* offices where Albert Parsons addressed them from the second floor window. He challenged the police that the next time they broke up a peaceful demonstration, the marchers would defend themselves with dynamite.

On Monday, May 4, 1885, troops marched into Lemont, Illinois, where quarry workers were on strike for a uniform scale of wages and restoration of last year's rates. Albert Parsons went to Lemont to report for the *Alarm*. It was alleged that the people had thrown rocks at the soldiers. "But the soldiery opened fire upon the people and killed two men on the spot, and bayoneted and stabbed two others, who have died from their wounds since," he wrote. When the American section of the I.W.P.A. met to condemn the militia's actions, the *Tribune* reported, "Citizeness Parsons, however, had a plan at once startling, unique, and redolent with gore." She was supposed to have made her now famous statement at that meeting:

Let every dirty, lousy tramp arm himself with a revolver or knife and lay in wait on the steps of the palaces of the rich and stab or shoot their owners as they come out. Let us kill them without mercy, and let it be a war of extermination and without pity. Let us devastate the avenues where the wealthy live as Sheridan devastated the beautiful valley of the Shenandoah.

She burned with anger at the murders of starving workers. On May 20, the American group resolved "to arm and organize into a company and become a part of the military organization now forming throughout the city" and "to establish a school on chemistry where the manufacture and use of explosives would be taught." They had Most's *Manual for Revolutionary Warfare,* if a German comrade would translate it for them.

Lucy and Albert's press was consistently bad. The *Inter-Ocean* wrote about one lakefront meeting, "Dynamite-eating Parsons and his wife were there and so were a lot of the rag, tag, and bobtail of the Communists from the Clark and Randolph St. resorts." At another lakefront meeting, Lucy was described as "a very determined looking negress" who put down her "anarchist sucklings" long enough to speak. Albert or Lucy or both were speaking on the lakefront every Sunday afternoon when the weather even halfway permitted it. They drew crowds of 1000 often, and up to 5000 people sometimes came to hear the I.W.P.A. speakers.

Mother Jones sometimes came to the lakefront to hear the I.W.P.A. speakers, but she thought the "anarchists" were too violent.

The press intensified the notion that anarchists were violent in the spring and summer of 1885. A simple meeting to protest the Russian-American extradition treaty was turned into a cloak and dagger affair.[12] The *New York Herald* alleged that the meeting featured the prominent "anarchists" Lucy Parsons, William Holmes, and Albert Currlin as a cover for a secret meeting in which all Chicago anarchists supposedly agreed to burn all their records, disband their organization, and re-form into cells in which each member would know only two other members—for the purpose of assassination and terror.

But it was not the "anarchists," it was the police who committed the real violence in Chicago that summer. Captain John Bonfield of the Chicago police force achieved notoriety for his brutality during the Westside streetcarmen's strike. On the morning of July 2, Bonfield viciously attacked several innocent people who were standing near Western Ave. and Madison St. One man was standing on that corner waiting for a wagon to ride downtown to his business; without warning Bonfield attacked him with his club. This victim saw Bonfield strike other people the same way. One was a 65 year old man who was standing on the corner when Bonfield ordered him to "fall back;" before the man could move, the police captain's club had smashed into his head, and he had to be taken to a drug store to have the wound dressed. A butcher on W. Madison St. was standing at the door of his shop when police ordered him to move on; he hesitated only a moment, and they threw him into the paddy wagon, leaving his store unlocked. The police also assaulted a brakeman and an engineer of the Chicago, Minneapolis, and St. Paul Railroad.

The next day, eight gas company employees were digging a ditch in the vicinity of a crowd of strike sympathizers. The crowd threw the loose dirt from the ditch onto the streetcar tracks. Bonfield ordered the ditchdiggers arrested. He shoved them into the paddy wagon and when one man stuck his head out of the wagon to ask someone to take care of his tools, Bonfield beat him and the man next to him senseless. Neither of the victims ever fully recovered from their injuries, and one died in January of 1889 from complications arising from his injuries; he had never been able to go back to work.

One thousand citizens who lived in the area of W. Madison St. signed a petition to the mayor asking for Bonfield's removal from the police force; Mayor Harrison agreed that Bonfield should be removed. However, several important men intervened on Bonfield's behalf, and he was promoted to Inspector.[13]

Other acts of violence on the part of Pinkertons, industrial spies, and police had roused the working class leaders to advocate forceable resistance. In 1885 Pinkertons fired into a crowd near the McCormick Reaper factory and killed several people. Four of the Pinkerton men were indicted for murder. The prosecutors were not interested in prosecuting the case; they allowed it to be continued a number of times, wore out the witnesses, and freed the murderers.

In September, 1885, the *Chicago Daily News* published a series of articles about corruption in the Des Plaines St. police station, whose commanding officers were Captains Bonfield and

Ward. The two officers were discovered to be running an extortion and bribery ring. They were involved in gambling in the district, and they forced immunity payments from prostitutes.

The summer of 1885 Albert Parsons went to Missouri, Kansas, and Nebraska, setting up I.W.P.A. sections. Lucy stayed in Chicago with the children, trying to keep the *Alarm* solvent. She was busy day and night.

Lucy Parsons and Lizzie Swank were two of the four women who carried the red flags from the Loop to Ogden's Grove on the northwest side of the city where the socialists held their picnics. The five miles were covered with the women gaily leading the way, followed by working men and women who brought their sack lunches for the festivities. Lucy spoke at the Labor Day festivities there in September.

In the fall of 1885 Albert Parsons and Michael Schwab went to the coalfields of Ohio and Pennsylvania to organize I.W.P.A. groups—the scene of the bitter Hocking Valley strike the year before. While they were gone, the I.W.P.A. held another Thanksgiving Day demonstration; Lucy Parsons and August Spies led the rally. In another part of the city, the militia was drilling to show its strength.

Lucy Parsons stepped to the front of the crowd, her black eyes flashing, her cloak wrapped about her to keep off the chill wind, and her dark face nearly blue with the cold. She began, "Fellow wage slaves: Why is the militia drilling—doing riot drill in time of peace? Are the money mongers so frightened over their evil deeds that they fear they will soon reap the fire of social revolution? Do they propose to shoot working people down in cold blood for no more crime than that they are hungry—their children sick?"

This time the marchers went to the South Side, along Prairie Avenue, ringing doorbells and insulting the rich. As they passed former ambassador to France Washburne's home, they pulled the doorbell, groaned and made cat-calls. They despised the man who had collaborated with the executioners of 10,000 Paris Communards.

Mother Jones thought the militant young Lucy Parsons too violent. "I thought the parade an insane move on the part of the anarchists, as it only served to make feeling more bitter. . . . It . . . only served to increase the employers' fear, to make the police more savage, and the public less sympathetic to the real distress of the workers." Mother Jones foresaw that police brutality would intensify and that the rulers of Chicago would use such demonstrations and incidents to generate a climate of hostility against all demands of the working class.[14]

Lucy's reputation spread. A Canton, Ohio, reporter quoted "To Tramps," called her a "veritable Louise Michel," and said, "She is a wonderfully strong writer and it is said she can excel her husband in making a fiery speech." Excelling Albert Parsons was no easy task. He was an eloquent and charismatic speaker who could hold an audience spell-bound for three hours as he recited statistics, quoted poetry and roused his listeners to rage over working conditions and the exploitation of labor. He was handsome and well-dressed with a carefully trimmed mustache; he kept his prematurely gray hair black with boot black. Lucy was intense and fiery; her earnestness converted many persons. Her dark complexion often contrasted with an all-white dress. She was pleased to be compared to Louise Michel, the "red virgin" of the Paris commune, and she was ready to die a martyr as the Communards had done. She would feel, as Michel had, that it was a great injustice to a revolutionary to deny her the heroic death of a martyr, because she was a woman. Lizzie Swank agreed.

Lizzie Swank, William Holmes, Lucy and Albert Parsons were the core group of writers for the *Alarm,* who expected and looked forward to American martyrs for freedom. Any of the four would gladly sacrifice his or her life in the name of economic freedom.

In November, 1885, Lizzie Swank and William Holmes were married, cementing their political compatibility into comradeship and struggle which would last until their deaths over 40 years later. Because of poor health, William Holmes had moved to Geneva, Illinois, in October, 1885, and opened a school of shorthand and elocution. Lizzie joined him there after their marriage.

An impassioned young woman, 32 year old Lucy Parsons had much to say about the injustices of her society. On occasion she used her vivid imagination to structure what she knew about Christian civilization. The childhood fable of Santa Claus caught her fancy for Christmas 1885. Her childhood illusions long gone, she decided to use a fictional letter from the gentle old man.

On his Christmas travels, he stopped on an idyllic island; there he met the natives, known in Christian society as heathens. A few years before a good Christian gentleman had been shipwrecked on their island. For the islanders' kindness to him, he arranged for them to come as his guests to the United States.

Their eyes were opened to steamships and trains, to the best of modern technology. They were wined and dined. But suddenly—at a lavish dinner in their honor at a downtown hotel—an "apparition" appeared. A young mother of five children who had no food or fuel for her family.

Accusingly, she pointed her finger at the elegant gentleman who was preparing a toast to the "heathen" visitors. The room seemed suspended in time. "That man is a murderer!" she shrieked. "My husband was crushed under the machinery in his factory. Now my children have nothing to eat!" The guests looked about with embarrassment. "Who let that woman in?" shouted the host.

Santa Claus reported that the heathens were more than happy to return to their beautiful island. They could not understand a society with such wonderful machines, which permitted a woman and her children to starve.

Lucy, too, was a "heathen" by the standards of white society. She had lost touch with the life of her Indian ancestors; her black forebears had been torn from the lush coast of Africa. White society had taught her the teachings of Jesus; she had learned about the equality of all people and how difficult it was for a rich man to enter the Kingdom of Heaven. But she was soon re-educated to how the rich used religion to justify the empires they had built.

Lucy's significant *Alarm* articles included "Our Civilization. Is it Worth Saving?" and "The Factory Child. Their Wrongs Portrayed and Their Rescue Demanded." Her son was now six and her daughter four, and she saw children not much older going into the shops and factories to supplement their families' incomes.

"The Negro. Let Him Leave Politics to the Politician and Prayers to the Preacher," published in the *Alarm* on April 3, 1886, is her most significant statement on the position of black people in society. She was responding to the massacre of 13 black people in Carrollton, Mississippi. Nearly every day the papers carried accounts of negroes who were lynched. Sometimes the violence against black people included mass murder.

In Carrollton, Mississippi, a young former state representative who had lost a recent election for the state senate (black voters numbered 300 more than white in the district), got into an argument with two black men. In the fray that followed, the white politician was slightly wounded. The blacks were jailed.

The incident first precipitated two lynchings. A lynching party went to the jail to get Ed and Charles Brown, who had fought with Lawyer James Liddell. But they had been moved, so the vigilantes lynched a young black boy instead.[15]

Shortly thereafter, a mob broke into the nearby jail at Monroe, Louisiana, and lynched a black man who had been jailed for defending a black woman from assault by a group of white men.

Ed and Charles Brown filed an affidavit against Liddell, charging that Liddell had assaulted them with intent to kill. On March 17, the Brown brothers, their witnesses, and black spectators were in the Carroll County courtroom for a hearing on the affidavit. Suddenly a mob of 50 to 100 whites rode up on horseback, dismounted, walked into the courtroom, and opened fire on the blacks. They systematically gunned down 13 black people; seven others escaped through the windows. Then the mob hopped back on their horses and rode leisurely away, knowing that no one would ever identify them or bring them to trial.

Charles and Ed Brown and 11 others were left dead. This was white racists' answers to black people who dared file an affidavit against a "leading" white citizen. The brothers' father had been killed by a white editor in 1871, because he had stood up for human dignity for blacks. The whites in the area expected that the massacre would put an end to rebellious blacks, as their leaders had been killed in the courtroom. No arrests were made, as no one could "identify" the attackers. This was Mississippi "justice."

Congressmen demanded an investigation into the massacre. The *Chicago Tribune,* a Republican paper, blamed the attack on Democrats. Lucy Parsons attributed the "awful massacre" to the fact that the blacks were poor. "Are there any so stupid as to believe these outrages have been, are being and will be heaped upon the Negro because he is black?" she wrote. "Not at all. It is because he is *poor*. It is because he is dependent. Because he is poorer as a class than his white wage-slave brother of the North."

Lucy believed that black people would have to work out their own liberation, and she offered some advice. She encouraged blacks to join "those who are striving for economic freedom" and she advised the friends of the massacre victims to take revenge. "You are not absolutely defenseless. For the torch of the incendiary, which has been known to show murderers and tyrants the danger line, beyond which they may not venture with impunity, cannot be wrested from you."

Lucy Parsons argued that all social ills stemmed from economic oppression. She argued that the oppression of black people was based on their economic position first as chattel slaves and then as wage slaves, and she argued that women were oppressed, because they were economically dependent upon men. Lucy Parsons recognized that racism and sexism are used to divide the working class and to reduce the living standard of the entire working class by providing a cheap or surplus labor force depending upon the demands of capital. She could see that ethnic groups were pitted against each other, that women were pitted against men, in fierce competition for jobs. However, Lucy Parsons did not see that racism and sexism have histories and existences independent of the economic structure of society, and she never had the chance to see racism and sexism under any other social system than the American capitalist system. She erroneously believed that the abolition of capitalism would automatically produce racial and sexual equality.

Lucy Parsons internalized the racism of white society to the extent that she denied her own black ancestry. Her burden of self-denial is a terrible indictment of a racist society. Her denial of her blackness, and therefore of her oppression as a black woman, made it exceedingly difficult for her to analyze her social position in relation to anything but her class status.

When Lucy wrote her article on "The Negro," the great movement for the eight hour day was rapidly building. The events of the following month would give her little time to think about racism for years.

After the economic crash in the early 1880's, Albert and Lucy Parsons took little interest in the eight hour day. The International Working People's Association turned its attention to the unemployed who had to concern themselves with immediate problems rather than the prospect of jobs eventually resulting from a shorter work day.

At the same time, however, the Federation of Organized Trades and Labor Unions of the United States and Canada (FOOTALU, which had been founded in 1881) met in Chicago in 1884 and set May 1, 1886, as the date for general strikes to win the eight hour day.

FOOTALU was a relatively small organization compared to the Knights of Labor or the Central Labor Union of Chicago, in which the I.W.P.A. had a strong influence. FOOTALU approached the Knights to ask for an endorsement of the eight hour strikes but was refused. Neither the Knights nor the Central Labor Union supported the movement. But because of a series of strikes by the Knights in 1884 and 1885, particularly the successful 1885 Union Pacific railroad strike led by Joseph Buchanan, many workers believed the Knights were organizing for the eight hour day. The demand spread like wildfire.

Workers who had never heard of FOOTALU rushed to join the Knights of Labor. The Knights' membership rose from slightly over 100,000 in July, 1885, to over 700,000 in July, 1886.

During the same period August Spies estimated that 10-12,000 people had joined the I.W.P.A. The organization had over 21,000 regular subscribers to its newspapers. Albert Parsons said that by May, 1886, there were at least 1300 I.W.P.A. members in Chicago organized into 17 sections. He claimed that the I.W.P.A. had organized sections in 97 cities and industrial centers outside Chicago.

In December, 1885, the *Alarm* had had this to say about the eight hour movement:

We of the International are frequently asked why we do not give our active support to the proposed eight-hour movement. . . . We answer: Because we will not compromise. Either our position that capitalists have no right to the exclusive ownership of life is a true one, or it is not. If we are correct, then to concede the point that the capitalists have the right to eight hours of our labor is more than a compromise; it is a virtual concession that the wage system is right.

Lucy Parsons had little use for the eight hour movement. "I say to the wage class: Strike not for a few cents more an hour, because the price of living will be raised faster still, but strike for all you earn [produce], be content with nothing less."

In a March, 1886, interview, Albert Parsons said,

The rate of wages . . . is regulated by what it takes to be one [a wage laborer]. A laborer is hired to do a day's work. The first two hours' labor of the ten he reproduces the equivalent of his wage; the other eight hours the employer gets for nothing. . . . Fewer hours mean more pay, the producers possessing and consuming a larger share of their own product.

Reduced hours would melt the wages or profit system out of existence and usher in the cooperative or free-labor system. I do not believe that capital will quietly or peaceably permit the economic emancipation of their wageslaves. The capitalists of the world will force the workers into armed revolution. Socialists point out this fact and warn the workingmen to prepare for the inevitable.

He believed that winning eight hours would mean that the capitalists would introduce labor-saving machinery to replace the workers. Then they would have to strike for six hours a day, and so on, for the same reason they struck for eight.

From 1879 to 1886 Albert Parsons believed that the peaceful reduction of the hours of labor, full employment, and payment according to the value of the labor product instead of a subsistence wage would automatically cooperatize the means of production and consumption. But by 1886 he had come to believe that this change would not come peaceably; all the evidence tended to substantiate his belief.

In March, members of the Knights of Labor on the Gould lines in the southwest declared a general strike, because several of their members had been fired for union activity. Terence Powderly attempted to arbitrate with Jay Gould; he thought he had an agreement from Gould and issued a back to work order. Gould denied that they'd reached any agreement, and the order was rescinded. Finally Powderly accepted terms which were nothing short of defeat for the workers and ordered them back to work; they defied his orders. The strike lasted two months, and the railroad bosses didn't hesitate to use violence against the workers.

Grand Master Workman Powderly was scared half to death by the militance of the southwest railroad strike and the organizing successes of the eight hour movement. The man who had been elected mayor of Scranton, Pennsylvania, on the Greenback ticket had little in common with the hundreds of thousands of uneducated and dirty workingmen who were joining the Knights. These men didn't share his concerns about legislation; they wanted eight hours NOW!

In March, Powderly issued a secret circular suspending the organization of new Knights Assemblies and stating that the Knights did not endorse the eight hour strikes. "No assembly of the Knights of Labor must strike for the eight hour system on May 1st under the impression that they are obeying orders from headquarters, for such an order was not, and will not be given." Powderly's order was ignored.

He urged the Knights not to strike, hoping to stem the growth of the "anarchist" movement. "Strikes are often the forerunners of lawless actions. One blow brings another, and if a single act of ours encourages the Anarchist element we must meet with the antagonism of the church. . . . I am ashamed to meet with clergymen and others to tell them that our order is composed of law abiding, intelligent men, while the next dispatch brings the news of some petty boycott or strike." He concluded, "Strikes must be avoided. Boycotts must be avoided."

Powderly wanted to be a labor statesman, not a militant organizer. He could barely keep from drowning in the rip tide of the eight hour movement.

In Chicago the eight hour movement was led by prominent members of the Knights of Labor. George Schilling was especially prominent in the movement and provided it with a socialist perspective. Joseph Gruenhut joined him. Robert Nelson, a machinist, was president and Dr. J. H. Randall vice president of the Chicago Eight Hour Association. Nelson became Master Workman of District Assembly 24 of the K. of L. in Chicago. Liberals like Judge Prendergast, Professor William Salter, and Mayor Carter Harrison participated in the movement for the eight hour day.[16]

In March, the Central Labor Union, I.W.P.A., *Alarm,* and *Arbeiter-Zeitung* all endorsed the May 1 general strikes for the eight hour day. The movement had the support of the working class, and the I.W.P.A. did not want to isolate itself. The workers quickly adopted the new slogans of the C.L.U. and the I.W.P.A.: "Eight Hours Work for Ten Hours Pay" and "Eight Hours With No Reduction in Pay." The I.W.P.A. members began signing people up in the Knights of Labor, of which they were also members, and in the Central Labor Union; they did not recruit to the I.W.P.A.

Lucy Parsons, Lizzie Swank-Holmes, and Sarah E. Ames began organizing sewing women into the Knights of Labor to strike for the eight hour day. Sarah Ames became Master Workman of Women's Assembly 1789, and Lizzie Holmes became statistician of the Knights of Labor Women's Assembly. Lucy Parsons planned to travel to St. Louis, St. Joseph, Kansas City and Leavenworth for the organizing drive, but she became ill under the strain of poverty, overwork, and little sleep, and could not go. She postponed her trip until after May 1; Albert Parsons planned to go to San Francisco as soon as the eight hour day was won.

Albert Parsons, August Spies, Samuel Fielden, Michael Schwab, and Oscar Neebe became very active in the eight hour movement. They organized cloakmakers, butchers, grocery clerks, and painters for the eight hour day.

At the end of March, the city announced that all city employees would get eight hours on May 1. Manufacturers began to concede the eight hour day. The packinghouse workers won eight hours.

On Sunday, April 25, 1886, the Central Labor Union held a massive rally for the eight hour day on the lakefront. Albert Parsons called the meeting to order, saying that its purpose was to achieve the eight hour day on May 1. "If the capitalists, by the lockout, raise the black flag of starvation against the producers of wealth, then the producers will raise the banner of liberty, equality, and fraternity." Parsons led three cheers for the eight hour day. Michael Schwab, Oscar Neebe, Sam Fielden, August Spies, and John A. Henry spoke.

Banners in English and German read "Eight Hours—Working Time May 1, 1886," "Liberty without Equality is a Lie," "Private Capital Represents Stolen Labor," "Our Civilization—the Bullet and the Policeman's Club," and "The Brewer Works All Day and Night and Hardly Gets His Rest."

By May 1 the syndicalists of the C.L.U. and the I.W.P.A. led the movement in Chicago. These men had been working class leaders for years, and they could bring out tremendous crowds.

The Haymarket Police Riot

By May 1, 1886, several hundred thousand workers had received the eight-hour day. Eight Hours appeared to be the tide of the times, which could not be turned back. Workers had marched in the streets for weeks singing "Eight Hours":

We mean to make things over, we are tired of toil for naught,
With but bare enough to live upon, and never an hour for thought;
We want to feel the sunshine, and we want to smell the flowers,
We are sure that God has will'd it, and we mean to have eight hours.
We're summoning our forces from shipyard, shop and mill,
Eight hours for work, eight hours for rest, eight hours for what we will!
Eight hours for work, eight hours for rest, eight hours for what we will!

The *Alarm* published its own song for the eight hour movement:

Come! sing me a song! that's sterling and strong,
No more of your mamby pamby verses,
Let dynamite down with the thing that is wrong,
No blessing be given to evil—but curses.
Act out, act out,
While your voices shout,
Iniquity to hell we'll leave her,
Into hell be he crammed,
With his "public be damned,"
Who pays a dollar a day for labor.
Come! sing me a song! that tells me of hate
And scorn for wrong where'er it be lurking,
Who'd live off the fruits of his neighbor's working,
Of death to the loafer, the thief the same fate,
Send out! send out!
An electric shout
And shock, my every honest neighbor,

> That shall powder the bones
> And stifle the drones
> Which "toil not nor spin" in the hive of Labor.

Lucy marched at the head of processions leading these songs, her dark hands motioning the crowds forward, her dark face full of the fire of indignation against capital.

May First dawned bright and sunny in Chicago. The eight-hour fever, spring fever, and a holiday spirit mingled in the air. The city had been shut down by the workers, and the factories were empty. On Michigan Avenue nearly 80,000 people gathered for the great parade. Leading members of the Citizens' Association watched throughout the day, wondering how they were going to save the city from "communism." If they could blame Albert Parsons and August Spies for any violence which might occur, perhaps they could break the movement. The *Chicago Mail* snarled,

> There are two dangerous ruffians at large in this city; two skulking cowards who are trying to create trouble. One of them is named Parsons; the other is named Spies. . . .
>
> These two fellows have been at work fomenting disorder for the past ten years. They should have been driven out of the city long ago. . . .
>
> They have no love for the eight-hour movement, . . . They are looking for riot and plunder. . . . .
>
> Mark them for today. Keep them in view. Hold them personally responsible for any trouble that occurs. *Make an example of them if trouble does occur.*

While the Citizens' Association thought about how to rid the city of "anarchism," Lucy and Albert Parsons led the thousands of singing demonstrators up Michigan Avenue. Lulu held her father's hand, and Albert held his mother's hand as they skipped along, filled with excitement.

May 1 ended peacefully in Chicago, as it had begun. None of the predictions of violence had been fulfilled. Albert Parsons left for Cincinnati to speak there. Lucy Parsons, Lizzie Holmes, and Sarah Ames remained in Chicago to work with the sewing women.

On May 3, the women's organizing paid off. Lizzie Holmes led a march of several hundred sewing women, whom the *Chicago Tribune* called "Shouting Amazons." "Between 300 and 400 girls and women were affected with a malignant form of the eight-hour malady yesterday morning," the paper reported. The marchers came running along Sedgwick and Division streets; they ran into one shop after another jubilantly calling their fellow workers to come out and march. Even the *Tribune* conceded that the marching women looked tired and overworked. Their "exterior denoted incessant toil, and in many instances worn faces and threadbare clothing bearing evidence of a struggle for an uncomfortable existence." The women were glad for even one holiday. They left behind the sign which said "No talking or laughing," and they laughed and talked and sang as they marched along.

At the end of the march they signed up to join the Knights of Labor. One women exclaimed, "We'll never give in. Never, never, until we get our demand. We want eight hours work with ten hours pay!"

On May 3, August Spies was invited to address a meeting of lumber shovers on Black Road near the McCormick Reaper works. The men at McCormick's had been locked out since February, and there had been some ugly incidents already. As Spies was finishing his speech, the police and Pinkertons fired shots. The strikebreakers were leaving the plant, and the detectives, Pinkertons, and police charged the pickets. At least one man was killed and up to six deaths were reported.

Spies rushed back to the *Arbeiter-Zeitung* and wrote a blistering attack on the police. The next morning—May 4—Adolph Fischer, a young militant compositor on the *Arbeiter-Zeitung* asked him if he would speak at a meeting that night to protest the police brutality at McCormick's. Spies agreed. But when he saw the leaflet for the meeting, he had second thoughts. It read, "Workingmen Arm Yourselves and Appear in Full Force!" He refused to speak at a meeting which had been advertised this way, but the compositors insisted that only a few "Revenge" leaflets had been printed, and Spies agreed to speak if the line were struck.

The same morning, Albert Parsons returned from Cincinnati, exhausted from his work there. He hurried home and collapsed into bed for a nap.

After the women's march on the 3rd, Lizzie Holmes had gone back to Geneva in the suburbs, where she and William had gotten a little bungalow. But the suburbs were boring and bourgeois, and she complained to Lucy about her new neighborhood; she wanted to be back in the noise and dirt and squalor of the city, where the action was.[1] The morning of May 4, Lucy urgently telegraphed her to come back into the city for a meeting she had scheduled that night about organizing the sewing women.

When Albert woke up rested from his nap, Lucy told him about the sewing women's meeting and he agreed to go. Lizzie joined them for dinner at home, and then the three adults and two children set off for the sewing girls meeting about 7:30 P.M. Albert was exuberant over his trip to Cincinnati; the women were elated with their recent successes, and the feeling of optimism filled the air. Albert mimicked a pompous trade union official he had met, and they were all laughing when they reached the corner of Randolph and Halsted streets. Two reporters met them and asked if they had any news. Albert said he didn't; he'd just gotten back to Chicago that day. They asked if there was going to be a meeting that night and he replied, "Yes, I guess so." They asked if he was going to speak at the Haymarket and he replied that he had another meeting. They joked around a little, and the reporter asked Parsons if he had any dynamite. Lucy laughed and interjected, "He's a very dangerous looking man, isn't he?" then took his arm, and they all ran for the street car and their meeting at the *Alarm* office.

Four or five women and twelve to fifteen men were already there, members of the American section of the I.W.P.A. Their meeting started at 8:30. Lucy had spent $5 to print up leaflets for the sewing women's demonstration. The American section voted to reimburse her. The section had just named Lizzie Swank-Holmes to head the sewing women's drive, when Balthazar Rau, the business manager of the *Arbeiter-Zeitung,* hurried over from the Haymarket meeting to ask Albert Parsons and Sam Fielden to speak there.

They adjourned and left for the mass meeting, which had gotten off to a slow start. The organizers had hoped for 20,000 people to crowd Haymarket Square. Instead only two or three thousand showed up. August Spies was just finishing his speech. Albert Parsons followed him. He referred to the depression, to its causes. He discussed the recent history of labor struggles, the 1877 railroad strikes, his travels through the eastern mining regions, and the eight-hour movement. He had facts and figures at hand to substantiate his accusations and assertions. He said the worker received only 15¢ out of every dollar. He challenged the ruling class to drive himself and Spies from the city, as the *Chicago Mail* had proposed that morning. "I am not here, fellow-workmen, for the purpose of inciting anybody, but to tell the truth, and to state the facts as they actually exist, though it should cost me my life." He knew there were persons in the city who would love to see him a corpse. He remembered the threats against his life in 1877. He wanted his speech to be as clear and to the point as possible, leaving no grounds for anyone to charge him with inciting to riot. He had talked for about forty-five minutes when he stepped down, and Samuel Fielden climbed up on the wagon which was being used as a makeshift platform. Then Albert joined Lucy and Lizzie and the children on another wagon.

Fielden talked about the law and the failure of legislation to meet the needs of workers—those without property. "The law is your enemy," he said. "It turns your brothers out on the wayside, and has degraded them until they have lost the last vestige of humanity." He continued, "I tell you war has been declared on us. People have been shot. . . . What matters it whether you kill yourselves with work . . . or die on the battlefield resisting the enemy?"

The sky had grown heavy and threatened a spring storm. Little Lulu and Albert were getting cold and tired; they wanted to go home. A few drops of cold rain splashed down. Their father suggested moving the meeting to Zepf's hall, on the corner, but a meeting was already going on there. Fielden assured Parsons that he was almost done.

Lucy, Lizzie, Albert and the children then walked the half block to Zepf's Hall to wait for the end of the meeting. Mayor Carter Harrison, who had come to the meeting to be sure that there was no disturbance, left at about 10:00 P.M., stopping at the Des Plaines St. Police Station to tell Captain Bonfield that the meeting was peaceable and that he should send his 176 policemen home.

Bonfield and Ward, known for their brutality in the 1885 streetcarmen's strike and for the corruption of the Des Plaines

St. Station, waited until the mayor had left to defy his orders. Bonfield may have been acting under direct orders from the Citizens' Association. He may have been paid by some wealthy industrialist to disrupt the meeting. Or he may have done it for the personal pleasure of cracking some radical skulls.

Almost as soon as Mayor Harrison had left, Bonfield marched the men into the square, and Ward ordered the crowd to disperse.

Fielden replied that it was a peaceable meeting, and that, in any event, he was nearly done. As he stepped down from the speakers' wagon, an unknown person hurled a bomb into the ranks of the police. The bomb came without warning, only a slight glow of the fuse in the air. It landed with a thud and detonated with an incredible blast.

Mayor Harrison heard the explosion at home where he was getting ready for bed. The Parsons heard it from Zepf's Hall. Albert was standing by the window. The women were sitting nearby watching the sleepy children, and yawning themselves, after a long, hard day. They were enjoying a beer with Adolph Fischer. For a moment the glare of the bomb lighted the room; a hail of shots followed. Some hit the outside of the hall. Albert hurried back to the table. "What is it?" asked Lizzie. "I do not know; maybe the Illinois regiments have brought up their Gatling gun," Albert replied. Frantic people came scrambling in; they all ran to a room at the back of the hall and shut the door. Total darkness filled the small, stuffy room, crowded with frightened people who wondered what had happened. Finally, they opened the door and cautiously went outside. Everything was quiet. No policemen were around.

Lucy, Lizzie, Albert, and the two children started up the Des Plaines St. viaduct for home, and Thomas Brown joined them. Lizzie urged Albert to leave Chicago. He hesitated but Lizzie urged him to grasp the chance to collect his thoughts— to choose the time and place to defend himself. At last he consented. Brown loaned him a $5 gold piece, and they decided Lucy shouldn't go to the train station with him. That would be too conspicuous.

"Kiss me Lucy. We don't know when we'll meet again." They held each other and kissed, knowing that some big change was about to occur in their lives, but not yet knowing what.

Then the two editors of the *Alarm* walked to the train station together. Lizzie bought the ticket, hoping that Albert would not be recognized. He insisted she take the change from the $5 to Lucy, knowing that she would need it for food. After the train had left, Lizzie returned to Lucy's place for the night.

William Holmes was waiting when Albert arrived in Geneva early the next morning, May 5. They carefully read the morning papers, trying to determine what was happening in Chicago. Holmes went out shortly after noon. Wild rumors abounded. The city had been set on fire and half burned. Anarchists had destroyed City Hall. Socialists and sympathizers were being massacred. Everyone scowled and glared at William Holmes; they knew he was a radical.[2] By the time William returned, Albert Parsons had written a scorching editorial for the next issue of the *Alarm,* an issue which would never appear. He denounced "the unprovoked and unlawful attack upon the Haymarket meeting by Bonfield and his uniformed ruffians." Neither dreamed that Lizzie, Lucy, and the editors and staff of the *Alarm* and *Arbeiter-Zeitung* had already been arrested and the *Alarm* completely suppressed.

The rumors of widespread destruction and massacre convinced Albert Parsons that the insurrection had begun; he wanted to return to Chicago and fight. "He did not doubt but that every Socialist in Chicago would be massacred, yet he hesitated not in making his choice—he would die with them," wrote Holmes. He calmed down, and Holmes persuaded him to wait for the news the next day; the two men agreed that if the rumors were confirmed, they would go to Chicago and join their wives on the barricades.

Albert thought Lucy might even be dead already, a martyr in the armed clash of social revolution. "He already thought himself alone in the world. He never doubted for a moment that, if the occasion required it, his heroic wife would sacrifice her life in the struggle for economic liberty." Ten years later Holmes could still hear "the startling rumors of wide-spread revolt in Chicago," and see "the pale set face, the flashing eyes and the impatient gestures of my comrade as he pleads the necessity of his immediate return to take his part in the revolution which he believes is already begun."

Back in Chicago, on May 5, 1886, events rushed forward.

Public opinion—fired by the daily papers—concluded that "anarchists" had thrown the bomb. The bombing was engineered by August Spies, Sam Fielden and A. R. Parsons who were trying "to incite a large mass meeting to riot and bloodshed," read a typical article.

However, the *Tribune* first reported:

Immediately after the explosion, the police pulled their revolvers and fired on the crowd. An incessant fire was kept up for nearly two minutes, and at least 250 shots were fired. The air was filled with bullets. The crowd ran up the streets and alleys and were fired on by the now thoroughly enraged police. . . . As the firing ceased they ventured forth, and a few officers opened fire on them. . . . When the firing had stopped, the air was filled with groans and shrieks. "O God! I'm shot." "Please take me home." "Take me to the hospital" . . .

Goaded to madness, the police were in the condition of mind which permitted of no resistance, and in a measure they were as dangerous as any mob, for they were blinded by passion and unable to distinguish between the peaceable citizen and the Nihilist assassin. For many blocks from the Des Plaines Station companies and squads of officers cleared the streets and mercilessly clubbed all who demurred at the order to go.

A telegraph pole in the middle of the scene of the riot was filled with bullet holes, all coming from the side of the police. The pole was removed within 24 hours "to improve service" and it was never again located. In a *Tribune* interview on June 27th an unnamed police officer stated,

I also know it to be a fact that a very large number of the police were wounded by each other's revolvers. . . . There was a blunder on the part of the man who commanded the police on the night of the Haymarket murders, or this fearful slaughter would not have occurred. Bonfield made the blunder, and is held responsible for its effects by every man injured there. . . . The whole thing was hasty and ill-advised, arising out of Bonfield's desire to distinguish himself.

The report which he recently made, six weeks after the riot, is laughed at by every man on the force who has any idea of the facts in the matter. He speaks of reorganizing the companies immediately after the bomb exploded, when every-

one knows that no such reorganization or "closing up" occurred. It was every man for himself, and while some got
two or three squares away the rest emptied their revolvers,
mainly into each other.

However, it became the commonly accepted view that the bomb
was the *signal* for the crowd to open fire on the police. A typical report: "The mob appeared crazed with a frantic desire for
blood, and holding its ground, poured volley after volley into
the midst of the officers."

The evidence demonstrates that it was the police, not the
"anarchists," who were the perpetrators of violence on the night
of May 4, 1886. Bonfield had been heard to say on several
occasions that he was waiting to get the anarchists alone, without the women and children, and that then he would make
short work of them. Chris Spies was wounded the night of
May 4 as he held off an assailant who attempted to assassinate
his brother August. Samuel Fielden was shot in the leg. The
Tribune reported, "There were several shots fired the night of
May 4 at a socialist who resembled A. R. Parsons, whom the
police were very anxious to make a target of."

The march of the police into Haymarket Square was probably a carefully orchestrated plot to create turmoil and confusion
in which the radical leaders could be gunned down. But the
bomb so disoriented the police that they were unsuccessful in
murdering their intended victims that night. August Spies,
Albert Parsons, and Samuel Fielden remained alive.

At least seven workers died of their injuries, and an untold
number were hurt. Many did not report their wounds or seek
medical treatment for fear of reprisals.[3]

One police officer, Mathias Degan died almost instantane-
ously. Six others died in the next six weeks.

Mayor Harrison, who had always insisted on the full rights
of socialists, anarchists, and communists to say whatever they
pleased, now issued a proclamation banning public meetings
and marches, citing the dangerous atmosphere in the city as
his reason. The Mayor came under heavy attack for having permitted such revolutionaries as Albert and Lucy Parsons to say
what they wanted, and now his conservative enemies blamed
him for the bombing.

Albert Parsons was sought as a fugitive.

Lucy Parsons and Lizzie Holmes had not slept well the night of May 4th; they got up early and hurried to the *Alarm* office. The police hurried to the *Alarm* and *Arbeiter-Zeitung* offices early that morning, too. They arrested August Spies and Michael Schwab on their first raid. The two women went back to work on the next issue of the *Alarm* as soon as the raiders had gone. Oscar Neebe heard about the arrests and hurried over, determined that the working people's papers would come out. Lucy Parsons and Lizzie Holmes quickly explained to him what had happened. Just as he and Lucy were beginning to discuss their situation, they heard the heavy tread of the law on the stairway again, and in rushed some of the roughest looking toughs that Neebe had ever seen, all detectives of the city of Chicago. Mayor Harrison was with them.

Harrison demanded, "Who is the manager of this paper here?" Neebe knew Harrison and asked him what the matter was.

"I want to have this thing stopped. There won't be any more inflammatory articles allowed in this paper." Neebe assured him he would read everything that went into the *Arbeiter-Zeitung* that day. Later in the day, Neebe was taken to City Hall to explain his connection with the *Arbeiter-Zeitung*.

Almost as soon as the Mayor and the second (at least the second) gang of detectives had left, another bunch of ruffians came running up the stairs. Lucy Parsons and Lizzie Holmes were sitting at the desk writing. An officer snarled at Lizzie Holmes, "What are you doing here?"

"I am corresponding with my brother. He is the editor of a labor paper," she replied.

The officer snatched Lizzie Holmes, and she protested loudly. "Shut up, you bitch, or I'll knock you down!"

Then another one of the mob grabbed Lucy and shook her. "You black bitch! I'm going to knock you down, too!"[4]

By noon, August Spies, Michael Schwab, Adolph Fischer, Gerhard Lizius , Oscar Neebe, Chris Spies, Lucy Parsons, Lizzie Holmes, and Mrs. Schwab had all been arrested at the *Arbeiter-Zeitung* office. The police released Lucy and hoped she would try to meet Albert. They arrested her two more times that day, but released her each time. For the next six weeks the police kept her under constant surveillance; they watched each house she visited, and immediately the occupants of the place became suspect. But their surveillance was not successful; she was still unintimidated and able to make contact with Albert without their detection.

The *Tribune* recalled that Lizzie Holmes and Lucy Parsons had carried the red and black flags in the front of the demonstration which "howled about the streets the night the new Board of Trade Building was opened." Their role had neither been forgotten nor taken lightly.

The police continued to return to the Parsons' flat on West Indiana St., but it was locked, and no one was there. They arrested Lucy the second time that day in a painter's flat on Lake St. Lulu and Albert Jr. were with her.

"I have been expecting you," she said calmly as she looked Officer Palmer in the eye.

"You still wear the red ribbon, do you?" he asked, when he saw the bright red handkerchief tied around her neck.

"Yes; and I'll wear it until I die," she replied defiantly.

The *Tribune* reporter who followed the officers to W. Lake St. reported that Mrs. Parsons "kept up a running abuse of the police department with her ill-tempered tongue while the officers were ransacking the premises." If the officers were following the usual methods of "ransacking" a place and pocketing the valuables, it's not at all surprising Lucy was "ill-tempered" about it.

The officers took her in, and Lieutenants Shea and Kipley tried to get information from her. "I am ready to die and I might as well die at once for the glorious cause," she snapped, her eyes flashing revolutionary fire and zeal. She refused to discuss Albert or the whereabouts of any comrades.

The police arrested Lucy with Sarah Ames for the third time that evening near the Fullerton Fish Market. The officers finally concluded that it was completely useless to question these women.

Lucy immediately sent out circulars to all I.W.P.A. sections across the country telling them what had happened in Chicago and asking for donations to defend the Chicago comrades.

When the news reached Albert Parsons and William Holmes that Lizzie Holmes was in custody and that Lucy had been arrested, they decided that Albert had to leave before the house was searched. He shaved his mustache and washed the shoe black from his prematurely gray hair. He took off his collar and neckscarf, and tucked his pants into his boots. At first he was determined to take a few enemies with him if he was arrested, but in the end he decided it was better to go completely unarmed. Thus disguised he set off for Elgin, Illinois, and then to Waukesha, Wisconsin. He was soon quite safe in Waukesha at Daniel Hoan's place, and he worked as a painter for the next six weeks.

On May 5, John A. Henry, a radical printer, published a mild leaflet asking for free speech in the face of the terror being waged against radicals; he then left for St. Louis, but was soon back agitating for the release of the prisoners.

On May 6, Lizzie Holmes and Adolph Fischer were arraigned. Holmes retained Kate Kane from Milwaukee as her attorney; her brother paid her $500 bond. Fischer was refused bond. Spies, Fielden and Schwab were held incommunicado. Lucy tried to get herself, Gretchen Spies (August Spies' sister), and Mrs. Fielden in to see them, but permission was denied. At Holmes' and Fischer's hearing, Lucy took charge of the situation for the radicals and let the attorneys know what she wanted done.

Reporters barraged Lucy with questions about the bombing and about Albert's mysterious disappearance (mysterious from their standpoint). She almost lost her composure once when she took a deep breath, bit her lips and replied, "We are not, any of us, laughing over this. It is terrible." In a whisper, she continued, "It is awful, but we were not to blame. We were-----" She stopped abruptly, quickly regained her reserved manner and refused further comment. She understood the gravity of the situation, and she was aware that it might cost some of her comrades their lives.

Lizzie Holmes appeared to be very tired. The reporter thought her "appearance did not warrant the charge preferred against her." It probably was her appearance as a small, unobtrusive fortyish woman which resulted in the charges against her being dropped. The state wanted an airtight case which would result in the execution of the most dangerous working class leaders. It would be difficult to secure a guilty verdict against a woman if there was a death sentence involved. By dissociating the women from the legal case, the state expected to execute the men.

Lucy Parsons was one of the first to publicly demand civil rights for the imprisoned "anarchists," arguing that they should not be condemned and executed without a hearing. To which the papers replied,

> It is the glory of the law which both Mrs. Parsons and her husband have so often scoffed at, outraged, and defied that it assures to every citizen—however guilty, however infamous, however dastardly—the right to a formal trial and an impartial judgment. . . . Mrs. Parsons need not fear but her fellow anarchists will get justice. It is the community that has reason to fear that they will not get their deserts.

On May 9, Albert Parsons' letter from hiding appeared in the papers. He said he would return when he was needed.

State's Attorney Julius S. Grinnell, who would prosecute the case, proclaimed, "Make the raids first and look up the law afterwards."

Captain Michael J. Schaack took charge of rounding up "anarchists," finding bombs, deadly weapons, and an untold number of "conspiracies." Schaack's imagination for anarchist plots ran wild, as did his calculations of the monetary rewards he could collect from the Citizens' Association for "saving society from anarchism." As soon as he had disrupted the radical organizations, he wanted to send his own men out as agents provocateur to form other organizations which he could expose. But Chief Ebersold refused to authorize the venture, deciding that, "I was satisfied that seven-eighths of this anarchist business was wind. He wanted to hire men to organize anarchist groups. I put my foot on that."

On the night of May 7, the police burst into Vaclav Djmek's house without a warrant; they intimidated Djmek and his wife, got the children out of bed, pulled the beds to pieces, and confiscated the pillowcases because they were red. Djmek offered no resistance on the way to the station, but was choked, roughed up, and had guns drawn on him. He was threatened and offered considerable money if he would turn state's witness. He was kicked, clubbed, beaten, scratched, cursed and threatened with hanging by the police while in their custody. The police abused his wife when she tried to see him.

The next day the police arrested Jacob Mikolando, an active I.W.P.A. member. They offered both Mikolando and Djmek jobs and money if they would testify in court as instructed by the police.[5]

Mikolando and Djmek both refused, and the police released them a few days later. The police offered Adolph Fischer immunity from prosecution if he would turn state's evidence; he absolutely refused.

The police also arrested 6'2" Rudolph Schnaubelt, Michael Schwab's brother-in-law and a friend of most of those arrested. They released him for lack of evidence, and he left Chicago. Later it became common belief that Schnaubelt had thrown the bomb, although there is absolutely no evidence that he did.

By May 10 hundreds of people had been jailed in a sweeping terror against socialists, socialist sympathizers and "foreigners." Lucy wrote the *Denver Labor Enquirer* describing the situation in Chicago. This was one of the first statements the labor movement had from any of the people who were accused of the bombing. She spoke out at the height of the hysteria, at a time when to be a dissenter was to insure arrest. "They have invaded the homes of everyone who has ever been known to have raised a voice or sympathized with those who have had aught to say against the present system of robbery and oppression. . . . This organized banditti have arrested me four times, they have subjected me to indignities that should bring the tinge of shame to the calloused cheek of a hardened barbarian."

The police had ripped open her mattress, stolen what few valuables she had and made a total mess of her apartment. They had threatened her six year old son, wrapping him in the rug and spinning him around on the floor. "Where's your daddy? We're going to string him up when we get him!"

Lucy viewed the bomb as the reply to the police order to disperse. She pointed out that it was not a conspiracy. "The bomb had been flung with such sudden and deadly effect that it had thoroughly disorganized and demoralized the police, and they became an easy prey for an enemy to attack and completely annihilate, if there had been any conspiracy or concocted understanding, as has been howled and shouted by the capitalistic press." In the meantime all the papers which would give the side of those in prison had been suspended or severely censured by police.

A reporter who went to her house for a visit found her a "self-possessed and fluent" speaker, whose "socialistic harangues are the most violent and vindictive of all the orators of that persuasion." He considered her well-educated in communist doctrine and capable of a tight, logical argument, but added "though her utterances are usually those of epigrammatic savagery. She is a remarkably strong-willed and determined woman of a fair education and no ordinary ability." She had scared him with the dangerous gleam in her eyes when she said, "That is my religion"—to run the machine which will guillotine capitalists.

After Albert Parsons' flight from Chicago, Texas newspapers picked up the story and recalled his and Lucy's past. The story of Lucy's marriage to Oliver Gathings came to light and added to the "scandal." She had to defend not only her political beliefs, but her integrity as a woman. The *Waco Daily Examiner* shrieked after its old enemy Albert Parsons: "BEAST PARSONS. His Sneaking Snarl From Some Moral Morass in Which He Hides. Miscegenationist, Murderer, Moral Outlaw, For Whom the Gallows Wait. More Dynamite Deviltry Unearthed in Chicago—the Scorpious Hide."

On May 14, Officer Schuettler arrested Louis Lingg, a handsome, well-built 21 year old carpenter. Lingg put up a strong resistence when surprised in his small room where he made bombs. Until his roommate, William Seliger, tipped them off, the police knew nothing of Lingg. The I.W.P.A. leaders did not know Lingg, a German who had been in the U.S. less than a year. In his short time in Chicago, he had become an organizer of the International Carpenters and Joiners Union, which elected him a delegate to the Central Labor Union.

Louis Lingg's father had died in 1877, the victim of a greedy boss.[6] His son developed a passionate hatred of capitalism and went to Switzerland to evade military service. But the Swiss expelled German evaders, and he was hounded from the country. He arrived in the U.S., a militant anarchist. Lingg was a spectacular catch for the police and prosecution who planned to scare the public with an actual bombmaker.

Lucy Parsons had never heard of Louis Lingg. "This Louis

Lingg," she announced, "is another police bugbear." She also said that the prisoners would have the best legal defense available, but she didn't think there was enough evidence to bring them to trial.

But the *Tribune* expected the men to be brought to trial, and it had a sequence of events planned for them, illustrated in a four part cartoon: 1) a radical speaker, 2) Spies, Fielden, and Schwab behind bars, 3) four waiting nooses, and 4) four graves marked A. Spies, A. Parsons, S. Fielden, and M. Schwab.

The Grand Jury was impaneled on May 17; it was not at all clear who would be indicted. Two printers from the *Arbeiter-Zeitung* who were in custody, Adolph Fischer and Anton Hirschberger, were the most frequently mentioned besides Spies, Parsons, Fielden, and Schwab.

On Tuesday, May 25, the Grand Jury voted on the indictments, but did not make the indictments public. The *Tribune* speculated that seven people had been indicted for murder: August Spies, Samuel Fielden, Michael Schwab, Adolph Fischer, Louis Lingg and perhaps George Engel and Anton Hirschberger. The *Tribune* reported that the cases of the missing Schnaubelt and Parsons had been left open.

When the indictments were made public on the 27th, the Grand Jury had indicted 31 men, ten of them as accessories before the fact in the murder of policeman Mathias Degan. They were August Spies, Albert Parsons, Adolph Fischer, Michael Schwab, George Engel, Samuel Fielden, Louis Lingg, Oscar Neebe, Rudolph Schnaubelt, and William Seliger. George Engel's name had first been mentioned in connection with the case only a few days earlier; he had edited an extreme German paper called the *Anarchist*. Oscar Neebe's indictment was a complete surprise. It was later learned that the brewery owners whose workers he had organized spoke with members of the Grand Jury and asked for the indictment to get him out of the way. William Seliger turned state's evidence. The police never relocated Schnaubelt, whom they had arrested several times but released.

All of the indicted men except Engel were members of the Central Labor Union. The ten men indicted for murder were not the most extreme advocates of propaganda by the deed. Lucy Parsons, Lizzie Holmes, J. P. "Dynamite" Dusey, John A.

Henry, Gerhard Lizzius, and Albert Currlin were all considered more "violent" than the men indicted.[7]

The State and propertied class were not interested in trying the most radical speakers. They were interested in executing or putting behind bars the leaders of the militant Chicago labor movement. Men like August Spies, Albert Parsons, Samuel Fielden, Michael Schwab, and Oscar Neebe were the real threats to their profits.

On June 5, the grand jury issued its final report. It found, in part, "That the attack on the police of May 4 was the result of a deliberate conspiracy, the full details of which are now in the possession of the officers of the law. . . ." and "that this force of disorganizers . . . was chiefly under the control of the coterie of men who were connected with the publication of . . . the *Alarm* and *Arbeiter-Zeitung*. . . ."

While the Grand Jury was in session, a defense committee was formed by Dr. Ernst Schmidt and George Schilling. They had a difficult task in front of them—saving their friends from almost certain execution, with an hysterical press and public screaming for blood, and with very little money. They had to find lawyers to defend their friends in court. The Central Labor Union retained its attorney, Moses Saloman, and his associate, Sigismund Zeisler, to defend the radical leaders. Both were young and inexperienced, and the defense committee looked for an older, more established lawyer to join the staff. Finally, Schilling persuaded Captain William Perkins Black, a liberal corporation lawyer, to defend the accused.[8] Black had little criminal law experience, and the defense filled out its legal team with William A. Foster, a criminal lawyer from Iowa.

Black first asked for a change of venue from Judge John G. Rogers' court, who had presided over the Grand Jury and was clearly biased against the prisoners. He hoped that Judge Murray F. Tuley would hear the case, but instead the change of venue was granted to the courtroom of Judge Joseph E. Gary.

The attitude toward the Chicago prisoners within the labor movement was mixed. People who knew them, like George Schilling and Joseph Gruenhut, stood by them. On May 12, Gruenhut opposed a resolution in the Trades and Labor Assembly of Chicago which condemned the "anarchist" leaders. On June 2, George Schilling opposed a resolution at the state

Knights of Labor convention offering sympathy to the families of the policemen killed or injured in the police riot. It took courage to speak out.

The *Chicago Express,* a labor paper which supported both the Knights of Labor and the eight hour movement, laid the blame for the bombing on the capitalists. "The crying sin of the age lies at the door of the rich, and the blood of the slain officers rests upon the souls of those who most vehemently denounce the Socialist and cry the loudest, 'Crucify him! Crucify him!'" The paper called Bonfield the "real author of the Haymarket slaughter" and charged that the seed of "anarchism" was "furnished by capital and sown by the Associated Press." Although the *Express* was highly critical of the radicals who were held responsible for the Haymarket bombing, the paper insisted that the ruling class was more guilty of the violence than were the radicals.[9]

The *Tribune* condemned Mayor Harrison's appointment of Gruenhut, saying, "The mayor knew that Gruenhut was a socialist when he appointed him. He put him in a position where he would . . . spread his subversive theories, and where he could juggle with statistics to enforce his communistic ideas. . . . If the man Gruenhut is a disgrace to the city, what shall be said of the person who has given him such large opportunities to disseminate his vicious and villainous doctrines?" The paper condemned the Mayor's appointment of Frances Hoffman corporation counsel; Hoffman had led the Relief and Aid Society demonstrations in 1873.

The mayor refused to bow to the arbitrary power of the police after the riot, and he vetoed a resolution to enlarge the police force on June 7. When the ordinance was passed over his veto, he refused to allow the Superintendent of Police to appoint any new men. The Grand Jury criticized the mayor and praised the police.

The more militant of those who attempted to support the hundreds in jail were jailed too. John Henry was jailed for speaking out against "the reign of arbitrary power" and calling for a lake front meeting. A lake front meeting called to discuss gardening would have been broken up if there was any hint of German or Bohemian involvement. Henry's wife intervened, declaring he was insane, and promised to take him out of

Chicago to avoid prosecution.

Some labor "leaders," like Terence Powderly, condemned the Chicago leaders. In New York only *John Swinton's Paper* out of all English language papers dared blame the Chicago police for the riot. The *Labor Enquirer,* the *Topeka Citizen,* the *Workmen's Advocate,* and the *Labor Leaf* were among the very few papers which bucked the revenge hysteria.

The police continued their search for Albert Parsons. They were soon convinced that Lucy had no idea where her husband was; they tracked her doggedly, to no avail. But both Lucy and the defense counsel were soon informed about both his hiding place and his disguise. Reports of sightings of Albert Parsons came from all points of the compass. Every time an I.W.P.A. section responded to one of the notices Lucy had sent out, some postmaster thought he had located Albert Parsons.

On June 4, Oscar Neebe was released on $17,000 bond. He was active at the Central Labor Union meeting on the 6th, and he worked tirelessly for the defense. Some weeks later he spoke at a C.L.U. benefit picnic held in Jefferson, just outside the Chicago city limits. In a ringing voice he declared, "The Central Labor Union is striving to realize a society without class or distinction. . . . We meet today in the cause of liberty, outside of the limits of the city of Chicago . . . and can freely say to the Chicago police. 'You can go to the devil.'" Captain Schaack had sent a few detectives to watch the proceedings. Lucy Parsons sat quietly watching.

Lucy received a letter from Albert asking her to confer with the defense attorneys and determine whether or not he should return for trial. He would return on her advice. On June 18 Lucy accompanied Black to the defense lawyers' daily conference for the first of two meetings with them. Black was enthusiastic about the idea, feeling sure that Parsons' voluntary surrender would help the defense and that they could assure him acquittal. Saloman agreed. Foster didn't believe a man's life should be endangered for idealism. Zeisler abstained. After the second meeting, Lucy communicated with Albert that he should come.[10]

They had agreed that Albert would surrender himself, and would appear in court with Captain Black on June 21, the opening day of the trial. He returned to Chicago undetected and went to Sarah Ames' home, where he changed his clothes, shaved his white beard, and dyed his mustache and hair its usual black. There he met Lucy, and they had a few hours to themselves.

Meanwhile, the trial was starting. Foster moved to separate the trials of Spies, Schwab, Fielden and Neebe from those of Lingg, Fischer and Engel. The motion was denied. At about 2:30, Captain Black quietly left the courtroom and walked outside.

A few minutes later, Lucy, Albert, and Sarah Ames got out of the cab they had hired and joined Black. As they hurried up the courtroom steps, a reporter said to a cop, "I'll bet a dollar to a nickel that man is Parsons!"

"Nonsense," the detective said, "not in a thousand years. Why don't you suppose I know Parsons when I see him? He isn't within five hundred miles of Chicago. Say, we detectives have been looking for him and . . ."

Reporters were running into the courtroom. State's Attorney Grinnell's lieutenant saw Parsons and told Grinnell. Grinnell jumped up, "Your Honor, I see Albert R. Parsons in the courtroom. I move that he be placed in the custody of the sheriff."

"Your motion, Mr. Grinnell," snapped Black, "is not only most ungracious and cruel, it is also gratuitous. You see that Mr. Parsons is here to surrender himself."

"I present myself for trial with my innocent comrades," Parsons broke in.

Judge Gary ordered him to take his seat with the prisoners. He rushed to the prisoners dock and shook hands with his comrades.

Lucy took a seat at the side of the courtroom and sat smiling at the consternation of the detectives. Reporters swarmed around her to find out where Albert had been. With a twinkle in her eye, she replied, "I can't tell you. If you want to find out for certain, go ask the detectives. They probably know all about it."

Headlines across the country proclaimed, "Parsons Walks Calmly Into Judge Gary's Courtroom!" The *Waco Daily Examiner* snarled, "BEAST PARSONS. The Chicago Crank-Anarchist Walks Coolly into Court to be Tried."

Parsons proclaimed his innocence of the charge of murder and said that he could not in good conscience remain free while his innocent comrades were tried.

Jury selection began with Albert Parsons in the prisoners' dock. The prosecution made every effort to secure a jury which would convict the defendants; the court, in the person of Judge Gary aided the prosecution. Prospective jurors who admitted to being biased against anarchists and socialists, who admitted to believing the men guilty, were accepted by the court as competent jurors. When challenged for cause by the defense, Judge Gary invariably overruled the challenge. The prosecution could thereby force the defense to exhaust their peremptory challenges and dictate jurors to them.

When the regular list of jurors had been depleted, the Court appointed a special bailiff to procure jurors. Bailiff Ryce said more than once, "I am managing this case, and I know what I am about. Those fellows will hang as certain as death. I am calling such men as the defendants will have to challenge peremptorily and waste their time and challenges. Then they will have to take such men as the prosecution wants."

It took until July 15 to fill the jury panel. No workingmen sat on the jury; the defendants were not to be judged by their peers, who were printers, brewery workers, teamsters, and carpenters, but by clerks and businessmen.

The courtroom atmosphere was that of a circus. Judge Gary surrounded himself with well-dressed, attractive women and laughed and talked with them as the prosecution and defense presented evidence. His mind was made up, and he didn't need to listen. The jury played cards through much of the proceedings. Spectators from far and wide came to see the celebrated case and observe the prisoners firsthand. The summer was hot and sweltering in the small courtroom. The families of the defendants often brought their children. Lulu and Albert Jr. might go and sit on their father's knees before the day's proceedings began.

In his opening statement, Prosecutor Grinnell said,

I will try and show to you who threw the bomb, and I will prove to your satisfaction that Lingg made it. There never was a conspiracy yet where some conspirator did not divulge the secret. In this case the man was Seliger. I have yet to see the first man who will deny that a conspiracy existed.

There are a great many counts in this case, but murder is the main one. It is not necessary to bring the bomb-thrower into court. Though none of these men, perhaps, threw the bomb personally, they aided and abetted the throwing of it, and are as responsible as the actual thrower.

The States Attorney did not claim the defendants threw the bomb or that they even *knew* who threw the bomb. He argued that their speeches and writings in the several years prior to the bombing inspired some unknown person to throw the bomb, and that they were, therefore, liable of conspiracy.

The state wanted blood. Seven policemen had died from injuries—though it had been conceded that some of them may have died from police bullets when the officers began shooting wildly. No mention was made of the seven or more workers who had been killed. The men were on trial for the first patrolman who died, Mathias Degan.

Captain Bonfield, the commander of the force which attacked the Haymarket meeting, was the first witness for the prosecution. As the testimony was given, it became clear that the prosecution's witnesses had seen many different things on the night of May 4. Dyer Lum in his history of the trial reported the various prosecution witnesses' testimony about Fielden's alleged gun:

> Whether Mr. Fielden was *on* the wagon, getting *down from* the wagon, on the *sidewalk,* back—*not quite behind* the wagon, in the *center* of the rear, or *under* the wagon when he was severally recognized, we need not concern ourselves, as no two agree. The wonder remains that Inspector Bonfield, who saw him descend in obedience to the order *before* the bomb was thrown, and to whom Mr. Fielden addressed the remark, "We are peaceable" while within touching distance of each other, and who was admittedly the nearest witness, should have failed to discover the murderous weapon aimed "directly at him," simultaneously, from so many points of the compass!

The testimony was typically contradictory.

For the most part, the prosecution relied on introducing "inflammatory" articles which had been written by the defendants or which had appeared in the *Alarm, Arbeiter-Zeitung,* or *Vorbote* over a period of several years. Lucy's "To Tramps" was introduced by the prosecution as "People's Exhibit No. 18."

Her husband was to be held responsible for everything which appeared in the *Alarm,* and perhaps also for her conduct, as women were often held to be legally incompetent.

Feeling that the evidence available in the papers might be insufficient, the prosecution manufactured testimony which was presented by perjured witnesses. M. M. Thompson testified to following Spies and Schwab as the two were discussing the conspiracy in *English.* Michael Schwab had left the Haymarket by the time of the alleged observation, and it was unlikely the two German editors would have discussed *anything* in English.

It was established that Louis Lingg made bombs, but that he made the bomb which was thrown at the Haymarket was never established. However, evidence about Lingg was used against all the defendants, despite the fact that they didn't even know him.

The most damaging evidence was given by Harry Gilmer. Gilmer testified that Spies lighted the bomb and Schnaubelt threw it from the alley. But Gilmer had told a different story a few weeks before! Ten persons testified to Gilmer's unreliable character, and in his final charge to the jury, Grinnell did not even bother to mention Gilmer's testimony.[11]

The prosecution tried to prove that the Haymarket meeting was unlawful and was called in order to attack the police and foment a riot. The prosecution tried to prove that a meeting held the previous Monday night was held to plan the beginning of the revolution, that the word "Ruhe" was inserted into a paper as a signal for the revolution to begin, and that this signal precipitated the bombing. Only Fischer and Engel had been at the meeting; 30 or 40 people were there, and it wasn't a secret meeting.

On Saturday, July 31, testimony for the state ended, and the defense began to present its arguments. Mr. Saloman said he expected the men to be tried for the crime for which they were indicted—conspiracy to murder—, not for their political beliefs in anarchism or socialism.

On August 2, 1886, the defense called its first witness: Mayor Carter Harrison. Though not a socialist, socialists had accepted positions in his administration, and he was generally regarded as a friend of working people.

The courtroom was packed to hear the mayor's testimony.

Lucy came in followed by Albert Jr. and Lulu just as Judge Gary was ordering the spectators without seats out of the courtroom. He gave Albert Parsons a few minutes with his children before the mayor's testimony began.

The Citizens' Association detested the mayor, and his testimoney for the defense didn't heighten their estimation of him:

Q. Did you attend the Haymarket meeting on Desplaines street on the 4th of May last?

A. A part of it, not the whole. . . . I believed that it was better for myself to be there and to disperse it myself instead of leaving it to any policemen. I thought my order would be better obeyed. I went there then for the purpose, if I felt it necessary for the best interests of the city, to disperse that meeting.

Q. Was any action taken by you while you were at the meeting looking to the dispersal of the meeting?

A. No!

Q. Do you recollect any suggestion made by either of the speakers looking toward the immediate use of force or violence toward any person?

A. There was none. If there had been I should have dispersed them at once.

A. I went back to the station and said to Bonfield that I thought that the speeches were about over; that nothing had occurred yet or was likely to occur to require interference, and I thought he had better issue orders to his reserves at the other stations to go home. He replied that he thought about the same way, as he had men in the crowd who were reporting to him.

Q. Did you see any weapons in the hands of the audience?

A. No, sir; none at all.

When the testimony was in, it was established that at the time of the bombing, Parsons and Fischer were in Zepf's Hall, Schwab was speaking at a meeting in Deering, Engel was home playing cards, Lingg was on the North Side, and Neebe was nowhere near the scene. Only Spies and Fielden were at the scene, and neither of them threw the bomb.

In closing Judge Gary made highly prejudicial remarks to the jury. "It has been decided that for a man to say that he is prejudiced against horse thieves is no ground for imputing to him any misconduct as a juror. Now you must assume that I know either that anarchists, socialists, and communists are a worthy, a praiseworthy class of people . . . or else I cannot say that a prejudice against them is wrong."

Although the indictment read "conspiracy to murder" Grinnell shouted in his final argument, "Anarchy is on trial! The defendants are on trial for treason and murder."

Captain Black objected. "The indictment does not charge treason, does it, Mr. Grinnell?" But Judge Gary overruled this and all other objections of the defense. Grinnell, who said in May, "Make the arrests and look up the law afterwards," shouted in August, "These men have been selected, picked out by the grand jury and indicted because they were leaders. They are no more guilty than the thousands who follow them. Gentlemen of the jury; convict these men, make examples of them, hang them and you save our institutions, our society."

Foster, for the defense, articulately argued that only the evidence which pertained to a conspiracy to commit murder on the night of May 4 should be considered by the jury.

Captain Black made an eloquent appeal for the defense, but his words were lost on a jury which had already made up its mind.

The court which had refused to permit the radicals to defend their philosophy in court, now permitted the prosecution to make it a trial for heresy.

Grinnell said that he did not believe Neebe should be condemned to death on the evidence. Then he listed the men as he perceived their order of guilt: Spies, Fischer, Lingg, Engel, Fielden, Parsons, Schwab, Neebe.

Tense anticipation gripped the city on the morning of August 20. Perhaps the "anarchists" would retaliate against the expected guilty verdict. Captain Schaack had persuaded the world that the "anarchists" had untold diabolical machines at their disposal. The courtroom was heavily guarded. When Lucy Parsons arrived shortly after 9:00 A.M., she was surprised to learn she could not sit near her husband. Police blocked the seats where the families of the accused usually sat. August Spies' mother and sister were already seated in the rear of the courtroom, where Lucy joined them.

Mayor Harrison had heard Grinnell say there wasn't enough

evidence to convict Neebe; the mayor had tried to persuade the prosecutor to drop the case. But Grinnell, fearing that dropping the case against Neebe at this critical point would jeopardize his case against the other defendants, refused. Neebe himself expected to be acquitted.

When the jury filed in, the courtroom was alive with excitement. Outside a crowd waited to hear the verdict. The defendants were escorted in at 9:50 A.M. They were tired and pale after the long ordeal of trial and imprisonment.

Judge Gary asked for the verdict. The handpicked jury had decided on the verdict in three hours' deliberation: guilty as charged in all cases, death for all but Neebe, who would get 15 years. The prisoners heard the verdict quietly. Parsons was smiling and defiant. He bowed to the crowd, then made a noose of the curtain cord and dangled it out the window. Black moved for a new trial, and the hearing on the motion was postponed until September. Schwab's wife, Schnaubelt's sister, became hysterical when she heard the verdict. Mrs. Black, Lucy Parsons, and the other women tried to calm her.

As the prisoners were led back to the jail, Fielden needed support. Lingg, Engel and Fischer were firm and composed. Parsons breathed defiance. Schwab and Spies were pale, but their inner strength saw them through. Neebe looked stunned.

Captain Black couldn't have been more shocked if he had received the death penalty himself. He had not expected *seven* death sentences! Lucy was angry. She had thought that Albert's voluntary return would stand in his favor and would help the defense. Instead, he had been condemned to hang by the neck until dead.

Across the nation, people rejoiced that law and order was vindicated, anarchism defeated. The *Tribune* was elated: "The Scaffold Waits. Seven Dangling Nooses for the Dynamite Fiends" was its cheery news. But the revolutionary spirit was not so easy to defeat. A few days after the verdict, papers asked, "Is It the Death Blow?" and noted, "Active Sympathy Shown for the Anarchists. A Bad Element Rampant."

The police still held three other radicals in jail, including Thomas Brown who had loaned Albert Parsons $5 the night of May 4. Others were free on $400 bond each; on August 20, police released one of the three remaining victims. As soon as the verdict was in, the prosecution and Citizens' Association wanted to try the others who had been indicted. Captain Schaack had been threatening for a long time to arrest the two most notorious women in the case, Lucy Parsons and Lizzie Holmes. He hoped he would have the opportunity to testify against them in trial. "Why not the women?" he asked. "Some of them are a good sight worse than the men." Even other socialists considered Lucy one of the most violent speakers; still, she was not indicted. Joseph Gruenhut pointed out, "Mrs. Parsons was the most outspoken advocate for utilizing the latest modern weapons of self-defense, and her husband was not near as rabid in his denunciations of the police outrages . . . but the State's Attorney never attempted to indict Mrs. Parsons for incendiary talk."[12] The States' Attorney did not find a woman as threatening as a man.

William Parsons, who hadn't seen his brother in 15 years, came to Chicago the last few days of the trial to support his brother. The presence of the former confederate general who was now a member of the Knights of Labor in Virginia added another dimension to the drama. General Parsons had become a reformer in his own right, though he did not share Albert's views; he had written a pamphlet, "National Depression— Cause and Remedy" which he addressed to the Congressional Labor Committee and distributed to members of Congress. He charged that financial contractions manipulated from Washington caused depressions and that a deliberate financial conspiracy had prevented the South from rebuilding after the war.

William Parsons denied reports that he had repudiated or disowned Albert. He condemned the forces which were preparing to execute his younger brother, "He is fighting for principle. . .; and his voluntary surrender to confront the scaffold proves his sincerity, and demonstrates that he has the courage of his convictions. . . . Among belligerents in actual war such an act of intrepidity would insure his honorable discharge; among savage tribes such a surrender would have insured his elevation to the chieftainship. It remains to be seen whether the class of selfish monopolists and their agents and tools are capable of appreciating an act that elsewhere would challenge the admiration of chivalrous adversaries."

General Parsons, a lawyer, was certain that the verdict would never stand up in a higher court. "I feel like saying that the right of peaceful assemblage is upon trial, and not these men. . . . It is a constitutional question of the right of the people to repel attack upon a peaceful and lawful assemblage. . . . This was not a case of homicide, but constitutional defense." He pointed out that the illegal interference with anarchist meetings was just the first step to illegal and arbitrary interference with any meeting.[13]

In September, a *Chicago Herald* reporter questioned Lucy about her marriage to Oliver Gathings. The reporter brought a picture of Oliver with him, which he showed Lucy. She insisted that they go to the jail and discuss the whole affair with Albert. As she entered the jail, she demanded of her husband, "Now, Mr. Parsons, tell what you know about this matter, and let's have it settled." Albert asked to see the picture, and explained, "I had something to do with his wife or the woman he lived with."

As he began to explain, Lucy broke in, "Now don't go beating about the bush. Tell the whole story as it is. I won't rest under this false imputation any longer."

Albert digressed on his political activities in Texas, his enemies in Waco, and accused Grinnell, Bonfield and Co. of being "at the bottom of all this." He continued, "The talk about my wife being a negro—now anyone—"

Lucy cut him off again. "Never mind about that matter. Let's have the story in question."

But he insisted on assuring the world of the purity of the Indian and Spanish blood in her veins and of her good character. "I feel very bad on account of my confinement here, and especially now since this slander has been started against my wife. I did live with a woman before I was married to Mrs. Parsons, in Waco, Texas, and I did take her away from the man Gathings, but she is not my present wife; I do not know what became of her. She may have had a child by me; I do not know. She had children, at any rate. But such things were common in Waco in those days." Albert attempted to take the blame and clear Lucy's reputation.

Lucy corroborated his story and snapped, "I have never in my life seen the picture you now show me, and never lived in Waco, and am not accountable for Mr. Parsons' wild oats which he may have sowed before I knew him. . . I don't consider myself on trial for bigamy at present. When the time comes I will substantiate what I say."[14]

On October 1, Judge Gary began to hear the arguments of the defense for a new trial. On October 7, he rejected the motion, and then offered the condemned a chance to explain why they should not be sentenced. The men denounced the judicial process which had sentenced them to death. They did not deny their belief that the capitalist system would be overthrown by violent insurrection, but they pointed to the conditions in society which had produced revolutionaries.

"I speak to you as the representative of one class to another," August Spies began. He pointed out that the violence of the capitalist class is greater than any violence he had ever advocated. He recalled his trip to the Hocking Valley mining region where he saw "hundreds of lives in the process of slow destruction, gradual destruction." He continued, "There was no dynamite, nor were they anarchists who did that diabolical work. It was the work of a party of highly respectable monopolists, law-abiding citizens, if you please. It is needless to say the murderers were never indicted. The press had little to say, and the State of Ohio assisted them."

Spies rose to his magnificent, articulate best: "If you think that by hanging us you can stamp out the labor movement . . . if this is your opinion, then hang us! Here you will tread upon a spark, but here, and there, and behind you, and in front of you, and everywhere, flames will blaze up. It is a subterranean fire. You cannot put it out. . . . You don't believe in magical arts, as your grandfathers did, who burned witches at the stake, but you do believe in conspiracies.

"You, gentlemen, are the revolutionists! You rebel against the effects of social conditions."

Michael Schwab reminded the court that the "anarchists" had used threats of violence no more frequently than had the most "respectable" men of society. "The president of the Citizens' Association, Edwin Lee Brown, after the last election of Mayor Harrison . . . called on all good citizens to take possession of the courthouse by force, even if they had to wade in blood. If seems to me that the most violent speakers are not to be found in the ranks of the Anarchists."

Oscar Neebe cited the police atrocities carried out in the name of "law and order." "They searched hundreds of houses, and money was stolen by searching houses, and watches were stolen, and nobody knew whether they were stolen by the police or not. Captain Schaack knows it. His gang was one of the worst in this city. You need not laugh about it, Captain Schaack. You are one of them. You are an anarchist, as you understand it."

He recited his "crimes." He had organized bakery workers, grocery clerks and brewery workers. He had kept the *Arbeiter-Zeitung* going after Spies and Schwab were arrested. He asked that he be given the honor of hanging with the other defendants, as it would be easier for his family than to watch him die by inches in the penitentiary.

Fischer spoke briefly, saying he had been convicted of anarchy, not of murder. He said that anarchists were always ready to die for their principles.

Louis Lingg, who had sat reading throughout the trial and had scorned the entire proceedings, arose to speak. His strong physique and captivating personality commanded the attention of everyone in the courtroom as he paced back and forth like a caged lion. He spoke with bitter irony, pausing as his words were translated into English. "Court of Justice: With the same irony with which you have regarded my efforts to win, in this 'free land of America,' a livelihood such as human-kind is worthy to enjoy, do you now, after condemning me to death, concede me the liberty of making a final speech."

"You have charged me with despising 'law and order.' What does your 'law and order' amount to? Its representatives are the police, and they have thieves in their ranks. Here sits Captain Schaack. He has himself admitted to me that my hat and books have been stolen from him in his office—stolen by policemen. These are your defenders of property rights!" He laughed at the court and its laws. "I do not recognize your law, jumbled together as it is by the nobodies of by-gone centuries, and I do not recognize the decision of the court." Nearly breathing fire, he held the audience in awe as he finished:

I declare again, frankly and openly, that I am in favor of using force. I have told Captain Schaack, and I stand by it, 'If you cannonade us, we shall dynamite you.' You laugh!

. . . but let me assure you that I die happy on the gallows, so confident am I that the hundreds of thousands to whom I have spoken will remember my words; and when you have hanged us . . . they will do the bomb throwing! . . . . I despise you. I despise your order, your laws, your force-propped authority. Hang me for it!"

George Engel explained how he became an anarchist. He pointed to the violence of the capitalist system. "I hate and combat, not the individual capitalist, but the system that gives him those privileges. My greatest wish is that workingmen may recognize who are their friends and who are their enemies." He spoke with a note of sadness, as workingmen had not unanimously rallied to the cause of the condemned men.

Fielden spoke at length, discussing his childhood as a cotton mill worker, the interests of capitalists and workers, and giving a lengthy review of the evidence against him. He was honest and sincere, and he spoke from the heart.

Albert Parsons was the last of the eight men to speak. He spoke for two hours on the 8th of October and for another six on the 9th. He had carefully prepared the text of his address. He knew it might be his last public speech. He explained the nature of capital, the theory of surplus value, and the labor theory of value. He reviewed the world history of working people, going back to ancient times. He offered statistics on labor and tenancy, on the number of women and children employed in industry. He reviewed the history of violence against working people since the 1877 railroad strikes. He believed that dynamite in the 19th century would play a role analogous to gunpowder in the 15th century. Gunpowder had brought down feudalism; dynamite would bring down capitalism.

He charged, "The law—the statute law—is the coward's weapon, the tool of the thief, and more—the shield and buckler of every gigantic villany, and frightful parent of all crimes." He charged the police with violations in the prosecution of the case. "They have violated free speech. In the prosecution of this case they have violated a free press. They have violated and denounced the right of self-defense. I charge the crime home to them."

He said that he had to stand trial with his innocent comrades, that his conscience could not have let him go free. "I have nothing, not even now, to regret," he concluded, exhausted from the two day delivery. He had wanted Judge Gary to take a recess until the next day; but Gary refused. He had been almost too tired to finish, and had had to condense much of the remainder of his speech.

The court was indeed on trial as the eight men made and substantiated their charges; for three days the accused were the accusers. When they had finished, Judge Gary sentenced them to hang on December 3, 1886.

As they waited on death row, the Haymarket defendants, who had fought the attack on First Amendment Liberties, could laugh grimly when the Statue of Liberty was unveiled in New York Harbor three weeks after their speeches.

Lucy had watched the consummation of the great trial, the incredible speeches in court, surrounded by the women who were her friends and comrades. Lizzie Holmes, Sarah Ames, Mrs. and Miss Spies, Mrs. Neebe, and Kate Kane—the attorney who defended Lizzie Holmes in May—were all there. Lucy was dressed in black, mourning the death of free speech in America and the coming executions of her comrades.

But she was not willing to give up so easily. While Captain Black would take the case to the Illinois Supreme Court, she would take the case to the American people.

Lucy Takes the Case to the People

When the sentencing was over, Lucy Parsons walked tall and erect to the prisoners' dock. She firmly took Albert's hand. "My husband, I give you to the cause of liberty. I now go forth to take your place. I will herald abroad to the American people the foul murder ordered here today at the behest of monopoly. I, too, expect to mount the scaffold. I am ready."

When the prisoners had returned to the jail, Albert sank into a chair on his side of the bars. Lucy collapsed into a chair opposite him, exhausted.

A reporter commented to her, "You are not standing it so well today as you did on the day the verdict was rendered."

She agreed. She and her children had been evicted from their apartment, because she didn't have rent money. She had worked her fingers to the bone for four weeks dressmaking, trying to keep body and soul together. She was to leave at 7 o'clock on the train for Cincinnati where she would begin her tour for the defense. "There is work to be done, and although nearly exhausted, I must be up and at it. The world must hear from me now. The voice of my husband has been silenced, for the present at any rate, and perhaps forever in this world, but his life will speak in eloquent terms in the cause of suffering humanity until the emancipation of wage-slavery comes. We are weak, tired, oppressed, but not discouraged nor disheartened. It is a day of struggle. Our cause is worth fighting for and worth dying for."

She was ready to go, and two hours after court adjourned, she was on the train to Cincinnati. Her little boy was staying with the Hoans in Waukesha, Wisconsin, where his father had found shelter in the spring. Lulu was staying with friends in another state. In the coming months she would be able to spend only a few days at a time with her children in Waukesha. Albert Jr. could play with Daniel Hoan Jr., the future socialist mayor of Milwaukee, who was his same age. The trial had completely disrupted their family life.

Tired, Lucy made her first speech on her seven week tour the next night. She rose to the occasion; her feeling that she, too, would soon be a martyr gave her even greater strength than her untiring character already possessed. The audience was in awe of this firm, strong, dark woman who stood before them, beautiful in her sadness.[1]

As she began to speak, her low, musical voice filled the hall. No one had to strain to hear her; she did not have to raise her voice to reach every single person in the hall. The women had arranged the meeting for her and she said to her comrades, "When the women take hold of a great and crying evil, you may expect revolution—not necessarily a revolution of blood and destruction, yet not necessarily one of peace."

With the execution set for December 3, the defense committee worked feverishly for a stay of execution and a new trial. Funds were desperately needed. They estimated it would cost $12,500 to appeal the case to the Illinois Supreme Court. Lucy Parsons was soon collecting $750 a week for the defense, but she considered that her secondary task. Her primary task was to tell the American people about anarchism.

From Cincinnati Lucy went to New York City, where she spoke at Cooper's Union. Her tall dark figure, her black dress, her copper complexion and piercing black eyes fascinated her audiences. She was a remarkable woman, in appearance and character. The press speculated wildly on her origins.

Her mellow voice captivated the audience at Cooper's Union. No one moved, scarcely remembering to breathe, in the two hours of her lecture. Her black eyes flashed, and her voice filled the auditorium. She denounced the factories of modern civilization as great slaughterhouses, where children went to die by inches. She contrasted the life of a child worker with the gems on every finger and the diamond tiaras in the hair of the great "society" women. Reporters who brushed away their preconceived notions were surprised by her remarkable intelligence and the coherence of her arguments.

The capitalists, she said, "grind little children's bones into gold." "Phil Armour is a slaughterer of children as well as of hogs." The bosses say, "Suffer the little children to come unto me, for of such is the contents of my factory." The word Anarchism evoked fear and images of bombs and daggers in the minds of many Americans; the press fanned anti-anarchist hysteria. But Lucy Parsons did not hesitate to use the word. To her Anarchism meant a beautiful condition of future society, an end to child labor, an end to the super-exploitation of women in the workforce. Anarchism "calls your children from the slaughterhouses and the factories, and put them at play in the kindergartens where they belong. Why is it that the tyrants take your children? I'll tell you. It is because children are cheap, and they send your wives and children to work in the factories to kill themselves."

She believed the final verdict would be rendered by the American people, not by the courts, which were the instruments of the monopolists. "You are the Grand Jury to pass on this case; you are to decide whether they are murderers or not; on this case hangs American liberty."

She rose to heights of oratory. "Then the onslaught of two hundred policemen, pistol in hand, murder in their very eyes. I appeal to you, the greater jury, the real American jury. There was somebody who did resent that onslaught of the two hundred armed police. Who it was nobody knows. Science has led every man to be a commander-in-chief, if necessary; it is science, not anarchism, that gave dynamite to the world." The crowd was on its feet, wild with applause. "Oh! when these seven death traps drop you will see the crime you have committed. A million people will then rise and cry 'Vengeance.' Aye, before the people are done they will seek the hiding place of the monopolists and the social revolution—(intense applause)—will be inaugurated."

Lucy, like many of her comrades, believed that the Haymarket bomb had been the beginning of the social revolution. They did not regret that revolution had begun.

Lucy spoke to Knights of Labor Assemblies, to I.W.P.A. locals, and to other socialist, anarchist, and labor gatherings. In Orange, New Jersey, she brushed past the armed guard and kicked in the door of the hall to speak. The police had put the muscle on the hall owner who tried to go back on his rental of the hall. In Bridgeport, Connecticut, 300 or 400 persons, including many Yale students, attended her lecture. She wrote to Albert, "I reached the above-named place in a drenching rain, which continued until midnight—I never saw such a rain." She was thrilled by the eagerness of the students to learn about anarchism; many stayed after her lecture to ask her what books to read. "My trip is having its effect," she wrote. "The powers that be don't know what to do with me. One New York paper suggests that 'Parsons be let out as a compromise to get Mrs. Parsons to stop talking.'" She found the article amusing; it stimulated her confidence in her ability to motivate crowds. Lucy enjoyed the fame her tour was bringing her, but even more she fervently believed that her tour might turn the masses of people towards "anarchism." On October 29, she spoke in Philadelphia, and on October 31, she was back in Connecticut to address a New Haven audience. The Yale students had a second chance to hear her speak. She told the audience, "My husband may die 'at the stake,' but his death will only help the cause . . . as it is a necessary thing in the early stages of any great reform that there be some martyrs. . . ."

Lucy shared with many of her comrades the mystical vision that martyrs would bring victory to their cause.

She looked forward to the time when the hours of labor would be reduced almost to zero. "A hundred years ago Franklin said that six hours a day was enough for anyone to work and if he was right then, two hours a day ought to be enough now." She cited a case in Augusta, Georgia, where 3,400 cotton mill workers were locked out, because a number of child employees had struck for sixty-two and one-half cents a week. The rich owner would give thousands of dollars to religion and charities, but not a cent to the working people who toiled in his mill. "For five years," she continued, "I have spoken against this civilization on the lake front at Chicago and I have said that any and all means are justifiable to destroy it, and by that statement I will stand or fall. . . ."

The means to achieve the society she envisioned might not all be peaceable. She believed that society itself was based on violence: the violence of the lockout, the strike, child labor, starvation and prostitution. If the revolution that she advocated ended these forms of violence once and for all, she would be happy. She believed that the bombing itself at Haymarket Square could be defended under the Constitution. "If the Anarchists had thrown the bomb at the Haymarket they didn't commit a crime nor violate any law. The Constitution gives the people the right to repel an unlawful invasion in any way they see fit." In this belief she was supported by her brother-in-law William Parsons and by the architect of propaganda by the deed, Johann Most.

The press had taken anarchist "advocacy" of violence and separated it from the rest of the philosophy. It caricatured the "typical" anarchist as bearded, wild-eyed, a dagger in his teeth, a bomb in one hand, a glass of beer in the other, and surrounded by flies (attracted by the foul odor he exuded.) The press omitted the anarchists' commitment to end child labor, starvation, and unemployment; to allow leisure time in which all persons could develop their interests and creativity. So when Lucy Parsons surprised her audiences by her appearance and the force of her arguments, she was defying the image in the press. In New Haven, she said, "You may have expected me to belch forth great flames of dynamite and stand before you with bombs in my hands. If you are disappointed, you have only the capitalist press to thank for it."

Lucy returned from her eastern tour in triumph. She had received tremendous acclaim. There was an added cause for elation; on November 27, the Chief Justice of the Illinois Supreme Court had granted a stay of execution. No anarchists would die on December 3. Lucy was jubilant; her tour had done its part in achieving the stay of execution.

She spoke at a gala socialist celebration; the socialists had a right to be happy; it seemed that the shadow might be lifting. Lucy's speech was unconciliatory that night. Emboldened by her trip East she said she believed the trial and its outcome would result in great achievements in the movement. The *Chicago Herald* reported the speech "was full of daring and showed very plainly that the misfortunes which have attended her husband have not in the slightest degree weakened her advocacy of the rankest principles of anarchy." An (unidentified) "prominent" police official said, "Mrs. Parsons' speech . . . was the most vindictive and defiant uttered in this city since the Haymarket massacre. It would appear . . . that she is striving to incite the reds to further deeds of violence, and, if need be, lead any movement against society. . . . The frantic cheers which greeted each revolutionary sentence show . . . that the pernicious doctrines of Spies and Parsons still obtain in certain quarters of the city." The police official did not want to identify himself; he continued, "Mrs. Parsons has returned with her head filled with bombastic notions. She is a woman who loves notoriety. Her trip East has had the effect of convincing her that she is the biggest Anarchist out of jail. . . . She invites arrest for the reason that she knows that in the event of such a procedure she will gain additional fame and be held up as a martyr. Mrs. Parsons is a dangerous woman." And indeed she was, from the standpoint of the police. For her part, Lucy was exhilarated by the role of martyr. "I am an Anarchist and a revolutionist!" She rose to her full height, her eyes shining, her low voice sharp, and cried to the audience, "I propose to continue so, even if I reach the gallows also (Prolonged applause.) I propose to . . . fight for justice . . . till I, too, am strangled."

Lucy fully expected to die a martyr; she would stand on her principles, never conceding an inch. "I propose to stand on these principles, and fight for justice for all the prisoners till I, too, am strangled. If I stood on the gallows with the noose about my neck, and a petition were placed before me for mercy, and I knew I could get mercy by the signing of my name, I would say, 'Spring your trap,' and would die before asking for mercy." Her principles were far more important than her life, or her husband's life. Again and again she said she could not accept a justice which permitted Albert to go free and which condemned her other comrades to death. They must all accept the same fate—uncompromising freedom, or death.

The next day she was reunited with Albert at the jail. She was stunningly beautiful in her dark dress; she beamed with joy at seeing her husband and lover. Her brother-in-law William Parsons accompanied her.

Lucy and Albert hugged and kissed each other—ecstatic over the stay of execution, the success of Lucy's trip, and the growing acceptance of their ideas. Albert's jailers hadn't seen such affection in a long time. A major victory had been won, and the case would go to the Illinois Supreme Court. Lucy left at the end of the permitted hour's visit, relieved that Albert would not hang on December 3, less than a week away.

But Lucy did not linger in Chicago. Her place was on the

road, taking the message to the people. After Thanksgiving, she went to St. Louis, Kansas City, and Omaha. In Kansas City she argued that the Haymarket bomb was a part of a Wall Street conspiracy to break up the eight-hour movement; she believed it was hatched by the same conspirators who drove impoverished women into prostitution and workers to drink and suicide, because they would not find employment to support their families. She called the police "vermin" and Judge Gary "Hangman Gary." She pleaded the innocence of her comrades to the murder charge, but she did not apologize for being a revolutionary. "I come to talk to you of those who stand in the shadow of their own scaffolds. I come to you an avowed Anarchist. I am a revolutionist, but I incite no one to riot, for I am not out on that mission; I hope to be some day." "You have heard a great deal about bombs. You have heard that the anarchists said lots about dynamite. You have been told that Lingg made bombs. He violated no law. . . . Had I been there, had I heard that insolent command to disperse, had I heard Fielden say, 'Captain, this is a peaceable meeting,' had I seen the liberties of my countrymen trodden under foot, I would have flung the bomb myself. I would have violated no law, but would have upheld the constitution."

In December, Terence Powderly ordered Knights of Labor Assemblies to stop collecting money for the anarchists' defense and to return the money which had already been collected. But the order didn't scare many Knights, particularly it didn't scare George Schilling and the other members of Labor Assembly 1307 in Chicago, the assembly which Albert Parsons, Schilling, and Tommy Morgan had organized.

Lulu Parsons was ill much of the fall; her illness was diagnosed as scarlet fever, but may have been the beginning of the lymph gland disease which killed her two years later. She was staying with "the kindest of people," said Lizzie Holmes, and she was back in Chicago. Lizzie thought she looked a bit thin and large eyed, and she still had a sore throat. But the people who were taking care of her had money and were doing everything they could for her. Dyer Lum and Lizzie Holmes responded to her imprisoned father's pleas to see her and give him a full report on her condition.

Instead of wishing Albert a Merry Christmas, Lizzie wished

him "strength and courage to endure your martyrdom." She said she would gladly trade her life for his if she could and reminded him, "Remember that millions of us know and appreciate what you are doing for the cause and are in danger of worshipping you for it. My heartfelt wishes and love be with you."[2]

Lucy was on the road again. In January she lectured in Detroit, Michigan, and in Buffalo, New York. Meanwhile, a mayoral race was shaping up in Chicago, with a very strong workingman's ticket offered by the United Labor Party.

In February Lucy went to Milwaukee to speak. The May Day violence in Milwaukee had been more serious than in Chicago; but in Milwaukee, 17 workers were killed, and no police. That was the difference. The radical leaders still had to pay the price. Paul Grottkau and Frank Hirth were jailed.

Hirth was still in jail in February, and he couldn't attend Lucy's lecture, but he sent a bouquet of red roses for his good friend. One of his children presented it to her before her lecture. By February Lucy had made 43 speeches in 17 states.

Lucy responded defiantly and sarcastically to the caricatures of anarchists in an article for the *Advance and Labor Leaf*. The police, the Citizens' Association of Chicago, and other enemies of social change had convinced a large segment of the population that anarchists threw bombs and ate babies. Lucy argued that all members of the labor movement who were struggling for a better society were really "anarchists." "WE ARE ALL ANARCHISTS" she said, and described how the ruling class portrayed them:

. . . to the average reader an avowed anarchistic society must be composed of beings somewhat resembling the human family, who hold orgies, which they have designated as meetings; having been *compelled* to come in contact with the human race enough (just enough) to learn a few words of the language.

. . . they invariably select only places that are dark, dank and loathsome, where no light is ever permitted to penetrate, either of sunlight or intelligence. . . . These "hysterics of the labor movement" (for these "fiends" have deluded themselves . . . that they have something in common with the labor movement) write their diabolical mandates upon grimy tables covered with bomb-slaughtered capitalists, these "fiends" having improved upon the capitalist method of starving said victims, and then taking their hides to make fine slippers for their daughters, etc.

And as these "foul conspirators" each in turn reaches a mangy hand under the table and takes therefrom a capitalistic infant's skull, each slowly raises bloodshot eyes, fills said skull with sour beer which is contained in the empty half of a dynamite bomb. At this signal, the whole crowd arise and straighten, as well as they can, their tatterdemalion forms, and with distended nostrils hiss from between clenched teeth, "BLOOD!"

Was this any more overdrawn than descriptions in the capitalist press? "No!" was Lucy's emphatic answer.[3]

In March 1887 Lucy again went east to raise money for the defense; the case had just gone to the Illinois Supreme Court. She arrived in Columbus, Ohio, on March 8, 1887, and was arrested that day. The mayor was determined that no anarchist was going to speak in Columbus! She was to have spoken in the Fourteenth Regiment Armory, but when Major Coit, the man in charge of the Armory found out who was to speak, he refused to rent the hall.

Lucy knew that her arrest in defense of free speech would draw attention to the cause; she could not let the opportunity go by and marched down to City Hall demanding an audience with the Mayor. She had told Major Coit, "If you understand that anarchy means violence and disorder, you, sir, are the only anarchist I know of in Columbus just now."

But Coit got to the mayor's office first, and whether or not he was the only anarchist in Columbus, he knew the mayor was on his side. Mayor Walcutt admitted Lucy and her friends Mrs. Lyndall and Urban Hartung after he had talked with Coit. Lucy's first impression of the mayor was that he had been drinking heavily. He abruptly cut off her request to use the hall. "I don't want to hear anything from you. There will be no meeting allowed in that hall tonight." The mayor, whose morals were constantly in question in the Columbus newspapers for corruption, bribery, supporting gambling houses and houses of prostitution, drew his line, however, at an anarchist speaking in his city.

"Sir, I come to you not as a dictator, but as a servant of the people." Before she could say anything else the mayor had turned to the detectives standing around him and ordered, "Take her down!"

She soon found out what "Take her down!" meant. Two burly detectives seized her by the arm. One yelled to the other to grab her other arm. They left a few imprints in her arms with their rough handling. They yanked off her shawl and tossed it to Mrs. Lyndall. Lucy screamed, "You scoundrels! Does it take two of you to carry one little woman?"

The charge against Lucy was "publicly contending" with one William White, "a delicate framed detective weighing only 280 pounds."

Lucy hastily telegraphed Albert. "Albert Parsons, County Jail: Arrested to prevent my speaking am all right notify press —Lucy." Albert fired off a telegram, "Lucy E. Parsons, in Prison: the poor have no rights which the law respects. The constitution is a dead letter to the people of the United States. A.R. Parsons."

For the first four hours of her imprisonment in the Franklin County Jail, Lucy was confined to the "Ranche." The "Ranche" was a long narrow corridor, four feet wide and 20 feet long. Heavy iron doors along the corridor opened into small, damp, foul-smelling cells. Lucy would never in a thousand years forget that first 24 hours in the Columbus jail. Around her were women, hauled in by the long arm of the law. A young woman lay on an incredibly filthy quilt. Sitting around on the cold, dirty, stone floor were four other women, and a rather pretty young woman, about 20 years old, sat on the only chair in the place.

As soon as the guards bolted the door, the women began to ask questions.

"What are you run in for?" asked one.

"Disorderly conduct."

"Is this your first time?"

"Yes."

"Oh, well, it won't go very hard with you, that is, if it is the first time."

"How hard do you think it will go with me?"

"Oh! If it's the first time $5 and costs, and if you can show them you never was in before it won't be that much."

"Well, do you think I can get out on bail tonight?"

"Yes, if you got about $10 to put up, and if you ain't got that much, I see you got a watch, put that up. Don't let 'em around here know you got money; if you do they'll soak you."

Lucy preferred to believe what the other inmates told her about bail. But the women who had been run in on drunkenness, prostitution, adultery, or just because their husbands got tired of them, had no conception that Lucy's crime was a political crime, not a simple disorderly conduct. It would take Lucy Parsons a lot more than $10 to get out of jail that night!

Lucy was getting hungry. She asked about supper.

"Bread and water and salt for breakfast, nothing, nothing for dinner, and bread and water and salt for supper."

"And is that all you have?" Lucy asked.

"Yep."

"So this is what you have? And you are put in here for punishment. Are you any better when you go out?"

"Ha! We are a sight worse. It only makes a girl worse to treat her like we are treated."

Once Lucy was over her initial indignation and fear at being thrown in the dungeon, she was eager to test her political theory out firsthand. The results confirmed her belief. She decided she would check out the rest of the place, especially the little dark dungeons which opened off the corridor. She started to walk into one of them, when the women shouted, "Don't go in there! You'll get full of bedbugs!"

She backed out hurriedly, puzzled. "Well, where do you sleep?"

"Out here on the floor."

"What! Do you sleep on nothing?"

A man came to the door and asked if they were hungry; Lucy asked the others if they would like sandwiches. They were enthusiastic and she sent out for seven sandwiches. The other women had no friends and no money with which to provide themselves more than the bread and salt jail fare. Lucy was better off; her friends commanded headlines, and she would not be forgotten in some small cell.

Later a guard came to the door. Lucy asked if there was any way she could get out that night. He thought $10 would get her out. She could leave it with the desk officer. The guard left, and never came back. He was told just who Lucy Parsons was and that she was not to be let out under any circumstances.

During the first three hours in the "Ranche," all sorts of men came down to the women's cell block, peeked in, teased, cajoled, and swore at the women. The women were accustomed to the daily game, and their tongues were just as foul. Lucy was shocked.

About 10 P.M. a guard ordered her to pick up her things and come with him. He carefully locked her into a 5' by 4' cell with oak slats held together by iron chains for Lucy to sleep on. The mayor didn't want to run any risks with his dangerous anarchist prisoner.

They kept her in lock up until 4:00 P.M. the next day. Thirty or forty friends and sympathizers came to see her, but only Mrs. Lyndall, who brought her meals, was allowed in. Despite the fact that none of her friends could see her, she had many "visitors." Every friend of the mayor, every petty employee of the prison, and any other man who heard about the great show down at the jail came in to laugh and gawk at her. They came in groups and lounged against the wall, peering through the iron grating as they would on a Sunday outing at the zoo. They asked how her health was and how she liked her new quarters. The parade of visitors lasted all day.

She was furious! All the detectives and drunkards and gamblers in the city could come and laugh, but none of her friends could come and talk.

She was taken to police court late that afternoon. The lobby was packed with newspaper reporters, detectives, police, and onlookers. Her attorney said "Not Guilty" when Mayor Walcutt called the case, but the mayor simply handed the lawyer a writ sending his client back to prison. He informed Attorney Watson he could read the writ, but that was all he could do and then proceeded with the other cases as if nothing had happened. The mayor had set bail at $300.

The Mayor acted on a section in the statutes which gave a magistrate the right to send a person to jail "without process or any other proof" if the incident took place in front of the judge. Lucy filed a formal demand for a trial by jury, but the mayor ignored it. She complained, "I found in the same indi-

vidual, complainant, prosecuting attorney, chief witness, all oc-
cupying the judicial bench to mete out impartial justice to me
. . . and thus preclude the possibility of my speaking in
Columbus that night. In other words a foul conspiracy to crush
free speech!

The horse-drawn paddy wagon came to return Lucy to the
jail. The crowd watched as Mrs. Lyndall kissed her good-bye.
Lucy stood in the back of the wagon as it started to move and
shouted to the crowd, "Your liberty is ended, American citizens! The right of free speech is refused!" Back to jail she
went, with no hearing.

Lucy's arrest caused a mixed reaction in the press. The
Cincinnati Enquirer headlined the event, "Lucy Parsons Raises
A Big Racket at Columbus, and is Promptly Lodged Behind
the Prison Bars. Her Terrible Invective Poured Out Upon the
Mayor and the City, the Cause of It." But the *Columbus Capitol* found her arrest altogether unnecessary and a threat to free
speech and assembly. The paper charged that it was a dangerous precedent for the police to legislate what meetings could
not be held. They knew Mayor Walcutt for his crooked administration, and believed they would receive the same arbitrary
justice Lucy Parsons received. "Indeed, it is possible that a
meeting to protest against the open gambling houses which are
permitted by Mayor Walcutt would be dispersed by the batons
of his officers, or a request to close the saloons on Sunday
would be received by his Honor as 'a personal insult.'" The
paper attacked the increasingly tyrannical acts of the city administration officials "some of whom but yesterday . . . discharged from custody men guilty of premeditated and felonious
crime" and expressed fear that the public had acquiesced in the
intensified level of political repression. The interests of the
Capitol were at stake; but its editors were quick to remind readers that their editorial policy abhorred "Anarchism and Communism" as much as "Mormonism and Mohammedonism."

On March 11th Lucy was out on bail with a court date set
for April 12. She headed for Cincinnati, then St. Louis and
asked the American people to consider the conspiracy against
free speech in Columbus. "Let the people of America read and
ponder, those of them who believe the laws are administered
alike for rich and poor, and in reading I hope they will lose

sight of me and simply see that it is not me on trial but free speech."[4]

Lucy had all the evidence she needed that justice was administered in opposite ways to rich and poor; her task was to demonstrate the evidence to the American people. She could lecture night after night on the miscarriage of justice in Chicago, but an object lesson in unequal justice—such as her arrest—brought attention to her campaign and sympathy to her cause.

She could politely ask the Mayor for her right to free speech. He could grant her rights, and she could speak to the public directly. Or he could refuse her rights, and she could communicate to the public indirectly through headlines.

She met roadblocks at every step of her way. Halls were closed to her at the last moment, detectives stood in every corner of the meeting halls, police kept her under constant surveillance. They knew exactly when Lucy Parsons was coming to town, and they were ready for her. In Columbus, Ohio, she had met a concentrated form of official tyranny.

Her tours for the defense brought herself and the case into the national limelight and kept them there for months. It acquainted thousands of people with radical ideas and helped to build the basis for the reform and radical movement of the 1890's.

Many labor historians have argued that the Haymarket bomb had an almost immediate disintegrating and conservatizing effect upon the American labor movement. Terence Powderly and Samuel Gompers both believed the Haymarket bomb had set back the labor movement for years. The *Arbeiter-Zeitung,* the *Chicago Knights of Labor,* and many other papers attributed the collapse of the eight hour movement to the bomb. Professor Norman Ware implied that Parsons' membership in the Knights of Labor resulted in a decline in membership. Professor Henry David successfully challenged this notion in *The History of the Haymarket Affair.*

It is, of course, true that Wall Street and factory owners used the bombing to rescind eight-hour gains and to disrupt the movement. It is also true that the Knights of Labor dwindled to almost nothing within a few years and that the eight hour demand was not won on a national scale.

In the aftermath of the bombing labor organizers turned to political activity rather than the economic agitation which Spies and Parsons had advocated. The day after the guilty verdict in the Haymarket trial, prominent labor leaders and socialists in Chicago met to plan a labor ticket for the next election. George Schilling, Fred W. Long, C. G. Dixon, William Gleason, Charles Seib, Joe Gruenhut, Tommy Morgan, and Paul Ehman were all there. The Central Labor Union endorsed the campaign and selected delegates to the Labor Party convention on September 25. They levied a 2¢ per member assessment on each union to finance the campaign; they could expect $400 on the basis of 20,000 members.

Meanwhile the Knights of Labor held their convention in Richmond, Virginia, in October. The election of George Schilling, Thomas Randall and William Gleason to the Chicago delegation was a victory for the socialists; most of the rest of the delegation was sympathetic to these three men. The Richmond convention almost unanimously passed a vote of sympathy for the condemned men, although Powderly viciously fought the resolution. Rank and file Knights supported Parsons, whatever the Executive Committee did.

At the Richmond convention, George Schilling announced the forthcoming publication of *Dawn of the Social Revolution* by his friend William H. Parsons. William Parsons intended to write a history of the Haymarket bombing and trial; he took an indefinite leave from his job and in a few months had written over 800 pages.

He planned to write the history from his standpoint as a Knight of Labor. Dyer D. Lum, an anarchist, later demanded that Parsons turn over his manuscript to him as he intended to write the history of the trial from an anarchist point of view. William Parsons refused.[5]

In June, 1886, it had been reported that 20,000 Chicago packinghouse workers, 10,000 clerks, and 15,000 building trades workers had won the eight hour day. Twenty five thousand cloak makers and men's garment workers had won nine hours. At least 70,000 Chicago workers had won reduced hours.

Very quickly, however, production at the packinghouses reached the level under the eight hour day that had been maintained under the ten hour day. Speed-up meant the continued slaughter of 2,500 hogs a day. Despite the fact that production had not gone down, the packers decided to take away the eight hour day in October, 1886. The stockyards workers struck to preserve their victories. George Schilling, who had organized 40,000 stockyards workers in the spring, fought tenaciously for them. Just as the workers were about to gain a complete victory, Powderly issued a back to work order saying that the strike had been lost. Confused over the conflicting orders, the strikers began going back to work. Powderly had broken the strike.

In the face of such defeats as the Southwest Railroad strike in the spring of 1886 and the Chicago stockyards in the fall, the Knights membership began a precipitous decline. In the six months after the disastrous stockyards strike, membership in Knights of Labor District Assembly 24 of Chicago dropped from 24,000 to 4,000.

In December, 1886, the American Federation of Labor was founded. Unlike the Knights, the A.F. of L. was strictly a trade union organization, and it challenged the Knights for the leadership of the working class.

The Knights of Labor had never accepted the theory of class struggle. In the leadership of the A.F. of L. were several prominent socialists, and even Samuel Gompers at one time considered himself a Marxist. The preamble adopted at the organization's founding convention focused on class struggle: "A struggle is going on in the nations of the world between the oppressors and oppressed of all countries, a struggle between capital and labor which must grow in intensity from year to year and work disastrous results to the toiling millions of all nations if not combined for mutual protection and benefit."

The new organization emphasized strikes; the Knights' leadership did not. The A.F. of L. favored the eight hour movement; the Knights' leadership did not. Most A.F. of L. trade union affiliates had socialist platforms and called for restructuring society. Formally, the American Federation of Labor was more radical than the Knights of Labor.

In Chicago the move towards a strict trade union base was reflected in a struggle within the United Labor Party. Certain Knights were strongly opposed when the U.L.P. closed its membership to all but members of labor organizations.

Perhaps the most remarkable feature of the Chicago labor

movement *after* the Haymarket bombing and trial was that it was still controlled by socialists. The radicals had captured the major labor organizations in the city: the three district assemblies of the Knights, the Central Labor Union, and the Trades Assembly. "Red and Redder" complained the headlines. "Socialists Now in Complete Control of all the Labor Organizations in Chicago." It was a frightening thought for the Citizens' Association that socialists dominated the labor movement and were not stopped by the threatened executions of seven "anarchists."

Mayor Harrison hoped to effect a fusion ticket between the United Labor Party and the Democratic party and insure his own re-election; he planned a Democratic invasion of the U.L.P., but Tommy Morgan was too shrewd for that. The mayor offered patronage; William Gleason, a bricklayer and member of the Committee of 21 (the executive committee of the U.L.P.) cooperated with Harrison. But Morgan, supported by the Central Labor Union and District Assembly 24 of the Knights of Labor fought fusion and won. For mayor the U.L.P. nominated Robert Nelson, a machinist, president of the Eight Hour Association of Chicago and Master Workman of D. A. 24.

If the rulers of Chicago thought they had defeated the labor movement and the radicals by the trial of the "anarchist" leaders, they would not have put so much effort into fighting the U.L.P. and capturing the labor vote.

By the end of February, Mayor Harrison realized that the Labor Party would result in a Republican victory. He refused the Democratic Party nomination and urged the Democrats to support Nelson. But most Democrats saw their class interest and voted for the other capitalist party candidate, John P. Roche of the Republicans.

For the time being Tommy Morgan would work with Lucy Parsons and other "anarchists" whom he despised in building the United Labor Party. But Morgan could be irascible and dictatorial, and his leadership did not inspire confidence or unity in the long run.

Albert Parsons had his public and private views on the election. He nominally suported the U.L.P. from jail, but he wrote to Dyer Lum that he didn't expect gains from political activity and the electoral process was meaningless. He didn't want his private views made public until after the election.[6]

Lucy was back in Chicago before the election, which was held in early April, 1887. The campaign was characterized by red-baiting. Candidate Roche offered voters the choice between the red flag of anarchism and communism or the American flag. The *Inter-Ocean* charged the United Labor Party with anarchism. The *Times,* the only Democratic paper in the city, cried "Remember the Haymarket!" a headline certain to evoke the Red Spectre and images of bloody massacre.

Lucy Parsons' prominence in the ranks of the United Labor Party substantiated the charges of anarchism. She was the center of attention at the U.L.P. rally the Saturday night before the election.

When the vote was in, Roche had won. But 23,500 people had voted for Nelson, nearly a third of the 75,000 votes cast. The United Labor Party had elected seven state assemblymen, one state senator, one alderman, and five out of the six judges it had endorsed. The party's congressional candidate lost by only 64 votes. The election was a victory for labor.

Albert Parsons told a reporter that the Republican mayoral victory was expected, but he was quite impressed that so many wage slaves "should stand up for their rights." Although the election did not give Nelson the mayor's job, the election demonstrated that the labor and socialist movement in Chicago had not disappeared in the bombing hysteria.

But immediately after what he considered the election defeat, George Detwiler, editor of *Chicago Knights of Labor,* blamed Tommy Morgan for the defeat and attempted to throw him out of the United Labor Party. The *Chicago Knights of Labor* charged the radicals with a variety of offenses which resulted in the defeat. "Blunder number one" was the exclusion of all persons who were not members of labor organizations, it charged. But their greatest offense was that they had achieved control of the party, nominated the mayoral candidate, and dictated the platform.

The paper charged that three rabid anarchists—Lucy Parsons, Albert Currlin, and Fred Long—had contributed to the defeat.

Added to a successive series of outrageous blunders was the crowning act of idiocy, a beer-guzzling jubilee on Saturday night before the election, with Mrs. Parsons as the most conspicuous attendant. Anybody has a right to hold a beer picnic whenever they please, and Mrs. Parsons or anybody else had a right to go; but when a central committee of a political party invests its money in beer and right on the eve of election opens out a saloon and gets up a political jubilee, than Mrs. Parsons' presence has a political significance, the results of which may be learned by contemplating Roche's majority.

Detwiler laid the blame on Lucy. But Ernst Schmidt had received nearly 12,000 votes for mayor in 1879, and that had been considered a peak of success. Eight years later, Robert Nelson, another workers' candidate, received nearly twice as many votes. Lucy's activities had profound political significance in Chicago, but her support of Nelson could not have subtracted a substantial number of votes; in fact she may have contributed to his total.

The Union Labor Party in Milwaukee was highly successful, and labor parties throughout the country made strong showings. The working people of New York City nearly elected Henry George mayor in the fall of 1887. He may have been counted out, and he ran well ahead of the Republican candidate, Theodore Roosevelt, who had called for the summary execution of all anarchists. George was the author of *Progress and Poverty* and the formulator of the single tax theory.[7] George, however, vacillated on the Haymarket issue, which he knew would affect his campaign. In January, 1887, he denounced the trial and conviction; in October he saw no reason to overturn the verdict of the courts. Lucy Parsons had thanked the Henry George Assembly in Detroit in January for its support; she would have to reverse her thanks.

After the mayoral election in April, Lucy was on the road again; in May she spoke to miners in Iron Mountain, Michigan.

The appeal to the Illinois Supreme Court dragged on through the summer. Lucy was in and out of Chicago, speaking at picnics and labor gatherings. She was also faced with the urgent need to sew as much of the time as she could spare to support herself and her children. She didn't even have money to buy underwear for Albert in jail, and he had to request socks and underwear from the Defense Committee.[8]

In July, Lucy appeared at the International Brewers and

Malsters picnic at Ogden Grove with George Schilling and a stack of books and pictures of the condemned men. She had Nina Van Zandt's life of Spies. The president of the union was furious that Mrs. Parsons should put in an appearance and threaten to make a speech; he demanded that she be thrown out or he would resign. However, she did not attempt to make a speech, and she spent the afternoon selling literature and pictures and talking with people about the case.

In August the defense held a mass rally in Sheffield, Indiana. They hired a special train, as they had for previous rallies, to go across the state border where the Chicago police could not disrupt their fund raiser.

It was a hot August day. When Tommy Morgan had finished his speech, the crowd shouted for Lucy. She was tired from the months of defense work; the sun was beating down on the speakers' stand, and she asked Tommy Morgan to hold an umbrella over her head. So as the man who detested her views protected her from the sun, she lectured on the inadequacies of the law and state socialism. She denounced the Henry George Assembly in New York for expelling socialists, after the socialists had made the movement as strong as it was.

By July, 1887, District Assembly 89 of the Knights of Labor, the socialist dominated Denver organization, had had enough of Terence Powderly's sabotage. They forced him to testify to them about his divisive roles in recent strikes: his opposition to the Great Southwest Strike of 1885 (led by Joe Buchanan), to the Southwest strike of 1886, to the general strike for the eight-hour day, and to the defeated Chicago stockyards strike in October, 1886.

Powderly feared Burnette Haskell, who questioned him, but not so much as he feared Joe Buchanan, the former organizer of the Rocky Mountain branch of the International Workingmen's Association and the editor of the *Chicago Labor Enquirer*. The questions were Buchanan's, and Powderly was preparing to go to Chicago, and, as he put it, "to meet that traducer in his own den. If he were here tonight I would cram the lies he has entered about me down his throat."

Buchanan and Haskell had more to ask Powderly than about his destructive role in Knights' strikes. They would make him defend his position against the Haymarket defendants; and they would make him defend the statements he had made about Lucy Parsons.

Under Haskell's incisive questioning, Powderly conceded that agents provocateur had used dynamite in the Southwest strikes to discredit the labor movement. Then Haskell asked the crucial question, "Do you not think it reasonable to suppose that the Haymarket bomb in Chicago was also thrown by detectives. . . .?" Powderly emphatically denied that the bomb could have been thrown by detectives. He then made the boldest accusation he had yet made: "I had from the brother of A.R. Parsons evidence enough to convict the men of Chicago of murder. . . . I kept silent from generosity although these men have slandered me in a horrible way. The Chicago men are assassins and can be proved so by me. I had the proofs of it long ago." Confusion and exclamations followed each sentence as Powderly spoke. A moment's stunned silence followed his charges.

"Then Sir, why do you not denounce them at once!" shouted Haskell.

Powderly had no answer for that question. He groped for a reply. "I am not a detective, and it was not any of my business."

Buchanan later charged that the reference to Parsons' brother "is a lie out of whole cloth." All the public statements which William Parsons made about the trial demonstrate that Powderly was telling a boldfaced lie.

After exposing Powderly's statement about the Chicago defendants for what it was, Haskell then demanded to know why Powderly had condemned Lucy Parsons.

The Grand Master Workman of the Knights of Labor replied, "Because she is not his wife because they only live together and are not married and because it is not my business to look after any woman of bad reputation, white or negro who tramps around the country as she does."

When Buchanan heard Powderly's accusations against Lucy, he made a written reply, saying that Powderly must have known that both Lucy and Albert were members of the Knights. He said he had taken the trouble to satisfy himself that "Albert and Lucy Parsons are regularly married." He continued the letter to Haskell, threatening Powderly for his accusations, "I have agencies at work to get the undeniable proofs and when

I get them, if you can furnish signatures (say half a dozen) to a document showing that Powderly made that assault upon Mrs. Parsons' reputation, he will be made to scorch for that as well as for other things."9

It still remains a question whether church and state sanctioned Lucy and Albert's relationship. They considered themselves married, and the "legality" of that marriage did not significantly affect their work. Lucy already labored under the triple oppression of being a woman, working class, and nonwhite. Her enemies used the question of her marriage to undermine her credibility in an era when women could not easily choose sexual freedom.

"Let the Voice of the People Be Heard!"

In September 1887, the Illinois Supreme Court upheld the verdict of the lower court. Albert Parsons wrote his "Appeal to the People of America." He reviewed the events which had brought him face to face with death; he denounced the verdict of the court. He left it to the American people to decide the verdict. "I leave it to you to decide from the record itself as to my guilt or innocence. I CAN NOT THEREFORE ACCEPT a commutation to imprisonment. I appeal not for mercy, but for justice. As for me, the utterance of Patrick Henry is so apropos that I can not do better than let him speak: 'Is life so dear and peace so sweet as to be purchased at the price of chains and slavery? Forbid it, Almighty God! I know not what course others may pursue, but as for me, give me liberty or give me death!' "

Lucy was arrested on the street distributing the "Appeal." Lucy and Albert were willing to commit their case to the very prejudiced American people; although the hysteria had died down somewhat, "anarchism" remained a highly charged word.

The next day Lucy went to the filthy Armory courtroom by herself. She sat quietly by the window reading the paper; the sorrow and trouble of the past year had brought lines to her dark face. Pretty soon the matron sat down, and they began to talk about Lulu, who had been sick again. Suddenly the judge interrupted the case which was in progress and called Mrs. Parsons. The judge felt kindly towards her and said softly, "Mrs. Parsons, there has been a technical violation of an ordinance on your part. There is not the slightest desire on my part to deal harshly with you, as I know the depth of your sorrow. I will fine you $5 and suspend the fine. You may go." Sadly and silently she left the courtroom.

Although their attorneys, who now included several very prominent Americans,[1] hoped to take the case to the U.S. Supreme Court, by October Albert and Lucy were telling reporters that they expected him to be sacrificed to the demands of capital.

The U.S. Supreme Court refused to hear the case on November 2, 1887—only a little more than a week before the scheduled execution date: November 11. By this time many liberals, labor leaders, and concerned citizens had spoken out against the verdict. They charged that the jury had not been impartial, that the defendants had been denied their civil rights.

The last resort was a petition campaign to Governor Oglesby for clemency or pardons for the condemned men. But not only did the city of Chicago deny the men their legal rights, the Chicago police attempted to deny the defense committee access to the mails. The defense committee had proof that most of the petitions they had mailed out of Chicago had never reached their destinations. Lucy's mail was opened, and much of it was never delivered.[2]

On November 2 Lucy brought Lulu and Albert to the jail. The jailers heard the children shouting "Papa! Papa!" before Lucy even came into the cell block with them.

Lucy had just heard the news that the Supreme Court had refused to hear their case; she was upset by the news, and her eyes were red. She had a sad smile on her face as she put her lips to the wire mesh cage and attempted to kiss Albert.

The children were wild with excitement, and the keepers let them into the cell. In an instant one was perched on his shoulder, and the other had happily settled into his lap, gleefully shouting "Papa! My Papa!"

"Give me a ride!" laughed Lulu. He quickly put her on his shoulders and ran back and forth in the cage while Albert followed at his heels shouting with delight. When their father was thoroughly exhausted, he put the kids down and turned to talk with Lucy.

They took the news from the Supreme Court calmly; they had expected weeks before that capitalism would demand Albert's blood, and they were prepared for the sacrifice which they believed would advance the cause of the working class.

Lucy strongly supported the four defendants who absolutely refused to petition for clemency: Albert Parsons, Louis Lingg, Adolph Fischer and George Engel. For over a year she had sworn that she would never ask for mercy from capitalists; she would die first. And she had repeatedly said that she would not accept a justice which set Albert at liberty and killed her other comrades. She and Louis Lingg were adamant that the seven men should stand together demanding liberty or death.

Lucy was furious when Schwab, Fielden, and Spies signed letters asking Governor Oglesby for mercy. Schwab and Fielden signed letters admitting they had not thought out what they said, and that it might have inspired violence. However, they denied they were a part of any conspiracy. Spies, after long deliberation and intense pressure from members of the defense committee finally signed a plea. As he took the pen, he said to Joe Buchanan and George Schilling, "I think I am making a mistake." The reaction to Spies' plea was immediate and fierce; the radical Germans denounced him as a coward.

George Schilling spent hours with Albert Parsons trying to persuade him to sign; but Parsons' mind had been made up for months. He had written his letter refusing clemency in the middle of October, and he made it public when Spies, Schwab, and Fielden appealed to the Governor.

Albert Parsons knew that Fischer, Engel and Lingg would go to the gallows whatever he did. He could not face waking up in the penitentiary each morning knowing that he had betrayed them. He was determined to hang with his comrades. "If the State of Illinois can afford to hang an innocent man, I can afford to hang," he declared.

Fischer's and Engel's families begged them to sign the petitions; Lucy absolutely refused to interfere with Albert's decision.

On November 3, Lucy, thin and haggard from months of defense work and the suspense of the appeals, faced the prospect of supporting her children alone. But her poverty would never budge her principles, and she was determined that Albert must die a martyr in the struggle for economic emancipation. She refused to take part in the amnesty movement or to sign appeals to the governor; she did her part appealing to people on the streets to buy General Matthew M. Trumbull's pamphlet "Was It a Fair Trial?" for a nickel each. The 20 page pamphlet read in part:

> Never before, except in burlesque, was the meaning of words reversed as in the Anarchist trial. Logic stood on its head, and reasoned with its heels. Facts absent from the theory of the prosecution were solemnly claimed as evidence

to establish it. It was averred that *if* certain events had happened which did not happen, they would have shown that the conspiracy and the tragedy were cause and consequence, therefore the connection is proved. . . .

The conspiracy which the prosecution attempted to show on the trial, and which it is pretended they did show, was not carried into execution in any of its essential details. . . . It was to begin by the throwing of bombs into the North Avenue station and into other stations in the city. Well drilled men, armed with rifles, were to be stationed outside to shoot the police as they came out; then the conspirators were to march inwards towards the heart of the city, destroying whatever should oppose them. . . . Nothing of the kind occurred; nothing of it was attempted. . . .

A scaffold for seven men is built of *"if"* and *"would have been."*

As many as 5,000 people crowded around Lucy as she sold the pamphlet, some out of curiosity, others out of a sincere desire to support her cause. The crowd blocked the streets; three out-of-breath policemen with flushed faces hurried up and shouted "Move On!" to her. But although she moved, the crowd followed, and continued to block the street. Two officers arrested her and took her to see Chief Ebersold, who released her saying she could sell books as long as she did not block the street. That was asking the impossible, because the crowds would not stay away—and Lucy did not want them to stay away.

She returned to the printers, picked up more copies of the pamphlet and walked briskly down the street selling pamphlets as fast as she could make change. Again a large crowd gathered around her. When a burly policeman rudely shouted "Move On!, she quickly moved, hurried up the stairway to the Defense Committee on Clark St., and sank down on the stairs exhausted. The police had harrassed and chased her through the streets for two hours, but she had still sold 5,000 pamphlets, bringing in $250.

The reporter who followed her up the stairway noted, "There was none of the old time defiance, not a sign of the wild, untamed lioness. . . . A year ago Mrs. Parsons would have turned on the bluecoated minister of despotism, she would have castigated him with fierce invective. Today she obeyed the by no means courteous order to 'Move On!' "

On November 5, Lucy was still selling pamphlets as fast as she could make change. She dropped by the jail with a basket of the pamphlets in their new green bindings slung over her arm and gaily chatted with Albert. She laughingly explained why the pamphlets were now bound in green, rather than in their original red. "It suits the police better."

Lucy and Albert had another reason to be happy that day. The first issue of the *Alarm* since April, 1886, came out edited by Dyer D. Lum. Lum was an active member of the Knights of Labor from New York. On the front page of the paper, Albert Parsons had written his parting message to comrades. "And now to all I say: Falter not. Lay bare the iniquities of capitalism; expose the slavery of law; proclaim the tyranny of governments; denounce the greed, cruelty, abominations of the privileged class, who riot and revel on the labor of their wage-slaves. Farewell. A.R. Parsons. Prison Cell 29, Chicago, Ill."

The following day, November 6, the police moved the men out of their cells and searched the cells. In Louis Lingg's cell they "found" four bombs.

When Lucy arrived at the jail for her visit, she was searched, as were the other visitors. Then they were forced to remain across the corridor under guard while talking with the prisoners. Lucy was furious and indignant.

When she heard that four bombs had been found, she sarcastically commented, "Why that's just one each for the boys." She no longer counted Spies, Schwab, and Fielden who had appealed for mercy.

"And are four bombs all that the detectives and deputy sheriffs could discover? My, my what a discovery it was, and how do the police or the powers that be explain the presence of those bombs in Lingg's cell?" Lucy was tired of the police finding bombs all over the city; Captain Schaack was capable of imagining bombs for any and all occasions.

Lucy was in the mood to have a little fun with the reporters. "I have it," she cried, "Eda Miller, his girl, brought those bombs to Lingg. Of late you will have noticed that she has been wearing a very large bustle, much too large for style or comfort. Then again, if you have watched her very closely, she always sits down very carefully and quietly. If she did not, why, she'd be blown to atoms!" Lucy solemnly continued her "disclosure." "She, then, must be the one who has furnished these bombs. There, you have an explanation of the mystery. Ha, ha, thank God, I don't wear a bustle at all, and therefore I cannot be accused of any complicity in this latest sensation."

Lucy was quite as good as the police in concocting fantastic stories about the latest bombs.

She went to the Amnesty Association and announced the news of the bombs. "If it is true, I know how they got there. They were placed there by the jail officials, who would do anything to stem the tide of public opinion which is now in favor of commuting the sentences of the Anarchists." But she didn't think they'd done a good job of it. "Why didn't they do a better job and make the conspiracy complete? They should have put a bomb in Lingg's cell, a fuse in Fischer's, dynamite in Parsons' and percussion caps in Engel's. That would have been a good job and would have made a complete conspiracy." On November 6, five days before the scheduled executions, Lucy could still joke about the antics of the police.

Albert Parsons was sure that the police had planted the bombs in order to put a damper on the amnesty movement. "Those bombs," he wrote, "if they were really found there, were put there by someone whose business it was to find them there." In any case, the openings in the wire mesh of the cages were too small to slip the "bombs" through—and the "bombs" could have been filled with molasses for all anyone knew. He and Lucy could barely touch each other with their little fingers through that wire mesh. It couldn't accommodate a bomb.

But George Schilling thought that Lingg knew the bombs were there,[3] and August Spies called Lingg a monomaniac with a martyr's complex and said he hadn't spoken to the young carpenter in nine months. He thought Lingg had had the bombs brought to him, and he was angry that Lingg was willing to sacrifice not only his own life to the cause, but the rest of the defendants' lives as well. Spies was probably equally perturbed with Lucy Parsons and her defiant attitude. "If anyone holds us, or any one of us, responsible for Lingg's deeds, then I can't see why we shouldn't be held responsible for any mischief, whatsoever, in the world."

George Francis Train,[4] who had said that if seven men had to be executed, society could more easily spare the seven justices of the Illinois Supreme Court than the condemned men, sent each a basket of fruit and $5. That $5 would help Lucy feed her children. Support and sympathy poured in from around the country.

Members of the defense committee, the men's families, and prominent citizens who wanted the defendants jailed—not executed—crowded the jail as November 11th approached, begging Parsons, Fischer, Engel, and Lingg to sign petitions.

On the 8th, Lucy paid her last visit to the jail; she was thrown out, along with the other women who had come to visit. She announced that her husband was dead to her and went home to her children to mourn for him. She swore she would never return to the jail and allow herself to be pushed around by the jail officials again. The authorities might think they had her where they could do what they liked, but she would not give them another opportunity to search her. "I spoke good-bye to him for the last time this afternoon, for I will never cross the threshold of the jail again to be insulted and humiliated. The other women can go there and grovel before the men who turned us out this afternoon, but I will never go until I can sit at the side of my husband and talk with him without an infamous guard at my side."

She continued darkly, threatening. "I want to live with the picture of my husband in a dungeon ever before my eyes. That will give me strength to bring up two revolutionists. The four men who will not belie their manhood are kept in dark dungeons, because they will not sign the petition. Mr. Parsons will never sign any begging appeal. He will die, and I hope they will make a clean sweep of it and hang the whole seven. Let them hang them all, and let the men who cry for blood have all they want of it. The blood of my husband be upon them."

Forty-one thousand names were collected on the petitions in Chicago between November 2 and November 9, when members of the defense committee met with Governor Oglesby. Another 150,000 names were gathered in New York, and 10,000 names came from St. Louis. All day the Governor held open hearings for petitioners. Samuel Gompers rushed to Illinois to petition the Governor on behalf of the condemned men. Terence Powderly, of course, refused to sign any petitions for mercy and hoped that "justice" would take its course and result in seven fewer anarchists on Friday.

After the public hearings were made before the Governor, Joe Buchanan, George Schilling, Henry Demarest Lloyd, and Professor Salter had a private meeting with the Governor.[5]

Buchanan had a second letter to the Governor from Spies. He and Schilling had brought five of Chicago's most radical Germans to hear Spies' letter.

In his second letter, Spies renounced his earlier appeal for clemency. He asked that if blood must be shed for blood, that only his life be taken, and the lives of his comrades spared. "I beg you to prevent a sevenfold murder upon men whose only crime is that they are idealists; that they long for a better future for all. If legal murder there must be, let one, let mine suffice. A. Spies." Silence reigned; Spies had redeemed his name in the eyes of the radical Germans. Lucy Parsons was by no means the only radical in Chicago who felt all the men should fight and die together.

Buchanan had another note for the Governor, which Albert Parsons had entrusted to him. "If I am guilty and must be hanged because of my presence at the Haymarket meeting, then I hope a reprieve will be granted in my case until my wife and two children, who were also at the meeting, can be convicted and hanged with me." Albert Parsons wanted to make the point that he was just as innocent of the bombing as were his two children. He hoped people would see how outrageous it would be to hang the children and realize that it was equally outrageous to hang him. Oglesby rang his hands. "My God, this is terrible!" he exclaimed.

Buchanan had one more petition to present, and he did it quickly, so he would not have to linger over Parsons' letter. It was an appeal for the lives of the "anarchists" from 50 delegates to the recent Knights of Labor convention.

It was the evening of Wednesday, November 9; Governor Oglesby had less than 48 hours in which to decide the fates of seven men.

The enemies of the defendants feared that the governor might commute Fielden's and Schwab's sentences.

Before 9:00 A.M. the next morning, the 10th, a blast

echoed through the Cook County Jail. People rushed to Lingg's cell where he lay with his face partially blown away. Lingg remained conscious until his death that afternoon. Whether he was murdered or committed suicide has never been resolved. But it was said that some unknown men had been seen in the jail early that morning.[6]

That evening Governor Oglesby announced his decision. Fielden and Schwab's sentences would be commuted to life in prison. Parsons, Spies, Fischer and Engel would die at noon the next day.

After she had heard the Governor's decision, Lucy Parsons decided to go to the jail. With two young friends she arrived at the jail about 9:00 P.M. The officer had strict orders not to let her in. "What time are you going to murder my husband?" she asked slowly, forcing the words. "Murder! Murder!" she pointed an accusing finger at the police. The policemen looked furtively about as they saw the heavy folds in her black dress. What if she had a bomb with her? Lucy Parsons scared them even in their dreams.

She became faint, and sat down, her two friends helping her. In a minute she was defiant and angry; the jail officials had refused her request. She got up, her eyes dry and flashing. "He is innocent of murder! They won't bring me one word from him!" she shouted as she walked out toward Clark St.

Inside the jail Albert Parsons was at peace with himself and his conscience. He seemed happy, even ecstatic, knowing that tomorrow he would die a martyr. He sang the Marseillaise and Annie Laurie in his rich, tenor voice. About 2:00 A.M. he went to bed, joking about the noise of the men hammering on the gallows. "How can a fellow go to sleep with that music?"

He had written his last request to Lucy, "**My poor, dear wife . . . . You, I bequeath to the people, a woman of the people. I have one request to make of you: Commit no rash act when I am gone, but take up the great cause of Socialism where I am compelled to lay it down.**" He feared that Lucy might follow her own advice to tramps, given three years before.

November 11th dawned bleak and gray in Chicago. The city was hushed and tense. The police had taken every precaution against a last minute jail break. Parsons' enemies in Texas offered to send 500 Texas riflemen to guard the jail. The offer was refused, but the roofs around the jail were black with riflemen, and troops were in the city. No one knew what the reaction to the executions would be. The Citizens' Association feared the worst. For many, Chicago would never be the same after November 11, 1887.

Albert Parsons and the other prisoners got up early, looking refreshed. They were calm and smiling. They had breakfast, wrote a few last letters to friends and comrades, and saw reporters. They would go to their deaths heroes, martyrs.

Lucy got up early, too. She thought she would be able to see Albert one more time. She washed and dressed little Albert and Lulu and hurried downtown through the blustery wind with William and Lizzie Holmes. She was dressed in black and had wound a long black crepe veil around her head, which trailed down her back.

William went to the Defense Committee office, while the two women and the children went to the jail. Ropes blocked off the jail at all corners, but Lucy was determined to get in.

At each corner of the jail, the police told her to "move on!" The children were turning blue with cold, crying and frightened. The police were having a game at their expense. Lucy moved back and forth on the sidewalk, trying to find a break between the police, but they always kept in front of her. She attempted to climb under the rope which blocked her way, but the police stood between her and the jail. Finally, she asked that just the children be allowed to see their father. This request, too, was refused. "Oh, you murderous villians!" she screamed. "You will forbid me to see my husband, whom you are about to kill, and not let him take a last look at the children whom you are about to make orphans!"

"Keep quiet," snarled an officer.

"I will not keep quiet. I have suffered your taunts and cruelties all morning, and I will keep quiet no longer. You murder my husband, and then ask me to keep quiet. I'll not do it!"

Suddenly she stopped, raised her arm defiantly and shouted with contempt and hate, "You must not follow me. I have no bombs about me now, but I could get them if I wanted to, and I could use them too!"

The officer grabbed the two women and two children and

hustled them off to the Chicago Avenue Station in a patrol wagon. At the station, a male officer watched with amusement as the matron stripped all four (even the children), searched them minutely for bombs, then locked them away naked.

"That woman is more to be feared than a thousand rioters," exclaimed one officer when he knew Lucy Parsons was safely under lock and key.

The hour of noon was drawing near. Albert Parsons was in his cell, crowded with reporters and curiousity seekers—people who had the credentials which would get them into the jail, which his wife and children did not.

Inside the jail the condemned men turned away a minister who had come to see them. At 11:30 the Sheriff came to their cells. He read the death warrants to the men, who were then prepared for the gallows, their hands fastened behind them, white shrouds and hoods over them. Parsons, Fischer, Engel and Spies said good-bye to Fielden and Schwab. (Neebe had been moved.) They walked resolutely to the gallows. As Albert Parsons stepped onto the scaffold, he appeared almost a saint; there was an unearthly goodness about him. The papers reported, "The moment his feet touched the scaffold Parsons seemed to completely lose his identity and to feel that his spirit was no longer part of his body. . . . The upward turn of his eyes, his distant, faraway look, and above all the attitude of apparent complete resignation . . . was by far the most striking feature of the entire gallows picture." Parsons knew that future generations would remember him.

The crowd of 200 watched in the small area behind the jail, with awe and wonder at the four men who were about to die. Suddenly the powerful voice of Spies broke the silence. "There will come a time when our silence will be more powerful than the voices you are strangling today!"

Engel shouted "Hoch die Anarchie!"

"Hurrah for Anarchy! This is the happiest moment of my life," shouted Fischer. He never regretted refusing immunity from prosecution.

Then, not like the request of a man about to die, but like a command or a warning, Parsons' voice rang out. "Will you let me speak, Sheriff Matson?" There was an agonizing silence. Muffled through his shroud, Parsons began as clamly as he ever had, "Let the voice of the people be heard. O---"

The trap had been sprung; four men were silenced forever.

At the Chicago Avenue police station only a few blocks from the scaffold, Lucy sat shivering in a cell with her two children. In another cell Lizzie Holmes could hear her moaning, knowing that Albert Parsons was dying.

At 3:00 P.M. the officer came to tell Lucy that Albert was dead and she could go.

As soon as they were released, Lucy and Lizzie went to claim his body. Lucy looked at the pine coffin which held her husband's remains; her piercing eyes never flinched. The women watched as the undertaker began to remove the lid from the plain coffin; when the lid was unscrewed, Lucy helped the undertaker lift one end; Albert's body lay there, exactly as it had been taken down from the gallows; only the white shroud had been removed. Lucy looked calmly at the body; Lizzie Holmes broke into tears as she looked at her dead comrade and fellow editor. Lucy looked intently at Albert, then bent over and kissed him passionately. She signaled the undertaker to close the lid.

Lucy would never forget how she was treated as her husband died. "Think of it! I was a prisoner with my children while my husband met his death, and they laughed when I cried out in my agony. This is the truth, and I shall not forget it!" She straightened up and her eyes flashed with grim determination. The interview was over.

Lucy had borne the strain of the last 18 months courageously, and she had worn herself out taking on additional sewing work to support her children. But she broke down completely on Saturday when Albert was brought home to her in a coffin. She began crying hysterically and fainted.

There was one last thing Lucy wanted to do for Albert. In their many searches of her flat, the police had missed the embroidered red flag she had made to carry at the front of the Board of Trade demonstration. She carefully got the flag from its hiding place, folded and braided it, and fastened it lovingly across Albert's body, from his left shoulder to his right hip.

Before 8:00 A.M., 5,000 people stood on Milwaukee Ave. outside Lucy's apartment with the simple sign "Mrs. Parsons, Practical Dressmaker." A squad of 24 policemen quickly cleared the streets in front and formed the line down the side of the street. The mourners glared at the cops, but obeyed the orders.

When the door was opened a few minutes before eight, the thousands of people began filing through the plain, poverty-stricken apartment.

Lucy sat in the bedroom crying uncontrollably, sometimes hysterical, surrounded by her women friends. Sarah Ames and Lizzie Holmes stayed with her all day. They tried to restrain her, but several times she broke through their arms in a frenzy and ran to the casket crying "Albert, you are gone; they have killed you!" and falling on the casket to kiss her dead husband, lover, and comrade.

Mrs. Fielden and her little girl came in through the side door. She was crying as she picked up Lulu and Albert and tried to comfort them. When everyone noticed the children, the whole room broke into tears.

Each time Lucy ran to the casket her friends helped her back to the bedroom; their efforts to console her were hopeless.

Close to 10,000 people had seen Albert's pale face with its half smile by 11:30 that night when the doors were closed. William Holmes and M. Walters from District 1307 of the Knights of Labor stood guard over the body all night. Lucy fell into a troubled sleep.

The defense committee had hoped there would be no funerals and had made no funeral plans, working for a reprieve. They quickly went to the Mayor with a request to hold a funeral procession.

Mayor Roche issued the permit for 12-2 P.M. on Sunday, November 13. No flags, no speeches, no music (except dirges), were permitted. The committee could not get permits to bury the dead men in the city, so they made arrangements to take the bodies to Waldheim Cemetery, outside the city limits.

The procession would start near Spies' house—from which the family had absolutely banned reporters—and move down Milwaukee Avenue, picking up the bodies of the five martyrs at their homes: Spies, Fischer, Parsons, Engel and Lingg.

Lucy's red flag was sealed in Albert's coffin. It would not fly in the wind as it had in the past—but it would be in the procession. Engel's and Lingg's coffins were covered with large red flags. Red flowers were everywhere.

As the procession moved down Milwaukee Avenue to the measured beat of muffled drums, Mrs. Ames and Mrs. Buchanan helped Lucy into the living room to have one last look at her most precious friend. She fell on his body with a shriek. No one dared touch her as she murmured "Albert," "husband," hugging and kissing him. Finally she passed out, and her friends carried her back to the bedroom to revive her.

A reporter who had made his way into the house commented, "The fearless Amazon who led the Anarchists in their march upon the Board of Trade, who had urged the use of torch and dagger stood weak, helpless, and fainting in the presence of death." Her bitter enemy Captain Schaack said that "Mrs. Parsons was in paroxysms of grief," but even in her sorrow, she did not forget the police. "Her curses were loud against the police."

Lucy would better have stepped defiantly onto the scaffold herself, than endure the death of her husband. She had the character of a martyr, not a widow.

She was completely shrouded in heavy black crepe as her friends helped her into the first carriage in Albert's funeral procession. With her were Lizzie Holmes, Sarah Ames, and Mrs. Fielden. Mrs. Buchanan, Mrs. Schilling, and Mrs. Oliver followed in other carriages.

Knights of Labor District Assembly 1307 was in charge of Albert Parsons' funeral; they defiantly opposed Terence Powderly. Joseph Buchanan, Dyer D. Lum, Dr. Randall of the *Chicago Express,* Lucien S. Oliver (president of the Amnesty Association), William Holmes, and M. Walters were Parsons' pallbearers.[7]

Lucy Parsons and Lizzie Holmes' grief-stricken, tear-stained faces peered out the carriage windows as the procession started to move; they were astonished at the tremendous crowd which had turned out to pay its last respects to their beloved comrades.

A quarter to a half million people lined the streets; four cops were stationed at each corner which the procession passed, and hundreds more were held in reserve at the police stations. The procession passed within half a block from the scene of the Haymarket bombing on the way to the depot to catch the train which would take them to Waldheim Cemetery. Seventy five policemen were stationed at the depot, but they were not prepared to deal with the 15,000 people who were going to the cemetery.

Three coaches were reserved for the families and close friends of the dead men. The first train was filled in minutes, and another train had to be made available.

The sun was a low, red ball in the winter sky when the mourners reached Waldheim. Lucy was helped from the coach after the 45 minute train ride. She walked behind her husband's casket, supported by two members of Knights Assembly 1307; Lizzie Holmes and Mrs. Fielden were with her.

At the cemetery, Captain Black spoke first, followed by Tommy Morgan, Albert Currlin, and Robert Reitzel. Black felt a personal responsibility to the men he had so ably defended in court; he felt the burden of Parsons' death especially, as he had been convinced that Parsons' return would help the defense. He never dreamed it would end in Parsons' execution. He told the crowd that we do not "stand beside the caskets of felons consigned to an unglorious tomb. We are here by the bodies of men who were sublime in their self-sacrifice, and for whom the gibbet assumed the glory of a cross." Black spoke quietly.

Thomas Morgan, who had fought bitterly with these men who had been mowed down by the forces of "law and order," followed Black.

Albert Currlin asked working people to avenge "the great crime which has been committed."

Robert Reitzel, the capable, sensitive editor of *Der Arme Teufel* (*The Poor Devil*) in Detroit, delivered a fiery address. Reitzel had come to Chicago a week before the executions, hoping there might be some way to liberate his comrades from jail. Reitzel, tall with a shock of blond hair falling over his high forehead, was a commanding figure. His youthful playful expression and dancing eyes were replaced by the compelling intensity of the sworn rebel.

"Friends of Freedom," he shouted in German. "My first word over these coffins shall be an accusation, not against the moneyed-rabble who thanked God today . . . but against the workers of Chicago. For you, the workers of Chicago have permitted five of your best, most noble and consistent representatives of your cause, to be murdered in your midst. . . . We have no cause to mourn for these dead comrades . . . but we must mourn for our own shame. . . . Let us part from these graves with the words of Herwegh in our hearts:

'We have loved long enough,

At last we will hate!' "

The committee had not secured a permanent grave site, so the caskets were placed in a temporary vault.

By December 10, even before Albert Parsons' final interrment, Lucy Parsons—with Lizzie and William Holmes' help—had finished editing and had published a collection of his writings. *Anarchism; Its Philosophy and Scientific Basis* contained Albert Parsons' writings, excerpts from Marx, Kropotkin, and other "anarchist thinkers" and articles by Lucy Parsons and Lizzie Holmes. The printer delivered three hundred copies of the book before the police confiscated the rest.[8] Early the next year, the volume came out in German.

"To My Friends and the Public," Lucy wrote. "With the aid of my friends, I am enabled to present for your perusal and consideration the last efforts of my dear deceased husband, to enlighten the seekers after truth and information upon the great and burning questions of the age: the relations of the wage-earner to the wage-absorber in society. . . .

"And now I speak as one who knows and has the right to speak: No nobler, purer, truer, more unselfish man ever lived, than Albert R. Parsons, and when he and his comrades were sacrificed on the altar of class hatred, the people of the nineteenth century committed the hideous crime of strangling their best friends. Fraternally yours, Lucy E. Parsons."

Lucy had rented an office on Washington St., in downtown Chicago, which became her headquarters for publishing and selling pamphlets and pictures.

On December 18, 1887, Albert Parsons, August Spies, Adolph Fischer, George Engel, and Louis Lingg were buried at Waldheim cemetery. A cold, desolate wind blew through the barren trees; snow and ice covered the ground.

It was another trying day for Lucy; she held her two children tightly, one on each hand. She had embroidered a pillow with the inscription "Our Papa" in blue violets, which she helped the children place on his coffin.

The lids of the coffins were removed, and the crowd once again looked upon the faces of the dead men. Lucy shrieked and fainted when she saw Albert. The crowd began crying in sympathy.

Joseph Buchanan was master of ceremonies, Captain Black eulogized the men, followed by Paul Grottkau and Albert Currlin. Grottkau was his fiery best; the crowd cheered after each sentence of the former *Arbeiter-Zeitung* editor's uncompromising speech.

By the end of the day the five martyrs were buried, and Lucy would have to live with her memories of Albert, their cause, and the great Haymarket conspiracy trial.

As newspapers wrote finis to the Haymarket case, and, they thought, to Albert Parsons, they had to remember that Lucy was an alive and capable revolutionary. "Mrs. Lucy Parsons was noted long before the Haymarket massacre as the inseparable companion of her husband in anarchistic meetings, where she preached the social revolution with even more vehemence than he," recalled the papers. By no means could they write "closed" on Lucy Parsons' case. Captain Schaack feared her more than ever. She renewed her revolutionary activities with a vengeance.

Albert R. Parsons was executed for "anarchism"
on November 11, 1887.

TO TRAMPS,

The Unemployed, the Disinherited, and Miserable.

A word to the 35,000 now tramping the streets of this great city, with hands in pockets, gazing listlessly about you at the evidences of wealth and pleasure of which you own no part, not sufficient even to purchase yourself a bit of food with which to appease the pangs of hunger now knawing at your vitals. It is with you and the hundreds of thousands of others similarly situated in this great land of plenty, that I wish to have a word.

Have you not worked hard all your life, since you were old enough for your labor to be of use in the production of wealth? Have you not toiled long, hard and laboriously in producing wealth? And in all those years of drudgery do you not know you have produced thousand upon thousands of dollars' worth of wealth, which you did not then, do not now, and unless you ACT, never will, own any part in? Do you not know that when you were harnessed to a machine and that machine harnessed to steam, and thus you toiled your 10, 12 and 16 hours in the 24, that during this time in all these years you received only enough of your labor product to furnish yourself the bare, coarse necessaries of life, and that when you wished to purchase anything for yourself and family it always had to be of the cheapest quality? If you wanted to go anywhere you had to wait until Sunday, so little did you receive for your unremitting toil that you dare not stop for a moment, as it were? And do you not know that with all your squeezing, pinching and economizing you never were enabled to keep but a few days ahead of the wolves of want? And that at last when the caprice of your employer saw fit to create an artificial famine by limiting production, that the fires in the furnace were extinguished, the iron horse to which you had been harnessed was stilled; the factory door locked up, you turned upon the highway a tramp, with hunger in your stomach and rags upon your back?

Yet your employer told you that it was over-production which made him close up. Who cared for the bitter tears and heart-pangs of your loving wife and helpless children, when you bid them a loving "God bless you" and turned upon the tramper's road to seek employment elsewhere? I say, who cared for those heartaches and pains? You were only a tramp now, to be execrated and denounced as a "worthless tramp and a vagrant" by that very class who had been engaged all those years in robbing you and yours. Then can you not see that the "good boss" or the "bad boss" cuts no figure whatever? that you are the common prey of both, and that their mission is simply robbery? Can you not see that it is the INDUSTRIAL SYSTEM and not the "boss" which must be changed?

Now, when all these bright summer and autumn days are going by and you have no employment, and consequently can save up nothing, and when the winter's blast sweeps down from the north and all the earth is wrapped in a shroud of ice, hearken not to the voice of the hyprocrite who will tell you that it was ordained of God that "the poor ye have always"; or to the arrogant robber who will say to you that you "drank up all your wages last summer when you had work, and that is the reason why you have nothing now, and the workhouse or the woodyard is too good for you; that you ought to be shot". And shoot you they will if you present your petitions in too emphatic a manner. So hearken not to them, but list! Next winter when the cold blasts are creeping through the rents in your seedy garments, when the frost is biting your feet through the holes in your worn-out shoes, and when all wretchedness seems to have centered in and upon you, when misery has marked you for her own and life has become a burden and existence a mockery, when you have walked the streets by day and slept upon hard boards by night, and at last determine by your own hand to take your life,—for you would rather go out into utter nothingness than to longer endure an existence which has become such a burden—so, perchance, you determine to dash yourself into the cold embrace of the lake rather than longer suffer thus. But halt, before you commit this last tragic act in the drama of your simple existence. Stop! Is there nothing you can do to insure those whom you are about to orphan, against a like fate? The waves will only dash over you in mockery of your rash act; but stroll you down the avenues of the rich and look through the magnificent plate windows into their voluptuous homes, and here you will discover the *very identical robbers* who have despoiled you and yours. Then let your tragedy be enacted *here!* Awaken them from their wanton sports at your expense! Send forth your petition and let them read it by the red glare of destruction. Thus when you cast "one long, lingering look behind" you can be assured that you have spoken to these robbers in the only language which they have ever been able to understand, for they have never yet deigned to notice any petition from their slaves that they were not *compelled* to read by the red glare bursting from the cannon's mouths, or that was not handed to them upon the point of the sword. You need no organization when you make up your mind to present this kind of petition. In fact, an organization would be a detriment to you; but each of you hungry tramps who read these lines, avail yourselves of those little methods of warfare which Science has placed in the hands of the poor man, and you will become a power in this or any other land.

Learn the use of explosives!

Dedicated to the tramps by

LUCY E. PARSONS.

☞ The above article appeared in "**THE ALARM**" October 4, 1884. "**THE ALARM**" is a Revolutionary Socialistic Newspaper published every week by the **Working People's International Association** at No. 107 Fifth Avenue, Chicago, Ill.

"To Tramps" by Lucy E. Parsons, first published in the *Alarm*, October 4, 1884 and later distributed as a leaflet.

SOCIALISM!

JUSTICE, EQUALITY, FRATERNITY.

MASS MEETING!

EVERY PERSONS' DUTY!

The Workingmen and Citizens of Columbus, O., will hold a Grand Mass-meeting

FRIDAY & SATURDAY EVENINGS, FEBRUARY 12 & 13,

At 7:30 o'clock, in the City Hall.

A. R. PARSONS, the Chicago Socialist,

Will address the meeting. Subject: "The Emancipation of the Wage-Slave; How to Achieve It." Every workingman and woman should be present. Free discussion. Everybody invited.

THE COMMITTEE.

Group No. 1, International Working People's Association.

SOCIALISMUS!

Alle Arbeiter u. Arbeiterinen von Columbus sind freundlichst eingeladen am Freitag u. Samstag-Abend, 7:30 Uhr, in der City Halle, zu erscheinen. Diseussion u. Eintritt frei.

Das Comite der Gruppe No. 1, J. A. A.

State Historical Society of Wisconsin

Albert Parsons and Michael Schwab made an extensive organizing tour of Ohio and Pennsylvania mining regions from November 1885-February 1886 before returning to Chicago to become involved in the eight hour movement.

Workmen, Bow to your Gods!

MUSIC.

ON TUESDAY EVE., APRIL 28TH

the Workmen of this City will celebrate the dedication of the new

Board of Trade Building.

The services will begin at 8 o'clock P. M. on Market Square, Cor. Randolph and Market Sts.

After the ceremonies and sermons the participants will move in a body to the grand temple of **Usury, Gambling** and **Cutthroatism,** where they will serenade the priests and officers of King Mammon and pay honor and respect to the benevolent institute.

All friends of the Bourse are invited.

Int. Working People's Ass'n.

Große Börsen-Feier!

bei Gelegenheit der Einweihung des hiesigen neuen

Börsen-Gebäudes,

am

Dienstag, 28. April '85, Abends 8 Uhr,

am

Market Square, Ecke Randolph- u. Marketstr.

Die Wohlthaten der Börse und ihr segensreiches Wirken für das arbeitende Volk werden von Rednern in verschiedenen Sprachen geschildert und gepriesen werden, worauf sich die Festtheilnehmer nach dem Tempel selbst begeben, um den hier bei Musik und Weingelage versammelten Mächtigen ein Ständchen zu bringen. Alle Börsenfreunde sind eingeladen.

Int. Arbeiter-Association.

State Historical Society of Wisconsin

Lucy Parsons and Lizzie Swank-Holmes led the April 28, 1885 march on the Chicago Board of Trade.

A. R. PARSONS,

THE GREAT LABOR AGITATOR, of Chicago,

Will Address the People of St. Joseph,

under the Auspices of

THE KNIGHTS OF LABOR.

At Turner Hall, Saturday Evening, July 18th, at 8 o'clock,

On the Labor Question.

All are Invited. Especially the Ladies.   **THE COMMITTEE.**

State Historical Society of Wisconsin

Albert R. Parsons spoke for the Knights of Labor in St. Joseph, Missouri on July 18, 1885.

George A. Schilling, leader of the 1886 Chicago
movement for the eight-hour working day.

Lizzie Swank-Holmes, organizer of the Chicago
sewing women for the eight hour day in 1886.

Chicago Historical Society

Chicago Historical Society

Two announcements for the Haymarket meeting. Note type "work-up" in hastily reset second version (right).

Lulu Eda Parsons, 1881-1889, was five when she heard Mayor Harrison testify in her father's defense.

Albert R. Parsons Jr., six years old, roughed up by Chicago police in May,

William D. Parsons

General William Henry Parsons came to Chicago in August, 1886, to support his younger brother Albert Parsons, who was on trial for his life.

MRS. PARSONS,

WIFE OF THE

Condemned Anarchist

WILL DELIVER A

FREE ∴ LECTURE

—AT—

KUMP'S HALL,

Tenth and Main Sts.,

Monday Evening, Dec. 20, 1886.

At 8 o'clock.

Everybody should avail themselves of this opportunity to hear the most Talented and Eloquent Woman of the age. FREE, FREE.

AMERICANS!

You have heard the verdict of an aristocratic judge and twelve "gentlemen" jurors against the Chicago Anarchists.

Do you sustain a class verdict?

Are you ready to hear the truth? If so, come to

TOWN HALL,

Wednesday Eve'g, Nov. 17, 1886

at 8 o'clock Sharp.

Mrs. Lucy E. Parsons

will appeal this case to the Grand Jury of the American people! Workingmen! Give your brethren fair play.

Admission, 10c. Ladies Free.

Lucy Parsons left for an extensive tour in defense of her condemned comrades in October, 1886. Lecture announcements from Kansas City, Missouri (left) and Meriden, Connecticut (right).

CHICAGO 1887

Louis Lingg, suicide or murdered.

Albert R. Parsons, hung.

Michael Schwab, life imprisonment.

George Engel, hung.

Samuel Fielden, life imprisonment.

Light Upon Waldheim!

L IGHT upon Waldheim! And the earth is gray;
  A bitter wind is driving from the north;
  The stone is cold, and strange cold whispers says . . .
  "What do ye here with Death? Go forth! Go forth!"

I S this thy word, O Mother, with stern eyes,
  Crowning thy dead with stone-carressing touch?
  May we not weep o'er him that martyred lies,
  Slain in our name, for that he loved us much?

M AY we not linger till day is broad?
  Nay, none are stirring in this stinging dawn—
  None but poor wretches that make moan to God
  What use are these, O thou with dagger drawn?

"G O forth, go forth! Stand not to weep for these,
  Till, weakened with your weeping like the snow
  Ye melt, dissolving in a coward peace!"
  Light upon Waldheim! Brother, let us go!

—Voltairine de Cleyre.

Adolph Fischer, hung.

Oscar W. Neebe, 15 years.

August Spies, hung.

The Haymarket defendants were immortalized as martyrs for working people.
A commemorative illustration from the *Labor Defender*, November, 1926.

State Historical Society of Wisconsin

bert Parsons Jr., 13 years old, pulled the cord which removed the red veil from the monument to his father and the other Haymarket defendants, June 25, 1893. Train ticket to the unveiling.

THE LIBERATOR

"COMRADES, LET US ALL UNITE."

2. No. 2.   CHICAGO, SUNDAY, SEPTEMBER 10, 1905.   Price, 2 Cents.

PRISONS AND PALACES.

New Study of the Conventional Lies of our Christian Civilization.

icial Moralities and Legalized Property Offc. a Premium for Criminal Acts.

se to the border of a beauti- own where nature herself n it a nest with her strong- ed, soft-verdured hills, where labor and intelligence have med wonderful things for s wants and loves, where civ- hm corrals men and women a mystical whole called "so , and where religion and hes take charge of the think- responsible part of man "for an good"—there frown the hard, gloomy walls of a nitiary. The whole world utiful around it, the sun falls ightly on its grim presence, t night the tender moon and stars above look as sweetly, ngly down as on the homes uth and innocence. Yet, ob

THE BALLOT HUMBUG.

A Delusion and a Snare;

A MERE VEIL BEHIND WHICH THE GAME OF POLITICS IS PLAYED.

Whatever we hear from all quarters we are very apt to be- lieve, whether it is true or not, especially if it requires some ef- fort to examine it. Of all the modern delusions the ballot has certainly been the greatest. Yet most of the people believe in it.

In the first place it is founded on the principle that the MAJORITY SHALL lead and the minority MUST FOLLOW.

No matter whether it will be any advantage to the majority to have the minority follow them or not.

Let us take a body of legis- lators, absolutely honest, and see what they can do. A, B and C have each a distinct principle to carry out, and there is no good reason why each one should not carry out his principle to a certain extent without interfering with the other.

THE CITY OF LIGHT.

Have you heard the Golden City Mentioned in the legends old? Everlasting light shines o'er it, Wondrous tales of it are told.

Only righteous men and women Dwell within its gleaming mall. Wrong is banished from its borders, Justice reigns supreme o'er all.

Do you ask: Where is that City Where the perfect Right doth reign? I must answer, I must tell you That you seek its site in vain.

You may come o'er hill and valley, You may pass o'er land and sea, You may search the wide earth over, 'Tis a city yet to be.

We are builders of that City, All our joys and all our groans Help to rear its shining ramparts, All our lives are building stones.

Some can do but humblest service, Here rough stones, or break the soil, While the few alone may gather Joy and honor from their toil.

While the few may plan the arches And the fluted columns fair, And immortal thought embody, And immortal beauty there.

But if humble or exalted, All are called to task divine,

THE FACTORY CHILD.

Where Do the Burdens Fall Heaviest--on the Strong or the Helpless?

An Earnest Appeal to Arouse Toilers from Their Apathy and Prove Themselves Men.

After reading a recent census late have patience amid the mur- report showing that children murs of discontent, which will be white children are toiling in waited back to you on every the cotton factories of the South breeze that kisses thy pale cheek for $1.75 per week one is con- in the struggle of the coming strained to inquire: Where do years. the burdens of capitalism press heaviest?

When we see the father who has kissed his loving wife and helpless little ones an affectionate "God bless you" and turns heavily upon his heel to seek employment, he knows not where, that he may furnish them bread, he knows not how much, we are tempted to say of this man pleasure has become to him a mockery, and misery a part of his being.

When we witness day by day the tired maiden wearing away

Toil on, toil on, thou victim of capitalism. Some day thy tears will be dried; some day thy chest will cease to heave. For brave hearts and strong arms will anni- hilate the accursed system which binds you down to drudgery and death. Only then will the factory door to tender childhood be for- ever closed, and the school house be flung open, and all the avenues of art and learning be opened up to children of the producing many.

Men! producers of the world's

Chicago Historical Society

y E. Parsons edited the *Liberator,* 1905-1906, which she named for William Lloyd Garrison's abolitionist *Liberator.* She wrote "The Ballot Humbug" and "The Factory Child."

CLUBS ROUT PARADE

WEST SIDE "UNEMPLOYED" PARADE RIOTERS UNDER ARREST

Mrs. Lucy Parsons, Haymarket Widow (Central Figure in Group), and Some of Her Followers Who Resisted Police. Below Is Policeman Defied by Marchers.

BREAD

SERGEANT NORE MILLS

"Dangerous rioters" under arrest; Jane Addams arranged bail for these wo arrested in the January 17, 1915 Hunger Demonstration near Hull House.

Types of Agitators Who Defied Miss Addams at Hull House.

"ARE WE MEN, OR ARE WE BUMS?"

MRS. LUCY PARSONS

RAIN PHOTO OF the MARCH of the JOBLESS

HUNGER

WORK NOT CHARITY

"WE GOT BEAT UP AN' BEAT UP GOOD." THE MAN FROM SAN DIEGO

GIVE US THIS DAY OUR DAILY BREAD

THESE TWO MEN PREFERRED JOBS, TO MARCHING IN THE RAIN —

SKETCHES FROM LIFE - HULL HOUSE

WORK NOT CHARITY

WE REFUSE TO STARVE IN THE MIDST OF PLENTY

THE CHAIRMAN

THE MAN WHO CHAMPIONED THE CAUSE OF THE WOMAN STRIKERS

ED POLICE ESCORT PARADE OF IDLE THROUGH LOOP STREET

[Continued from first page.]

statements, but also underestimate the sincerity of your cause?, tried to turn the marchers from the street | program, demonstrating our povert

Irwin St. John Tucker Papers, University of Illinois at Chicago Circle

Labadie Collection

Lucy Parsons led the January 31, 1915 demonstration of the unemployed of Chicago through rain and slush. (top) Lucy Parsons behind bars after January 17, 1915 Hunger Demonstration. (left)

Chicago Ill. 6/11/36

Dear Comrade

Tom Mooney;

I received your most welcome letter some days ago and would have replied sooner but was not well. Regarding the data of the trial, I sent about all I had on hand to universities.

I mailed you a copy of the Life of Albert R. Parsons. It contains much valuable information which you wished. I am sending under another cover copies of the "Alarm" that Parsons published. In your lonely prison cell. it will take you back to other days of our movement.

Well dear Comrade I have been active in your cause to liberate you, have spoken in many meetings both here and in the east. I am not discouraged in the belief that justice will be done you and I can clasp your hand a free comrade, vindicated; my vision is becoming so dim it is difficult for me to write legibly any more

I am yours Fraternally yours

Lucy E. Parsons

Lucy Parsons' letter to Tom Mooney, who was held political prisoner for over 20 in San Quentin penitentiary, California.

Lucy Fights for Free Speech

On December 15, 1887, the Pioneer Aid and Support Association was formed. Its official purpose, as stated in the original charter from the State of Illinois was "to aid and support the families and dependents of persons who lawfully uphold the interests of labor and in consequence thereof such families and dependents become deprived of the aid and support of which such persons would otherwise be enabled to afford."[1] The Pioneers' principle function was to support the families of the Haymarket martyrs. The widows received $8 a week plus $2 each for the first two children and $1 for a third. Lucy received $12 a week. The Pioneers continued to support the families for eight years after the executions.

In March, 1888, Lucy left Chicago for a speaking tour in the East; she was now the widow of the Haymarket martyr, the mark she would carry for the rest of her days. One ordeal was over; another had begun. It was her task to do the work of two —her own and her dead husband's.

In the East her freedom of speech was respected more than in Chicago. But when she returned home, the Chicago police arrested her twice in June for selling copies of *Anarchism* on the streets. She was assessed a five dollar fine the first time; the second time Judge White dismissed the case after accepting a copy of *Anarchism* and promising to read it.[2]

She was violently angry at the police. When they arrested her friends John Hroneck and Frank Chapak that same summer, she told a reporter, "They haven't murdered any Anarchists since November last, and they seem to be thirsting for more blood. . . . If Grinnell and Gary are not killed very soon, I will kill them myself, and you can rest assured I will not make a botch of it." She pointed to her little boy. "What do you suppose I am raising him for? I shall teach him that his father was murdered, and by whom! Those red-handed butchers had better look out!" The rhetoric should not be interpreted as program, but it was frightening for a small child.[3]

Lucy was already at work in 1888 on a volume of letters and writings of Albert Parsons, to be titled *The Life of Albert R. Parsons*. A fiery, good looking, young German printer, Martin Lacher, was helping her. He moved in with her in 1889. They kept two large watchdogs to warn them if police agents or saboteurs were coming to disrupt their work. Their way of life gave the "avant-garde" of the proletariat plenty to gossip about. Robert Steiner, who later married Gretchen Spies, wrote, "Comrade Lacher is a nice young man. However, since he does not live in the city but in the country with Mrs. Parsons, I have no contact with him. His lifestyle has—considering the moral inhibitions among the "Avant garde" of the proletariat—given occasion for lots of small talk." Lacher became the secretary of the Pioneer Aid and Support Association.[4]

The five "anarchists" were hardly buried before factionalism again erupted in the movement. The group which had supported Mayor Harrison in 1887 kept the name United Labor Party. On January 28, 1888, Tommy Morgan, the Central Labor Union, the *Chicago Labor Enquirer,* and the *Arbeiter-Zeitung* united to form the Radical Labor Party.

By summer the movement was rent by internal divisions. George Schilling, Joseph Buchanan, and Ernst Schmidt among others endorsed the Democrats and the tariff reform movement. Tommy Morgan went back to organizing for the Socialistic Labor Party, which had been virtually nonexistent in Chicago since 1881. He could not hold together a broadly based labor party, but he could dominate a small sectarian socialist group.

The people who control factions in political organizations are not necessarily the same people who bring out crowds for rallies; in fact, the two kinds of "leaders" are often very different in character. The kind of political sectarianism and ideological struggle needed to control a faction or organization is time consuming and often incompatible with organizing masses of people on issues like wages, hours of labor, working conditions, living conditions, and unemployment.

The Chicago "anarchists," Albert Parsons, August Spies, and Samuel Fielden, had been masters at motivating crowds. Their friends George Schilling and Joe Buchanan were trusted by huge crowds, but neither Schilling nor Buchanan had the personality to beat Morgan at his own game, and neither were as committed to ideological purity as was Morgan.

The power of men like Tommy Morgan comes from their willingness to spend endless hours to control some small faction or organization. They can hold up mass organization for years. Morgan's power was derived from organizational sources, while Albert Parsons, August Spies, Lucy Parsons, Joe Buchanan and George Schilling's power was derived from popular support.

The alleged "anarchists" also called themselves "socialists." Their first priority was speaking to the needs of the working class—as they saw them. Morgan's scheme was to control the organization by claiming exclusive right to the use of the term "socialist" and through it the mass movement which the "anarchists" had built.

Joseph Buchanan attempted to work out a synthesis of the six or more labor and radical parties around a single platform: "Government ownership and operation of the railroads and telegraph." But there was little interest in unity, and in August, Morgan decided to expel Buchanan from the Socialistic Labor Party for his position on the tariff and his work for Frances Hoffman, a Democratic candidate. Buchanan wrote, "The self-constituted liberators of the enslaved human race had not any patience with any one who dared exercise the rights of a freeman. The boss of the Socialistic Labor Party had decided that I must be 'crushed.'" Morgan had tried to control Buchanan's *Chicago Labor Enquirer.* He didn't succeed, but Buchanan was forced to suspend the *Enquirer* in August, 1888, for lack of money.

In October Morgan viciously attacked George Schilling, who was leading the Chicago streetcar strike. He claimed Schilling was unpopular among unionists, and he assured the citizens of Chicago that socialists had nothing to do with the streetcar strike. "The socialists, neither collectively nor individually," declared Morgan, "have had anything to do with this disturbance. Schilling is not a socialist. He is an anarchist."

The seventeen members of the Socialistic Labor Party went off to pass a resolution calling strike leader Schilling "an enemy to socialism and unworthy of the confidence of the workingmen."

Schilling was not surprised at Morgan's attack, but he was surprised that the socialist "leader" was willing to sacrifice 2,000 workers to sectarian ambitions. "No pimp of corporate power, no Pinkerton hireling, no assassin or informer could have surpassed Mr. Morgan's attempt to defeat the interests of the men."

Schilling recalled his own record as the organizer of the stockyards for the eight-hour day and contrasted that with the record of Morgan who had retired to Woodlawn after factionalizing and destroying the Socialistic Labor Party in 1880-81 and who had sat home during the entire eight hour movement. "Had the eight-hour movement been started simply to resolute no doubt Tommy would have been willing to take a contract to furnish all the resolutions required. But to organize men in work shops and factories to prepare for a general strike if the demand is not acceded to, to meet corporate power direct and tell the boss class 'we must have eight hours or quit,' to risk jobs and become boycotted—for such work Mr. Morgan is not available." The Haymarket police riot brought Morgan out of retirement. With Albert Parsons, August Spies, Samuel Fielden, Michael Schwab, and Oscar Neebe out of the way, he hoped to take over the movement.

When Morgan tried to take over the name "socialist" claiming that "socialists" had to have brains, George Schilling remarked, "But if we are to believe his other statement [that only S.L.P. members are socialists] then it is clear that it is not brains, but ten cents per month, a red card, and the willingness to vote for all the resolutions Mr. Morgan will introduce" which makes a person a socialist.[5]

Morgan charged that the Central Labor Union "was controlled by a lot of anarchists against political action, but were secretly working in the interest of the Democratic Party." His charge had some validity, though there was little secrecy in the fact that George Schilling, the business manager of the *Arbeiter-Zeitung,* was working for several Democrats. The *Arbeiter-Zeitung* was conducting the campaigns of Joseph Gruenhut and John M. Palmer who sought public office as Democrats.

Lucy Parsons saw people she respected like George Schilling and Joseph Buchanan supporting Democrats. She would never agree to work for candidates from either of the two capitalist parties. At a meeting on September 30, the working class leaders who supported the Democrats were vigorously denouncing the Republican Party.

Lucy Parsons stood up and aggressively marched to the platform; the crowd roared with approval. "Have the Democrats committed no sin?" she shouted. "Have the Republicans been guilty of everything?" She charged that President Cleveland had been elected by the shotgun, that the South had been carried for the Democrats "by the most shocking outrages and crimes."

"I have seen the Ku Klux in the South myself. I know something about them, and they were every one Democrats. The negroes of the South are no longer in physical slavery, but the Democrats of the South intend to keep them in economic slavery!"[6]

In 1888 the men who commanded the respect of the workers —George Schilling, Ernst Schmidt, and Joe Buchanan—directed the independent labor movement into work for tariff reform and the Democratic Party. Lucy Parsons, who shared Tommy Morgan's opposition to work with the Democrats for different reasons, was unable to keep the Chicago working class movement out of the Democratic Party.

The political victories of the independent labor parties in 1887 were lost in collaboration with the Democrats across the country in 1888.

At the end of October Lucy sailed from New York to London. The voyage was an exciting new experience for her—after she recovered from the initial seasickness. She made friends with the other passengers, played games, and thoroughly enjoyed herself. Lucy was on her way to address meetings of the Socialist League of England on the first anniversary of the executions and the first anniversary of the murder of three workingmen in Trafalgar Square in England. She was the guest of the Socialist League, and she met William Morris and Peter Kropotkin.

Lucy, however, alienated Annie Besant, the leader of the match girls' strike, who charged that she was stumping the country in the interest of the "physical force party." Mrs. Besant refused to have anything to do with her.

At her welcoming meeting, Lucy commanded her audience; her physical appearance dramatized her cause. She was dressed in deep mourning, the blackness accentuated by the small gold chain she wore on her breast. Her full lips, black hair, warm complexion and shining black eyes captivated the English audience. Her strange beauty fascinated them with thoughts of her mixed ancestry. But it was her voice that fixed each person to his seat. She had complete control of that voice. Rich, clear, and low it filled the room; ten times the volume could not have produced the same effect. She shaped her voice to each mood of her speech. "I have been treated with the greatest indignities in American prisons; but I do not complain," she began. "I have thrown myself in the path of established order, and we who do so must expect to take the consequences. . . . Let none of us, . . . say 'I suffered this; I have done this.' The cause is above you and me." As she began to speak of the cause, her voice took on a supernatural fire, and she shouted with triumph, "The cause robbed the scaffold of its ignominy!"

She was confident that the revolution was on its way, in the vital forces of all human beings. "What is the revolution?" she asked. "Why, it is the very breath of life, that stupendous struggle for relief. I hear that voice in the cold dank mines of Siberia; I hear it in the sunny clime of Italy; I hear it across the mighty Atlantic's waves; I hear it in the prison of Joliet, in the State of Illinois;—wherever there is a man or woman beneath the sun who wants better homes, better clothes, better food."

She talked about the common blood of humanity which flows in black Africans, workers of Europe and in her own ancestors —the real native Americans. Poverty was their common enemy and they must fight it together.

In subsequent speeches, she shared the platform with William Morris, leader of the English movement and author of *News from Nowhere* and with Peter Kropotkin, the world famous geographer and gentle anarchist theoretician of non-violence.

A big brass band accompanied her to the pier and gave her a grand send-off for her return voyage. She returned to America well satisfied with her trip and inspired to carry on her work. She addressed large crowds in New York before returning home to Chicago and her children.[7]

Lizzie Holmes had taken the children to the November 11 commemoration at Waldheim Cemetery where George Schilling read the letter which Albert Parsons had written to his children two days before his execution.

To my darling, precious little children, Albert R. Parsons Jr. and his sister, Lula Eda Parsons. As I write this word I blot your names with a tear. We never meet again. O, my children, how deeply, dearly your papa, loves you. We show our love by living for our loved ones; we also prove our love by dying, when necessary, for them. Of my life and the cause of my unnatural and cruel death you will learn from others.

Your father is a self-offered sacrifice upon the altar of liberty and happiness.

To you I leave the legacy of an honest name and duty done. Preserve it, emulate it; be true to yourselves, you cannot be false to others. Be industrious, sober, and cheerful. Your mother—O, she is the grandest, noblest of women— love, honor and obey her. My children, my precious ones, I request you to read this parting message on each recurring anniversary of my death, in remembrance of him who dies not alone for you, but for the children yet unborn. Bless you, my darlings, Farewell. Your father,

Albert R. Parsons.

Lizzie Holmes held each child by a hand as they listened solemnly to the letter.

William Holmes, who had been elected president of Parsons' Knights of Labor Assembly spoke, as did Robert Reitzel and Paul Grottkau. Fifty children from the Northwestern Social School sang songs between the speeches. Four thousand people had come to the cemetery to pay their respects.

In late December, 1888, Labor Assembly No. 1, now called the Albert R. Parsons Assembly of the Knights of Labor announced a lecture by Lucy E. Parsons: "Review of the Labor Movement in Europe."

When Police Chief Hubbard saw a leaflet for the meeting he notified the owner of Waverly Hall to cancel it. "Mrs. Parsons can advertise herself as much as she wishes to, but not with the aid of the police. I have received information that Mrs. Parsons intends to make an anarchistic harangue and that her sole purpose is to get arrested," said the chief.

At 6:00 P.M. the evening of the lecture, a police captain and a squad of plainsclothes detectives arrived at the hall; the Captain got the key, stationed two men at the door, and then waited with the rest of the men in a nearby restaurant.

At 7:45 Mrs. Parsons, Mrs. Holmes, Mrs. Davidson, William Holmes, L.S. Oliver and a number of other radicals arrived. Forty people had arrived when Lizzie Holmes, the Secretary of Albert R. Parsons L.A. No. 1, and Mrs. Davidson, the Treasurer, went to the police officers and formally demanded the hall. The cops said they had orders not to let anyone in. Then the two women went to the Captain who said he was acting on orders from the Chief of Police. Lizzie Holmes decried the police action as an unconstitutional outrage.

The people complained of "The Tzar," the police chief "to whom the people must bow." "Free American Citizens! The Stars and Stripes!" sneered Lucy as the police cleared the stairway to the hall. The people gathered at the corner where Martin Lacher termed the incident an outrage and called for restraints on the police. An officer ordered him to stop, but he refused, and the officer threatened to arrest him. When he defied the order again, the officer grabbed him by the collar and dragged him away. Robert Burns, a molder, went to the station to demand that Lacher be booked on some charge so that he could be bailed out. The police tossed Burns behind bars for his efforts.

The next morning Lucy sat quietly in her rocking chair at home when a reporter came to visit. The Christmas tree was still covered with toys and candies and the children had left some clothing on the floor beside her when they left for school. She answered questions slowly and quietly, unlike the Lucy who was known as a violent agitator who brought out huge crowds and large numbers of police.

She contrasted the relative freedom of speech she had seen in England with the systematic repression of free speech in Chicago. She condemned the system which permitted one person to profit from the work of another and contrasted capitalism with anarchism which meant "that the world and its wealth and its treasures and its happiness should, like the air and the sunshine, belong to all mankind, and not to the few . . ."

She was disappointed in her friends' inaction the night before; she asserted that free speech must be defended at all cost.

They should have thrown themselves against that door, broken it open and entered that hall, cost what it might. Trouble?

Of course there would be trouble. Half a dozen or so would probably have been killed by the police, and I was perfectly willing to be one of the number. Some of us would have been killed, but we would have emphasized our claim to the privilege of free speech and free assemblage in a way that would not have been forgotten.

She was eager to join Albert as a martyr to the cause.

She didn't blame the police and the mayor for the suppression of the meeting as much as she blamed their financial backers. "You see Roche was elected . . . to save the city from the anarchists . . . and the record as savior must be kept up. Otherwise the Citizens' Association and the rich men who boss Roche will say: 'How is this? The city hasn't been saved; the anarchists are meeting the same as ever.' "

Martin Lacher's hearing came up that day. His exceptional good looks, intelligence and good manners thoroughly impressed Judge White. Lacher's sensitive brown eyes, rimless glasses and neatly trimmed black mustache gave the appearance of an educated, gentle man. The favorable description of Lacher in the press was vastly different from the portrait of the bomb-throwing, dagger carrying, bearded, beer-drinking, filthy wretches who were usually depicted as anarchists.

Lacher had been charged with disturbing the peace. When he came to trial Detective Nordrum who had arrested him testified that he had made threats against Inspector Bonfield and had exclaimed, "America is worse than Siberia." The detective charged Lacher with being an anarchist—in his view, a disturbance of the peace in itself.

Lacher testified in his own defense. He attributed his arrest to personal spite on the part of Detective Nordrum. He related an incident in which he and his wife, Helen, were walking on the north side; he pointed Nordrum out to her as a detective. Nordrum overheard and turned on him cursing viciously.

After the testimony was in, Judge White asked Lacher if he plead guilty to disorderly conduct.

"Yes," replied the prisoner quietly.

"But you have declared you were not disorderly. Why do you now wish to plead guilty?"

"I recognize the forces I have to contend with, and that is why I plead guilty," replied Lacher.

"But you ought not to debase yourself by so doing. You are mistaken if you think you can not get justice here."

The judge refused to accept his plea; he wanted to dispel the feeling that anarchists never got a fair hearing in a court of law—a belief that was in Lucy Parsons' and Martin Lacher's interest to promote and exemplify.

Lacher told the judge he'd been a citizen for eight years. Judge White dismissed the case against Lacher and let Robert Burns go with a $5 suspended fine.

Nordrum was furious at the turn of events and especially incensed that Lacher had dared tell the story of their encounter on North Clark St. He saw the young man standing quietly talking with reporters at the back of the courtroom. He stormed back, "Get out of here!................. .... you," snarled Nordrum, grabbing Lacher by the collar and nearly yanking him off his feet. Lacher quietly walked out of the courtroom. Even the usually anti-anarchist press defended Lacher's right to remain in the courtroom as long as he behaved himself.

Two important events took place in Chicago in early 1889 which affected the climate for radicals in the city. One was the ruling by Judge Tuley that "anarchists" have the right to freedom of speech just like other citizens. The other was the exposé of corruption in the Chicago police force which resulted in the dismissal of Inspector Bonfield and Captain Schaack, the two principal enemies of "anarchism" on the force.

On January 5, the "anarchists" appeared in Tuley's courtroom, ironically, to argue that the police had interfered with their property rights by denying them the use of halls they had rented—interfering with the purchase of the halls "for a certain length of time." Their complaint stated that police "had threatened to strike, pummel, arrest and otherwise forcibly prevent the petitioners from so meeting."

Certain newspapers were disturbed that "fifty frowsy-headed and sinister-looking men" had spent the day in court. These "seditious foreigners" were actually suing for an injunction against further disruption of their meetings by the police. The *Chicago Tribune* complained that it is "wildly ludicrous of Mrs. Parsons and the Red gang that hangs on her skirts to say it is unconstitutional to stop 'free speech' when its admitted aim is the abolition of all law, all government, and all rights."

Lucy Parsons' civil rights had indeed been violated; the order had come down from on high that she was never again to speak in the city of Chicago.

Judge Tuley's ruling in favor of free speech was a tremendous blow to the Chicago police force and a great victory for Lucy Parsons. Tuley wrote in his decision, "The Anarchists have the same rights as other citizens to assemble peaceably for the discussion of their views; . . . the police have no right to presume an intention on their part to break the laws; . . . their meetings must not be prohibited or interfered with until a breach of the law is actually committed; . . . in no other city of the United States except Chicago have the police officials attempted to prevent the right of free speech on such unwarranted pretenses and assumptions of power, and . . . it is time to call a halt."

Bonfield's men responded by threatening to revoke the saloon licenses of halls which rented to socialists. As Waverly Hall had no saloon, it was virtually the only hall available to radicals.

Coupled with the exposé of the Chicago police force, Tuley's ruling had tremendous impact. During a scuffle the Fall before, Mrs. Mabel Lowenstein had shot and slightly wounded her husband, Policeman Jake Lowenstein. She retained the firm of Dwight and Kern as her attorneys, the lawyers for the *Arbeiter-Zeitung*. Mabel Lowenstein released police documents regarding the conduct of the police during the Anarchist trial to her lawyers, who in turn gave the material to George Schilling and Joe Gruenhut for the *Arbeiter-Zeitung*.

These police record books were incontrovertible evidence that witnesses had testified exactly the opposite in court to what they had testified when first taken into police custody. Mrs. Lowenstein was prepared to testify to the corruption of the police officials. She charged that Captain Schaack and her husband had stolen and fenced considerable property, which they had stored at her house. Captain Schaack had even stolen Louis Lingg's brooch and cuff-links. The proof for Lingg's and Neebe's charges against the police was now available.

The *Arbeiter-Zeitung* printed these charges, and a month later the *Chicago Times* published the charges. Bonfield had Jens Christiansen, editor of the *Arbeiter-Zeitung,* and the editors of the *Times* arrested for libel. Bonfield and Schaack retained

lawyers Furthman and Ingham, who had prosecuted the anarchist case with Grinnell, as their attorneys. Schaack's detectives
beat reporters from the *Times* when they ventured into his
northside territory.

Not only did Bonfield deny civil liberties, he promoted crime
for his personal gain. It was established that he had accepted a
five pointed gold star—and even wore it—as protection for a
keeper of a house of prostitution. When this had been revealed
five or six years before, he had returned the star and managed
to stay on the police force.

In 1889, Bonfield and his detectives couldn't seem to find
any gambling in Chicago—despite the fact that everyone else
in the city knew about it. In January, 1889, one of the men
Bonfield had attacked in July, 1885, died. Bonfield still faced
court suits over the incident.

The *Chicago Times* had had enough of autocratic police rule.
"The arbitrary conduct of the Chicago police" is a "more real
danger to the republic than either the mouthings or the acts of
the handful of anarchists who may be considered revolutionary
in their designs. People who uphold lawlessness upon the part
of public officials must expect that it will be combatted sooner
or later in an equally lawless manner. The Chicago police department is not preventing, it is creating anarchy. This is a
free country; free speech is guaranteed by the constitution, and
even Mrs. Parsons is entitled to her full rights."

The *Times* charged that Bonfield's word was accepted as
"Holy Writ" by the city administration and by certain newspapers. "The willingness . . . to condone . . . violation of the
Constitution on the mere statement of a man like Bonfield . . .
is amazing. . . . The statement of this man concerning anarchists is no more trustworthy than his judgment concerning civil
liberty is sound." The fact that police officers who couldn't
spell their own names were allowed to interpret the meaning of
civil liberties dismayed the editors of the *Times*. "A star on
the bosom of a burly thing does not authorize him to interpret
the law."

Captain Schaack was exposed as a slum landlord who had
evicted an elderly woman in the dead of winter with no place
to go. She was a hardworking Irish washwoman whose house
was being sold for debt; the creditors tried to get a grocer who

knew her to buy the property, but he refused to obtain the woman's house this way. Captain Schaack readily agreed to buy the property. In 1879 he paid less than $1,000 for a house which was worth over $5,000 ten years later.

Captain Schaack obtained his farm by similar means. The desk officer who worked at the station with him had a farm, but was badly in debt due to medical bills of his family. Schaack first threatened to fire the man, then persuaded him to give the farm to him in exchange for paying the $1,400 in debts. The man had no choice, as Schaack controlled his job. Schaack detailed three police officers to fix up his new property at city expense. He sent them off in a wagon with a keg of beer for three weeks to put up fences and replaster the house.

After these revelations Governor Palmer of Illinois was forced to denounce the Chicago police as despots. Bonfield cried, "Anarchism!" in a last effort to save himself. But it was too late. On February 6, Mayor Roche removed Bonfield, Schaack, Ward, and Lowenstein from the police force.

It was a victory for the "anarchists" who had charged police corruption all along. Now the characters of the men who had persecuted the men were fully revealed. The reign of the police was checked briefly. They did not commit another major act of aggression against the radicals until November 12, 1891.

At the same time as a more liberal attitude was beginning to infiltrate Chicago, Lucy Parsons and Tommy Morgan prepared for a showdown. Only two days after the arrest of Lacher and the suppression of Lucy's speech, the two protagonists faced each other at Waverly Hall. L.S. Oliver chaired the meeting, but Morgan had packed it with S.L.P. members. Morgan had decided that Spies and Parsons had been dead long enough to denounce them and "the doctrines of physical force."

When the floor was opened for comments on Morgan's speech, Honoré Jaxon got up. Jaxon, a French-Canadian Indian, had been convicted of treason in Canada for inciting an Indian insurrection and had been sentenced to death. Louis Riel, the leader of the revolt was executed, but his lieutenant Jaxon escaped and made his way to Chicago, passing up the opportunity to die a martyr. Jaxon arrived in Chicago in early 1886 and quickly became a leader of the Carpenters Union organizing for the eight hour day.

He recalled a conversation he had had with Albert Parsons. "Our late comrade reminded me that every reform had its martyrs. He felt as if he would rather die fighting for freedom than die a slave." Jaxon disagreed. "I told him it is better to live and continue to fight for freedom than it is to die before you are free. Dead fighters, I told him, could not fight. A dead martyr is not worth a .... as a warrior." The crowd hissed and booed Jaxon back to his seat.

Lucy Parsons angrily made her way through the crowd to the front of the room. The hall echoed with applause. She denounced Morgan as the room shook with cheers.

I would like very much . . . to answer the assertions Mr. Morgan has made about those who are dead. But the ukase has gone forth from Roche and Lord Bonfield that I am never to make another speech in Chicago . . . but I can not sit here quietly and hear it said that those who are dead had anything to do with the throwing of the Haymarket bomb, though in the war against tyrants all things are justifiable. Those who say anything else are curs. They were miserable curs who last Sunday night allowed themselves to be driven away from this hall by police!

"God forbid that any country should be for twenty years without a rebellion," she quoted Thomas Jefferson. "Did Parsons or Spies ever utter anything more revolutionary than that?" Glaring at Jaxon she shouted, "It has been said that dead martyrs are no good, but their memory is dear to us and a perpetual inspiration because they died before they would ask pardon for deeds they did not do." The crowd roared its approval.

A little more than a year after the executions the question of force and arming which had split the movement in 1880 again divided the ranks. The partisans of Albert Parsons and August Spies believed the sacrifices had contributed to the revolutionary movement; their detractors wanted to discredit the "martyrdom." Tommy Morgan's association of the "doctrines of force" with the Haymarket bombing did not differ significantly from Prosecutor Grinnell's allegation of conspiracy.

On January 7, the conflict between Lucy Parsons and Tommy Morgan commanded front pages in Chicago. After Professor Charles Orchardson's address advocating the purchase of private property from its owners and the Australian or secret ballot as reforms, Lucy's voice rang out from the back of the hall. Few had seen her come in inconspicuously after the meeting had begun, but the sound of her familiar voice brought cheers. "Neither prison bars nor scaffold shall ever prevent me from speaking the truth. The ballot is useless as a remedy, and a change in the present condition of the wage slaves will never be brought about peacefully. Force is the only remedy, and force will certainly be used."

She told the people to go on voting if they thought it would work, but that they should back up their vote by taking guns to the polls. "Men who are armed are bound to be free, and you are all wage slaves today, because you are not." The applause was deafening. Lucy paused and gazed triumphantly around the room. "I do not possess the right of ballot, nor do I want it under the present system of wage slavery," she proclaimed.

"It makes no difference to me if the room is filled with cops or if the newspapers can make sensational headlines. . . . Any and all means are justified in order to get rid of the present system of wage slavery." The overwhelmingly enthusiastic response to Lucy's speech demonstrated that the majority favored her open advocacy of force to Morgan's and Orchardson's "socialism" which called for similar ends, but whose "policy" was not to admit that force might have to be used.

On the night of January 23, 1889, the regular meeting of A. R. Parsons Assembly No. 1 of the Knights of Labor met in Waverly Hall. The meeting was packed for Lucy Parsons' speech and the celebration of Judge Tuley's ruling. It was a personal victory of Lucy over the police, because Chief Hubbard had said she would never be allowed to address another meeting in Chicago.

She was dressed in black and she had brought seven year old Lulu with her, dressed in a pretty red dress with a bright red silk handkerchief tied around her neck. Lizzie Holmes was secretary of the Assembly, and William Holmes, president of Albert R. Parsons Assembly No. 1, called the meeting to order at 8:00 P.M. Fifty of the best known members of the American Section of the International Working People's Association and over half the members of the board of the *Alarm* crowded around the speakers' stand to celebrate the victory for the International and the revolutionary movement. Tommy Morgan stayed home.

Professor T. H. Garside, who had recently come to Chicago as the official lecturer for the S.L.P., sat in a chair near Secretary Lizzie Holmes' desk. He was Scottish, the leader of the cloakmakers strike in New York and had been a lecturer for the Knights of Labor. He was tall, pale and gentle, and he sat stroking his curly auburn hair, quietly pleased with the scene. William Holmes appeared elated and dreaming of future revolutionary victories.

The chairperson introduced Lucy Parsons, as a person "who had not only the intellectual qualifications but also the moral courage to defy the minions of hell." The crowd applauded as she began her lecture, "The Religion of Humanity."

"The Christian civilization of Chicago . . . permits the heart's blood of your children to be quaffed in the wine cups of the labor robbers. . . . Socialism is the 100-cents-on-the-dollar religion. (Cheers) . . . . We have heard enough about a paradise behind the moon. We want something now." She denounced the mansion in the skies in favor of homes here and now. "We are tired of hearing about the golden streets of the hereafter. What we want is good paved and drained streets in this world."

She called charity "hush money to hide the blushes of the labor robbers." Charity could not free people; they would have to do that for themselves. Neither could a small group of isolated revolutionaries act in the name of the masses. "He who would be free must himself strike the blow." But the struggle was irrepressible. "You may as well try to kindle a fire in the ocean waves or sweep back the tides with a broom as to stop this great tide of discontented humanity."

She denounced racism and attacked the church and state as Siamese twins. She paid her respects to Dr. Thomas "who stands up every Sunday and tickles the ears of the Board of Trade robbers. When the First Regiment went to the Stock Yards last year this saintly man stood up and gave them his blessing." She was sick of "religious leaders" who opposed the struggles of working people for a decent existence. "I want my immortality in this world, and if there is any in the next world we can look after that when we get there," she concluded.

Professor Garside followed her 90 minute speech with a half

hour lecture. The members of the International found him much more acceptable than did his ostensible comrade of the S.L.P., Tommy Morgan, a fact which was beginning to concern Morgan. Morgan had anticipated an ally in Garside, but Garside quickly sided with Lucy Parsons, the Holmes, Martin Lacher, George Schilling and other "anarchists."

Garside started out saying he disagreed with anarchism and physical force; but almost immediately he called the ballot box worthless and described law as both written laws and the natural impulses of the people.

Morgan jumped to his feet. "I won't allow Socialism to be imposed upon. Socialism means one thing and anarchy another. . . . Mrs. Parsons spoke in this hall last Wednesday night, and she used the word socialist every time she should have used the word anarchist. Mrs. Parsons has no right to call herself a socialist. She is an anarchist and has avowed herself as such. If there is any odium attached to it she ought to have it."

When the meeting was over, Morgan was humiliated, and Lucy Parsons led her followers to West Twelfth Street Turner Hall for the first of three major benefits that winter for the martyrs' families sponsored by the Pioneer Aid and Support Association. The *Chicago Inter-Ocean* called it a "Beer Guzzling Free and Easy Concert in Aid of Lucy Parsons and Others: Beer, Profanity, and Anarchy." From 3:00 P.M. until midnight 10,000 persons came and went; a third of the crowd was women. There was never an empty table or chair. Cartoons representing capital's exploitation of labor decorated the walls.

Morgan declared war on the anarchists, while Chicago's rulers looked on with amusement. There was standing room only at the next Sunday meeting. Morgan began his attack on Garside, but the crowd interrupted him with an ovation for Garside. He solemnly began again. "I want you anarchists to understand that you will not be allowed to parade yourselves as socialists. . . . Garside has disgusted all the socialists while the anarchists roared with delight, and Mrs. Parsons openly twitted them about the wonderful progress that was being made in Chicago." Lucy thoroughly enjoyed Morgan's discomfort, and he feared that she would lead the Chicago movement instead of him.

Morgan introduced a resolution asking that the National

Executive Committee suspend Garside as official organizer for the S.L.P. L. S. Oliver tried to rule Morgan's motion out of order. It was discussed briefly, and then passed at the next meeting of the local executive committee.

At the next public meeting, Morgan felt he had defeated Garside. He wanted to end Lucy Parsons' power as well. He charged that anarchists would destroy education, that state socialism stood for cooperative ownership and control of public utilities and transportation companies. "I am threatened with the terrors of the *Arbeiter-Zeitung*," he exclaimed, "but I will fight that paper to the bitter end, and if we had the power we would kill it."

Morgan's friend, Professor Orchardson, accused Garside of associating with Paul Grottkau and inviting that advocate of force to speak at a socialist meeting. Lucy Parsons' dark eyes flashed as she stood up to protest Orchardson's anti-anarchist resolutions.

"Mr. Chairman, those resolutions contain certain strictures on anarchy that are outrageously false. You never give me a chance—"

"Order!" shouted Morgan.

"You can't dictate to me. . . ."

"Somebody get a policeman!" yelled Tommy Morgan. "Mrs. Parsons, get out or be put out."

"I won't!" shouted Lucy Parsons defiantly.

She walked to the front of the room and faced the audience. Morgan pounded his gavel and yelled "order!" with each blow as he tried to drown out her voice.

"Morgan!" shouted the Socialists.

"Parsons!" thundered the "anarchists."

"I loathe and detest dictators!" screamed Lucy.

Morgan summoned his strongarm men who hustled her to the rear. The meeting was in an uproar. Morgan, who alleged that he didn't like Lucy Parsons because she stood for force, didn't hesitate to use force to expel her from the meeting.

The compelling problem for Morgan was that Lucy Parsons' followers were increasing, not decreasing. "They are certainly not decreasing. Physical force instead of an appeal to the ballot is being strongly advocated yet" he wrote in the S.L.P. press.

The suspension of Garside did not end the controversy. On

February 10, 1889, Lucy again debated with Morgan and his followers. She was asked what would happen if some individual infringed on the liberty of someone else.

She thought for a moment and replied that a policeman on the corner could not prevent someone from breaking into her house to steal. "Each individual act must be tried on its own merits. If some one commits murder, that will be overstepping natural law, and it will be so understood and be treated accordingly."

None of her critics asked what natural law was or what human being was capable of saying what natural law was. Morgan asked who the judge of a crime would be—the victim or someone else.

Her response was syndicalist. "I claim that a trades union and the Knights of Labor are practical illustrations of the feasibility of Anarchism. These men come together for a common purpose and each one subscribes to certain by-laws or rules. If a member violates those rules the society then and there decides what the penalty shall be."

On February 17 the anarchists and socialists again clashed at Waverly Hall. Martin Lacher contradicted Professor Orchardson's position that socialists would not oppose 1 or 2% interest rates.

Lucy Parsons then objected to the S.L.P.'s endorsement of the postal system, which, as she pointed out consistently tampered with her mail and charged her 36¢ to mail a book while the private express company charged her only 9¢ per book. She discussed the decentralization of power and said she did not want to become a slave to the state.

On February 24, Garside made a victorious return to Chicago. He had been reinstated as official lecturer for the S.L.P. in Chicago at the demand of the German socialists. Garside arrived at Turner Hall with Paul Grottkau—who had been anathema to Tommy Morgan since at least 1880.

The crowd at Turner Hall cheered Garside and his allusions to Morgan's dictatorship. Back in Waverly Hall, Mr. Morgan was presiding over his usual Sunday afternoon meeting. Lucy Parsons was there to keep him in check.

On March 3, 1889, the socialists met in Waverly Hall to decide what to do in the coming city elections. Morgan could do nothing without the German members of the party and the support of the *Arbeiter-Zeitung,* which he had so recently threatened to destroy. It was decided that a committee would approach the editors of the *Arbeiter-Zeitung* to see if they would support a socialist ticket. If they agreed a ticket would be nominated; if not, the plan would be dropped.

Morgan had tried to get rid of Lucy Parsons, Martin Lacher, William and Lizzie Holmes, Paul Grottkau, and their followers before the election decisions would be made. But he had failed, and ironically he was at the mercy of these same people, some of whom did not believe in the electoral process at all, to decide whether or not he could run a ticket.

The *Arbeiter-Zeitung* opposed Morgan's candidates, and the campaign was ineffectual due to lack of money and support. Lucy Parsons and Tommy Morgan continued their struggle for the leadership of the Chicago movement through the spring and summer of 1889.

The conflict was to determine who would control the Chicago movement, but it was couched in the rhetoric of anarchism vs. socialism. The same rhetoric of hyperbole and exaggeration which prosecutor Grinnell had used to convict the Haymarket defendants, Tommy Morgan now used to try to discredit their friends.

Lucy Parsons' vision of a future society was not of a society with no regulations whatsoever, but of a society of voluntary association in which the members of trades unions would voluntarily agree to regulations governing their behavior and which would be enforceable by members of the association. She chose to call this system "no government," but in reality, she advocated a syndicalist theory of society. She advocated workers' ownership and control over the means of production and distribution through their unions.

Tommy Morgan, on the other hand, advocated state control of the means of production and distribution by a "socialist" political machine. He was interested in working through the electoral process to achieve state power, and he wanted the respect of the establishment, something which William Holmes assured him he would be no more able to achieve than would Lucy Parsons.[8]

By March, 1889, Lucy Parsons and Martin Lacher had fin-

ished *The Life of Albert R. Parsons,* and it was ready for distribution. George Schilling, who wrote the introduction, was
handling orders. He expected that his introduction would make
Powderly "squirm."[9]

The growing liberal tendencies in Chicago, reflected in Judge
Tuley's ruling and in the police exposé, also produced a series
of Economic Forums the winter of 1888-89. The forums were
structured to bring together representatives of labor and business. George Schilling and Dyer D. Lum both spoke for labor.
Judge John P. Altgeld, author of *Our Penal Machinery and Its
Victims,* delivered a lecture in March.

Lucy Parsons was there to question his reforms. "Judge
Altgeld," she demanded, as soon as the discussion started. "Will
you deny that your jails are filled with the children of the
poor, not the children of the rich? Will you deny that men
steal because their bellies are empty? Will you dare to state
that any of those lost sisters you speak of enjoy going to bed
with ten and twenty miserable men in one night and having
their insides burn like they were branded?"

Shouts of protest interrupted her; some hissed. Altgeld gave
her the floor, and she continued. She criticized Altgeld's limited reforms—end to striped convict uniforms, rewarding work
for prisoners, reading material and large, clean cells. She said
she agreed with Altgeld's horror at clubbing. She had firsthand
experience at the receiving end of the club.

"But I will not rise to your reform bait," she continued. "This
is your society, Judge Altgeld; you helped to create it, and it
is this society that makes the criminal. . . . And if the workers
unite to fight for food, you jail them too. . . . No, so long as
you preserve this system and its ethics, your jails will be full of
men and women who choose life to death, and who take life
as you force them to take it, through crime."

Altgeld responded that the American system was the best that
people had yet devised. "I don't deny the evils; but I face them
practically, and I recommend the same practical course to those
utopians who would prefer that everything be cast in the waste
basket."

Lucy Parsons and her supporters continued to question Altgeld. In the papers the next day the liberal Altgeld was praised
for his responses to Lucy Parsons.

Another aspect of the liberalizing trend in 1889 was the beginning of the settlement house movement in Chicago. That year Jane Addams and her friends founded Hull House on Halsted St., just southwest of the Loop in a center of dirty neighborhood tenements, small sweatshops, and the light industry district of Chicago. Garbage lay strewn on the streets of the new home for Italian, Polish, Bohemian, and Russian Jewish immigrants. Jane Addams responded to the same oppressive conditions which Lucy Parsons had already fought in Chicago for over a decade, but Jane Addams' style of work was more acceptable to the property owners of Chicago than was Lucy Parsons'. Moreover, Jane Addams was white and upper middle class.

In 1894 Mary McDowell founded the University of Chicago settlement house in the back of the yards district of Chicago. In 1894 as well, Graham Taylor, a minister and faculty member of the Chicago Theological Seminary, founded the Chicago Commons in a large house at 140 North Union St.

Lucy set up her little stand with books and papers and pictures here and there in the city—for as long as she could evade the police in one place. Or she trudged miles through the city handing out leaflets, talking to people and selling socialist papers. She walked picket lines with strikers day in and day out, even in the most bitter cold, then walked home after dark, her thin cloak wrapped tightly around her to keep off the biting wind. She was becoming as much a part of Chicago as the Board of Trade or the stockyards. Travelers to Chicago made it a point to see Lucy Parsons, either for inspiration or out of curiosity.

The recollection of the Haymarket bombing and trial dominated political and social life in Chicago for years; those who had been involved could never dissociate themselves from Haymarket as long as they remained in Chicago.

On October 6, 1889, Lucy Parsons wrote to Joseph Labadie that she planned to speak at the second anniversary November 11th demonstration in New York. She asked him to arrange meetings in Detroit for her on her way there—before November 3.[10]

One week later her little daughter Lulu Eda was dead. Eight year old Lulu died at home the morning of October 13th of lymphodenoma, a disease of the lymph glands. It may have been brought on by the scarlet fever she had had in 1886.

Lucy did not go to the New York meetings as she had planned; she had lost half her family in less than two years. Only she and her son were left.

Lulu was buried at Waldheim cemetery in an unmarked grave near her father. A dozen carriages followed the carriage carrying the little white hearse. In the first was Lucy Parsons, Albert Parsons Jr., Martin Lacher and William Holmes. Martin helped Lucy down from the carriage, and she leaned on his arm as they walked to the hearse. Lizzie Holmes was one of the four women pall bearers. Bright red ribbons hung from several of the wreaths which decorated the flower-covered casket.

Lucy stood supported by Martin as the four women carried the casket of her little girl past her to the grave. She sat down quickly for the simple secular ceremony. William Holmes gave the address, and Mrs. Kinsella sang "Annie Laurie," which Albert Parsons had sung on the eve of his execution.[11]

Lucy Parsons' personal life was seldom without trauma. On the morning of July 16, 1891, Chicagoans were titillated by newspaper articles describing Lucy's troubles with her ex-lover, Martin Lacher. "Mrs. Lucy Parsons . . . known far and wide as the Goddess of Anarchy and would-be destroyer of all existing forms and institutions of government, has sought the services of the representatives of law and order to protect her from the attacks of a former lover."

Lucy's and Martin's relationship came to a stormy conclusion in police court that day. She had sworn out a warrant against Martin Lacher, and she appeared as the prosecuting witness at the West Chicago Avenue Police Station. When the case was called, Martin was ushered into the prisoner's box. His shock of black hair and draggled mustache suggested that the accommodations at the jail had not been adequate. He wore a bright red neckscarf with a small gold gallows as a scarf pin.

Lucy took the stand, her eyes aflame. She claimed that Martin had been a boarder in her house. "This man came to my house and began to abuse me, claiming that I was holding some of his property," she charged. "I put him out once, but he returned and broke in both the front and rear doors of my house with an ax, and also smashed up my ornaments and furniture.

He has made threats against my life and property, and I have no recourse but to appeal to the law."

Martin nervously fingered his miniature gallows as Lucy denounced him. They were a long way from the day he had appeared in court to respond to charges resulting from his defending her right to free speech. He spoke in his own defense, refusing to be sworn because of his anarchist beliefs. He told the court that he and Lucy had lived together for two years and that he had loved her more than his own life. He stated that his wife Helen, who lived two blocks from Lucy, had threatened to prosecute Lucy for adultery, but that he had given her a folding bedstead to drop the case. He said that two weeks earlier Lucy had invited someone to a party at her house whom he couldn't stand and that was the cause of the fight.

Martin was shocked that Lucy Parsons, whom he loved and whose ideals he admired, had had him locked up. "Your honor," he pleaded, "after all this she had me arrested and thrust into a common police station."

He read a list of money he had advanced to her and bills he had paid for her. He said that he was unemployed and that "Mrs. Parsons has seen fit to transfer her favors to someone better able to pay for them."

The courtroom scene was vicious. Lucy had her honor as a woman to defend. Lacher charged her with "various gross offenses against the moral law." She burst out furiously, "If you say that again, I'll kill you!" waving her umbrella at him.

"Your honor," she continued, "it is an unwarranted attack on me. He has threatened me repeatedly with this exposure if I left him, and the reason I have endured his company so long was because I was afraid of him." She stormed out of the courtroom.

Everyone had seen Lucy's black eye. Now it was Martin's turn to show the court his wounded arm which he declared was "the outcome of a combination of Mrs. Parsons and a flatiron." With Lucy out of the courtroom, he continued his defense. Yes, he had broken the furniture. But he could prove that it was *his* furniture. He claimed that during the time he and Lucy had lived together, he had supported his wife and family, too. Since the "trouble occurred," he had been living with Helen and their two small children.

Lucy returned to the courtroom and said she had another statement to make. But Judge Severson ruled that enough had been said, dismissed the malicious mischief charge against Lacher and fined him $25 plus costs for disorderly conduct.

The proceedings that day left no doubt about legal discrimination against women, even in the case of a male anarchist vs. a female anarchist. Reports said that Lacher had paid her bills "to protect her from the exposure and shame that threatened her through her disinclination to meet her just and legal obligations." No one denied that Lacher had chopped up the furniture or threatened her. The responsibility for the incident was laid at the door of the woman—Lucy Parsons, the notorious advocate of social revolution—and she was cast in the role of whore.

Parsons, not Lacher, was really on trial; she was being tried for choosing to enter a relationship without sanction of church and state. The man was "prisoner," but his moral integrity was not questioned; he was commended for paying his lover's bills.

The story made the rounds as movement scuttlebut. Emma Goldman recalled the incident nearly 40 years later and complained that Lucy Parsons had "dragged a man she had been living with into court over a couple of pieces of furniture."[12]

New Directions in the Movement

By 1890 Chicago's population had reached one million, more than triple its population when Lucy and Albert Parsons first arrived on that urban, industrial scene. In 1890 40% of Chicago's population was foreign born and another 38% were the children of immigrants. That is, nearly 80% had been in the United States less than a generation. Fourteen thousand blacks had moved to Chicago from the South. In the 1890's the Russian Jews began arriving by the thousands to escape the vicious pogroms in the Pale of Settlement of Tzarist Russia. During the 1890's Chicago's population grew another 600,000 to reach 1.7 million by 1900.

The vast increase of people brought incredible sanitation problems in the working class neighborhoods where the city seldom thought to provide garbage disposal services in any case. Outdoor privies were outlawed, but their use persisted and with it serious health hazards. Chicago pumped its sewage out into Lake Michigan, then pumped it back diluted as drinking water. For good reason Lucy Parsons talked about clean streets and neighborhoods.

By 1890 Chicago was the second largest American city, the second most important manufacturing center, and the leading railroad center. By 1887, 27,000 people rode the suburban trains to and from Chicago each day. In 1882 the first cable car had been built on State St., and by 1890 the cable car was fast replacing the horse-drawn public transportation system. By 1893 Chicago had over 500 miles of street railway tracks, and the first elevated railroad had been opened in 1892 to take visitors to the Columbian Exposition. Charles Tyson Yerkes had taken over the city's street railroad system.

In the 1890's, the U.S. became the world's leading industrial power. U.S. industrialists began to export their capital, and the age of overseas imperialism began. In 1890 the frontier was closed; the modern era had begun.

Technological progress had provided refrigerated railroad

cars for transporting meat and other perishables thousands of miles to markets. Mechanization in the mines and in the factories and the demand of the modernizing industrial society for vast numbers of unskilled, lowpaid workers further diminished the power of the skilled craft unions. The 1890's brought major defeats to craft unionism, which was met by the rise of industrial unionism designed to meet the strength of consolidated capital.

By 1890 the divisions in the "anarchist" movement were clear. The trade unionists of the International Working People's Association who had been more "syndicalist" than "anarchist" allied themselves with other unionists. Men like Joe Labadie, George Schilling, Joe Buchanan, and Dyer Lum tried to take over the Knights of Labor shortly after the 1887 executions. Many became active in the American Federation of Labor.

The 1889 debate between Tommy Morgan and Lucy Parsons had demonstrated that the "anarchists" would ally with social democrats and other reformers against people like Morgan who wanted to build a tight party structure and work for state control of the means of production.

In 1886, 16 year old Emma Goldman, a Russian Jewish immigrant, had arrived in the U.S. At the height of the eight hour day movement she went to work in a Rochester, N.Y., sweatshop for $2.50 a week. She was a rebel in spirit; news from Chicago of the great Anarchist trial made her an anarchist.

Emma Goldman went to her boss as an individual and demanded more money. The boss told her if she got a raise, everyone else would want one. Emma quit her job and went to New York City in 1889 to work closely with Russian radical exiles. Lucy Parsons would never have gone to a boss as an individual. Her class consciousness would have told her to organize the workers first, then tell the boss that they were getting a raise or striking. There was a major difference between Emma Goldman and Lucy Parsons on the basic question of class consciousness.

Many of Goldman's friends in New York styled themselves after the Russian nihilists, as did her lover Alexander Berkman. Goldman first followed Johann Most and his ideas of propaganda by the deed. But she broke with him on certain ideas and refused him as a lover, and he became embittered towards her.

Lucy Parsons and Emma Goldman came from very different social and political backgrounds. Parsons developed in the context of the militant Chicago working class movement of the 1870's and 80's. Goldman developed in the immigrant radical intellectual circles of New York.

By 1890 socialism was a powerful force in the American labor movement. At the 1890 A.F. of L. convention a resolution calling for "the collective ownership by the people of all the means of production and distribution" was defeated by a narrow margin. In the referendum which followed, a dozen major unions endorsed the resolution. The 1893 A.F. of L. convention passed the resolution.

Lucy Parsons, Hugh O. Pentecost, and Johann Most had expected to speak at a commemoration for the martyrs in Newark, New Jersey on November 7th 1890. They were met by police at the door to the hall.

When Lucy attempted to speak on the street the police used their clubs to disperse the crowd. They arrested eight people and took Lucy to the station in a closed carriage so that the crowd could not attempt to free her.

Three days later she was released on one thousand dollars bond and the trial date was set for November 17th. When the trial opened Lucy refused to plead either guilty or not guilty. But on November 28th she defended herself in a special court session and was acquitted of inciting to riot.[1]

The Chicago police had suffered a serious setback in 1889. By 1891 they were again ready to make a raid on the radicals. The monetary remuneration from the Citizens' Association had slowed down to a trickle, and the police hoped to revive the anarchist scare to help line their own pockets. On November 12, 1891, the police broke up a stockholders meeting of the *Arbeiter-Zeitung* on the pretext that they were plotting to avenge the executions of their comrades.

Two "reds" were brought to trial and fined $50 each. Lucy Parsons sat quietly through the proceedings reading letters. The papers had even begun to find the prosecution of the anarchists amusing.

"The prosecution [tried] to make the most of the affair and to let no dramatic incident escape. . . . [but] dramatic incidents were scarce. . . .Assistant City Prosecutor Hines . . . made the comforting statement that the only fact he cared to establish was that the defendants carried revolvers, and then he forgot . . . and tried to prove that the prisoners all read the *Arbeiter-Zeitung* and had applauded at the meeting . . . Wednesday night."

In 1891, Lucy Parsons began to edit *Freedom, A Revolutionary Anarchist-Communist Monthly.* She and Lizzie Holmes took on the bulk of the editorial tasks. The police were at it again; they tried to suppress the 1892 Paris Commune celebration in Chicago. Lizzie Holmes mocked the scene. "Authority . . . began to rear and plunge—some working people were going to hold a ball and festival, and the city was in danger! The Chief of Police sprang to the rescue and planted companies of his men all about the place of the festivities. He rushed a hundred or so policemen, detectives, and sluggers in citizen's clothes into the hall." The detectives tore down the decorations, and the Police Chief ordered that no beer be sold.

The meeting was held, but the lack of beer and decorations dampened the celebration; the hall looked like an armed camp. The Jewish I.W.P.A. had a more successful celebration without police interference, and Lucy Parsons delivered the main address.

Working people suffered four major defeats in 1892: in the silver mines at Coeur d'Alene, Idaho; in the Carnegie steel mills of Homestead, Pennsylvania; in the railroad yards of Buffalo, New York; and in the coal mines near Tracy City, Tennessee. The defeats of 1892 demonstrated the tremendous power the industrial capitalists had gained since the Civil War and the extent to which they owned the American government.

The Coeur d'Alene miners had the support of the local community and government. One thousand federal troops were sent to Idaho to put down the rebellion. They imprisoned hundreds of strikers in a "bullpen," a barbed wire concentration camp, where they were ill-fed, ill-clothed, and beaten. The mine owners won.

At the Homestead steel mills, Andrew Carnegie and Henry Clay Frick decided to break the back of the skilled craft union. The company locked the workers out and declared that it would not negotiate with the union. The night of July 5, 1892, barges of Pinkertons hired by the Carnegie Steel Company headed up the Monongahela River to try to break the control which the locked out workers had over access to the plant. The Pinkertons were roundly defeated in a fierce gun battle.

Radicals like Lucy Parsons believed these labor struggles meant the revolution was just around the corner. Her *Freedom* welcomed the Homestead workers' victory over the Pinkertons. "The first real battle between Labor and Capital in which force was met with force has been fought and won by Labor. Hurrah!" But the editor was disappointed in the strike leader's action after the victory; he had telegraphed the governor to find out what to do with the captured rifles!

At the time, Emma Goldman, Alexander Berkman, and their comrades were living communally in Worchester, Massachusetts, running an ice cream parlor. They had been saving money to send Berkman back to Russia to commit a revolutionary act there, but when they heard about the defeat of the Pinkertons, they decided the time had come for an *attentat* in America. They were sure that the workers would follow them into revolutionary activity.

On July 23, 1892, Alexander Berkman walked into Frick's office and shot him. Frick was only wounded, and Berkman was arrested.

In Chicago, Lucy Parsons applauded the *attentat* and organized meetings for Berkman's defense. "For our part we have only the greatest admiration for a hero like Berkman," wrote the editor of *Freedom*. Berkman's assassination attempt was the first *attentat* in the U.S. However, many people believed that an anarchist had thrown the 1886 Haymarket bomb, and the two incidents were linked to re-fuel the anti-radical, anti-labor hysteria.

Carl Nold and Henry Bauer were arrested in Allegheny City and charged with conspiracy. They had known nothing of Berkman's plans, and, in fact, Bauer belonged to Johann Most's faction which was at odds with Berkman and Goldman. In February, 1893, Lucy Parsons delivered a fiery address on behalf of Nold and Bauer at a Chicago defense meeting.

Johann Most, who had been considered the architect of propaganda by the deed, suddenly turned on Goldman and Berkman, renounced terrorism, and suggested that Berkman was actually an agent for Frick who had used a toy pistol to gain public sympathy for the unpopular Chairman of the Carnegie Steel Company.

Goldman heard him speak; she sprang to her feet and demanded that he retract his statement; he refused. With Berkman facing years of prison in addition to charges from other anarchists, Goldman gave Most one last chance to retract his statement. She attended his next lecture with a horsewhip carefully concealed under her cloak. She asked him again, but he only called her an "hysterical woman." With that, she pulled out the horsewhip and gave Most the beating of his life. When finished, she broke the whip, tossed it at his feet and left the hall.

Lucy Parsons was shocked at Most's reversal. She was surprised and disappointed that Berkman's action did not spark the workers to revolutionary action. The incident marked a turning point away from the *attentat* in the radical movement.

Berkman could legally have been sentenced to a maximum of seven years for his assault on Frick. However, he refused legal counsel, and the charges against him were multiplied to yield a 22 year sentence. He served nearly 14 years before he was released in May, 1906. Nold and Bauer each got five years. Emma Goldman realized the futility of acts of terror from this experience.

Activists of the Chicago movement were going divergent directions by 1892. Dyer Lum had gone back to New York City with bitter feelings toward the Chicago radicals; the *Alarm* had ceased publication in New York on February 2, 1889, and Lum sold the subscription list. William Holmes called it a "dastardly act" and said Lum's act made it almost impossible for the Chicagoans to issue another paper. Holmes himself was studying law, and Schilling reported to Lum that Holmes had become an individualist. Lum wrote to Voltairine de Cleyre, who, like Emma Goldman, had become an anarchist after the Haymarket trial, that George Schilling was "Democratic rainbow chasing again" and that Lucy Parsons was publishing *Freedom* in Chicago. No admirer of Lucy Parsons, Lum remarked, "However it will probably do as little hurt as it will good."[3] Tommy Morgan was still busily denouncing "anarchism". When the women of the Municipal Order League and other reformers met to discuss cleaning Chicago streets, Morgan discovered a "tinge of

Anarchism." "The old denunciations of the authorities are here, couched in more elegant diction," he declared.

Schilling became active in the People's Party, which was formed in Omaha the summer of 1892, and he worked for reform Democrats in the campaign that year. William and Lizzie Holmes were becoming more theoretical in their approach to anarchism, and they were coming to adopt the theories in addition to the name. Dyer Lum had become a morphine addict, and he felt that Chicago had killed him for all literary purposes.[4] Lum became Samuel Gompers' personal secretary and speechwriter in the A.F. of L.

Dyer Lum and Lucy Parsons exchanged polemics in the colums of *Freedom*. Gompers' secretary did not want to be identified as a communist, and he objected to the paper calling itself "A Revolutionary Anarchist-Communist Monthly." Lucy assured him that he was welcome to contribute to the paper without feeling the tag of "communism" applied to him, and she argued that he had written "communist" pieces for the *Alarm* and that the *Alarm* had also been a "communist" paper.

Part of the animosity between Lum and Lucy Parsons might be attributed to Lum's racism. Lucy dealt with racism in the paper. She condemned the crimes against black people in the South as as vicious as any of the pogroms against the Jews in Russia. "Women are stripped to the skin in the presence of leering, white-skinned, black-hearted brutes and lashed into insensibility and strangled to death from the limbs of trees. A girl child of 15 years was lynched recently by these brutal bullies."

On March 30, 1892, the *Chicago Tribune* reported that three negroes had been convicted under the vagrancy laws and had been sold on the auction block at Fayette, Missouri, because they were unable to pay the fines. One man went to a farmer for $25, another to a stock-dealing firm for $5 and the third to a cattle feeder for only $1. Black residents of Fayette met at a nearby church to protest the sale. "Some people said the auction block was abolished with Lee's surrender to Grant!" was *Freedom's* comment.

On March 27, 1892, black people of Chicago met to protest racial violence in the South. One speaker declared, "The White race furnished us one John Brown; the next must come from our own race." *Freedom* predicted that revolution would soon sweep the South. "The whites of the South are not only sowing the wind which they will reap in the whirlwind, but the flame which they will reap in the conflagration."

In his opium- and morphine-induced stupor Dyer Lum might be forgiven some indiscretions, but it is remarkable that his racist views were tolerated in a "progressive" movement. He couldn't stand hearing Lucy Parsons denounce burning "outrages." In March, 1893, less than a month before his death, Lum wrote to de Cleyre about a black man who had been burned at the stake, "I would have carried wood myself if I had been there. 'Awful' ! ! ! ! ! ! ! Yes, and so was the offense, of which every week some similar proceeding at the hands of niggers—to shoot him would only have made a county sensation. Burning him made the flesh of every nigger brute in the South to creep."[5]

The racism of the society was reflected in the radical movement. Lucy Parsons was persecuted for her color and could not admit that some of her ancestors were black. Yet she defended the rights of black people on principle.

In 1893 the A.F. of L. dropped its commitment to organize black workers and formed Jim Crow locals when it organized blacks at all. The A.F. of L. did not follow in the anti-racist tradition of the Knights of Labor.

In 1892 Judge John P. Altgeld ran for Governor of the State of Illinois. There was reason to believe that he might consider pardoning Michael Schwab, Samuel Fielden, and Oscar Neebe, who remained in Joliet Prison. Clarence Darrow, a young corporate lawyer who had come to Chicago in 1887, became active in the Amnesty movement. Many leading citizens of Chicago became involved in the movement, feeling that the hysteria was over, and the three living victims could be released with little harm to society.

William H. Parsons, Lucy's brother-in-law, hoped that the Amnesty movement would succeed; he was in contact with George Schilling. He tried to find Lucy during a quick visit to Chicago in 1892, but he couldn't locate her street.[6]

Altgeld was elected Governor. When he took office, he appointed George Schilling head of the Illinois Bureau of Labor Statistics. But he didn't act right away on the Amnesty question. When Schilling and Darrow pressed him on the issue, he said he was studying the case and would make his judgment on the basis of the record.

On June 25, 1893, the working people of Chicago gathered at Waldheim Cemetery for the unveiling of a monument to the Haymarket Martyrs. Five special trains carried 8,000 people to the cemetery. With his mother directing, 13 year old Albert Parsons Jr. drew aside the red hood which covered the monument. At her neck Lucy Parsons wore the small golden gallows which had become the symbol of the movement. William Holmes and Ernst Schmidt delivered the addresses.

The trial was still a source of controversy, and only a few months before the monument was unveiled, Judge Gary had written a defense of his conduct of the trial for *Century Magazine*. Sarah Ames prepared a reply to Judge Gary for distribution at the June 25th ceremony. In this *Century Magazine* article Gary had admitted that Gilmer and Thompson were probably perjurors. On November 8, 1887, he had written to Governor Oglesby on behalf of Samuel Fielden, saying in part, "He was the honest, industrious and peaceable laboring man. . . . There is no evidence that he knew of any preparation to do the specific act of throwing the bomb that killed Degan. He was more a misguided enthusiast than a criminal."

Sarah Ames reminded Judge Gary that he had just thrown away the two keys to the prosecution's conspiracy theory and to the conviction of the men. However, he still dared to defend the conduct of the trial. "If you could be candid in this case would you not have to admit that without the perjury in the case the men could not have been convicted?" she asked the Judge.

According to the prosecution, it was Fielden's speech which had made it necessary for the police to break up the meeting. Sarah Ames argued that if Fielden's speech had somehow violated the law, it was the "duty" of the police to get a warrant for his arrest, not to break up the meeting. "Are there any detectives and policemen in your large acquaintance that you would consider capable of passing upon questions of rhetoric, belles-lettres, oratory, illustration and simile?" she asked the Judge. "Nowhere have you shown that it was the duty of the police to disperse the meeting," she concluded.

Although a growing number of people had come to accept Sarah Ames' position in the seven years since 1886, the public was not prepared for what Governor Altgeld did the next day, June 26, 1893. He unconditionally pardoned Samuel Fielden, Michael Schwab, and Oscar Neebe, and he condemned the judicial errors and prejudicial evidence which had convicted all eight men.

A storm of protest broke. Altgeld was depicted as a bloodthirsty anarchist from coast to coast. He had support in a few quarters, however. In July the Chicago Trades and Labor Assembly adopted a statement supporting Altgeld's pardon. Mayor Harrison, who had become the owner of the *Chicago Times*, personally drafted the *Times* editorial in support of Altgeld.

Eighteen ninety three was a fruitful year for radicals; in February the vultures of speculation and over-capitalization came home to roost with the failure of the Philadelphia and Reading Railroad. Four million were out of work by summer. Hundreds of thousands applied for public assistance. Historian Richard Hofstadter wrote, "No other panic had elicited such fears of revolution."

The ruling class was scared for good reason. At the Columbian Exposition Chicago millionaires displayed the opulent majesty the city had attained in the 22 years since the Chicago Fire. A few blocks from the World Fair thousands of homeless men, women, and children camped in tent colonies and shacks. Two thousand people slept in City Hall corridors each night. The Exposition itself had been built at great cost in workers killed and injured.

Workers were angry and bitter after the defeats in 1892. The government had taken the side of the bosses more and more. An employer could almost always get an injunction against strikers. Now in 1893 people found themselves with no jobs at all. They turned to socialism and syndicalism for answers.

"Voices of Anarchy. Known Characters Talking Again" read the headline on August 21, 1893. The particular "known character" was Lucy Parsons, whom all the forces of "law and order" in Chicago had failed to silence. A crowd of thousands of unemployed overflowed Metropolitan Hall; the Chicago press raised the spectre of anarchism.

Lucy Parsons walked forward, her dark face alive with excitement. Waving arms filled the air, and the windows rattled with the applause. More threatening than the content of her speech was the welcome she received from the audience; the Chicago police knew she could excite thousands to action. They feared the "worst." She began in a low voice, "Now is my harvest time. I attempt no concealment of the fact that I, with other true hearted anarchists, will take advantage of your present condition to teach you the principles of the true faith."

Her voice rose in a crescendo. She continued amid shouts of applause. "You are the sole producers; why should you not consume? . . . Your salvation lies in stirring you to desperate action. The present social system is rotten from top to bottom. You must see this and realize that the time has come to destroy it."

Her voice fell to low, threatening tones which filled the auditorium. Had she stopped, not another sound could have been heard in the densely packed room. "Oh fools—fools that you do not grasp it."

She separated each sentence. "Let our streets run with gore but let us have justice." "Capitalist lives swept away are so much gain to us."

"That is why I am a revolutionist!" she shouted. With the determination of one prepared to act, she told the crowd, "You must no longer die and rot in tenement houses. . . . Shoulder to shoulder with one accord you should rise and take what is yours." Lucy was exhausted when she returned to her seat amid a cyclone of shouts.

The name Spring Valley, Illinois, was infamous among miners. The Spring Valley Coal Company advertised high wages and good living conditions; when miners responded to the ad, they found unemployment and intolerable living conditions. The company was notorious for its use of black strikebreakers, and Spring Valley had been the scene of many long, bitter strikes. Henry Demarest Lloyd's *The Millionaires Strike Against the Miners* exposed the brutal practices. As director of the Illinois Bureau of Labor Statistics, George Schilling conducted an investigation into conditions in Spring Valley.

A strong and militant I.W.P.A. section had been organized in Spring Valley, and Lucy was invited there for Labor Day 1893 to agitate among the miners. She told the miners that anarchists tell capitalists "to get off the earth;" she said that if they didn't do so peaceably, they would be forced off. The *Spring Valley Gazette* had heard rumors of another meeting "that was not so well tempered and abounded in blood and beer, dynamite and destruction" to which "none but the faithful were admitted."

Lucy sent her friend George Schilling a copy of her speech; he returned it with critical comments. He said he knew nothing about the men at Spring Valley who were ready to chop down the door with an ax in defense of her right to free speech. He felt she was making a mistake in agitating primarily among the foreign born rather than choosing to work with native Americans. "Their threats and vituperations against the American people and their institutions . . . will again and again culminate as did the Haymarket tragedy. . . . When you terrorize the public mind and threaten the stability of society with violence, you create the conditions which place the Bonfields and Garys in the saddle, hailed as the saviors of society." He said that without a "new conscience" [consciousness] all violence is reactionary.

He criticized the martyrs. "At Waldheim sleep five men . . . who died in the hope that their execution might accelerate the emancipation of the world. . . . They worshipped at the shrine of force; wrote it and preached it; until finally they were overpowered by their own Gods and slain in their own temple. . . . The public mind, terrorized by fear . . . swept away the safeguards of the law and turned its officers into pliant tools yielding to its will."

He felt that her agitation conducted "with great vigor and more than ordinary intellectual power" had been wasted on the foreigners.[7] But as Lucy saw it, she worked with the most downtrodden elements of society. After all, only a few generations back the self-righteous "natives" had been foreigners too.

Lucy's own experience as a black and Indian woman brought her close to the experience of the recent immigrants. Years later Agnes Inglis commented on the exchange between Schilling and Parsons. "Lucy seems to have seen them where they lived and worked. Theoretically he was right . . . but yet there is nothing theoretical about hunger."[8]

George Schilling had been one of Albert Parsons' close friends and comrades. He spearheaded the defense committee and later the amnesty movement. Yet six years after the executions and only months after Altgeld's pardon he wrote this private letter to his friend Lucy Parsons. He believed that his friends' discussion of violence had led to the reaction of Gary, Grinnell, and Bonfield, but he would never have criticized them publicly.

Enthusiastic with the revival of radicalism, the Chicago "anarchists" began to plan a conference for September 20, 1893. Peter Kropotkin was expected to attend. But when the cops got wind of the impending meeting, they issued a ukase against it. So the anarchists gave up the idea of meeting in the Art Palace and resolved to meet clandestinely.

Honoré Jaxon, the man who had escaped martyrdom in Canada, offered his office in the *Times* building, owned by Mayor Carter Harrison, as a suitable meeting place. Earlier in the year, Jaxon had succeeded in seating himself among the foreign diplomats at the opening ceremony of the Columbian Exposition and then presented himself as the representative of the Metis Indian nation of Canada. Jaxon became an important spokesperson for Native Americans.

Jaxon's office was fixed up to resemble a tepee. Here the anarchists met, right under the mayor's nose, so to speak. Lucy Parsons; Voltairine de Cleyre; Lizzie Holmes; William Holmes; C. L. James, the "anarchist" alderman from Eau Claire, Wisconsin (who got nervous about the police and left abruptly); and Van Ornum, author of "Why Government At All?" were all there.

The police learned of the meeting a month later, from New York papers. The papers reported the usual: that the anarchists had decided to cut the fire alarm, telegraph and telephone systems before setting fire to the city while covering their scheme with a peaceful public program for agitation. The police were unable to find out whether or not Peter Kropotkin had been there.[9]

In October Mayor Harrison was assassinated by a disappointed office seeker. He had been mayor of Chicago for four terms from 1879 to 1887, and he had won a fifth term in 1893 so that he could preside over the Exposition.

On November 11, 1893, Lucy Parsons had a confrontation with the new mayor over whether or not she would be allowed to speak. After promising not to denounce the mayor or otherwise threaten the security of society, she was let into the hall where she promptly denounced the mayor at a tzar. The detectives decided it would be better not to interfere. At the ceremony at Waldheim that November 11th, Michael Schwab and Samuel Fielden spoke before the graves of their comrades. Lucy did not often show her sorrow openly, but as she gazed at the monument, tears trickled down her cheeks.

The very next day Tommy Morgan found himself in tremendously hot water for his suggestion of the use of dynamite. William T. Stead, a British journalist and reformer, had brought together a coalition of reformers and called a mass meeting to discuss unemployment, the depression, corruption in city government, and other social problems. When Stead finished his speech, trying to answer the question, "If Christ came to Chicago today, what would he think of it?," Tommy Morgan spoke. "If you well-to-do people do not listen . . . a desperate man . . . will kill, will destroy. . . . And if the pleadings of editor Stead, in the name of Christ and for justice, cannot shake you out, may someone blow you out with dynamite." Graham Taylor unsuccessfully tried to explain that Morgan had been misunderstood. Lucy Parsons chuckled over the affair.[10]

In January the anarchists prepared to hold a parade; the Chief of Police had in hand a "verbatim" report of the meeting of 300 "anarchists" from the previous week. The report indicated that "extremely incendiary language was used. . . . The horrors of Barcelona and Paris were commended as worthy of emulation." Chicago policemen quaked in their boots whenever they thought of Lucy Parsons leading a parade through the city.

Charities offered thin soup and sometimes a place to sleep; the city offered a limited number of jobs sweeping the streets. But this was not enough to prevent major social unrest.

By the spring of 1894 Coxey's Army was gathering on Chicago's South Side to prepare for a march on Washington. These victims of the depression listened to Lucy Parsons tell them they "were belched up from the hearts of the people and indicated a good condition."

In the fall of 1892, Eugene Victor Debs began organizing a new industrial union. The 1892 defeats had convinced him that craft unions were antiquated and that industrial unions would have to confront the new industrial machine which relied on unskilled laborers. Eugene Debs was the kind of man who gave his overcoat to someone who needed it more than himself, who frequently gave his last dollar to a down and out tramp. Debs was tall and lanky. He was an eloquent speaker, and he became the living symbol and leader of the American workers' socialist movement for over thirty years.

Six days before Altgeld's pardon of the Haymarket Martyrs, the American Railway Union was formally organized. In 1893 it scored a major victory against James Hill and the Northern Pacific Railroad.

In the spring of 1894 workers at the Pullman Palace Car Company outside Chicago, hit by one wage cut after another, began signing up with the union. In George Pullman's "model industrial city," rents were higher and wages lower than in Chicago. Jane Addams had investigated and publicized conditions in Pullman.

When organizers were fired, the workers at Pullman walked out; they appealed to the A.R.U. for support. A boycott of all Pullman cars by railroad workers began on June 26, 1894—exactly one year after Altgeld's pardon. The boycott was successful beyond expectations. However, President Grover Cleveland and Attorney General Richard Olney were eager to crush the strike, as was the General Managers Association, the organization which represented the railroad owners. Olney had been a railroad lawyer for years and held substantial railroad interests.

In cooperation with the Attorney General, the General Managers Association deliberately attached mail cars to Pullman cars in an effort to get workers to violate federal law. Attorney General Olney ruled that the strike was interfering with the federal mails and secured blanket injunctions against the strike. President Cleveland ordered Federal troops into Chicago over the protests of Governor Altgeld and the mayor. Troops were called back from South Dakota where they were fighting Native Americans to fight the Chicago strikers.

Eugene Debs was jailed, and six months later he emerged from jail a socialist. Clarence Darrow quit his lucrative job as a railroad lawyer to become the lawyer for the American Railway Union. The Pullman workers, who sometimes had only 3¢ a week left in a check after George Pullman had deducted the rent and fees in the company town, had lost to the combined force of big government and big business. The Pullman defeat virtually killed the A.R.U.

Eugene Debs had noted that in 1892 a Republican President, Benjamin Harrison, crushed the Coeur d'Alene miners' strike with the army. In 1894 he saw the Democrat Grover Cleveland (whom he'd supported in 1892) crush the Pullman workers with the army. He knew something had to happen. Debs, with Henry Demarest Lloyd, Darrow, and Joe Buchanan, were among the prominent leaders who tried to bring the labor movement into the Populist movement.[11]

Lucy Parsons was impressed with Debs' leadership of the strike. She thought that Debs might be the new revolutionary leader.

The American Federation of Labor never supported the A.R.U. and the Pullman strike. By 1895, the A.F. of L. was taking a conservative turn in the face of the Homestead, Coeur d'Alene, and Pullman strikes. The A.F. of L. would cling to the area it already controlled—high wages for a few skilled workers in selected trades—and enter into a tacit agreement with the bosses not to organize immigrants, blacks, or unskilled workers in exchange for preserving its own domain.

Late one fall afternoon in 1894, Lucy was in Milwaukee for a lecture. Arthur Boose, a Wisconsin farm boy who had been left lame from a lumbering accident, was sitting in front of the boarding house where he lived talking with the old union men about workers' struggles, when he saw people streaming into the hall across the street. Several of his friends got up to go to the meeting; then an old German man came over and told him that he should come along to hear Lucy Parsons.

After her speech, Arthur Boose was so moved that he got up and said he was one of the people who had helped kill her husband. "Why no young man. You were too young to do so," Lucy replied.

"Well, I thought he was guilty and therefore I helped to kill him as much as the jury who found him guilty."

"No," she said. "You were too young." Arthur Boose had been only 10 or 11 in 1887.

Boose later recalled, "Had it not been for Lucy Parsons, I may of been a rank 'scissor-bill,' who knows?"[12]

Arthur Boose was only one of the many young men and women whom Lucy Parsons inspired.

In 1895, William and Lizzie Holmes moved to La Veta, Colorado. Samuel Fielden and his family moved there about the same time. The following year the Holmes went to Denver. Lizzie was seriously ill for several years.

William Holmes had become a lawyer, which drew hostile comment from many comrades. Lizzie defended his decision to become a lawyer and argued that had the comrades in the Haymarket trial had good anarchist lawyers, the outcome of the trial might have been different. Lucy Parsons was outraged that Lizzie would make such a comment. She vehemently declared that the trial was a class trial and that nothing could have changed its outcome.[13]

The Holmes more closely identified with the emerging intellectual streams of American anarchism, while Lucy Parsons stayed in the mainstream of American working class radicalism, following such leaders as Eugene Debs and Bill Haywood. The Holmes wrote voluminously on theoretical questions, and Lizzie wrote extensively on the women's question.

In 1897 they became involved in the Denver Labor Exchange, a cooperative effort to circumvent the capitalist economy. Through the Labor Exchange people could exchange work with each other without exchanging money. It was an attempt to set up a microcosm of what they believed the ideal society to be within the structure of the capitalist system. In 1898 the Holmes formed the Labor Exchange Co-operative Publishing Company and put out the *Labor Exchange Guide*.[14]

The visit of English anarchist Charles W. Mowbray to Chicago in 1895 provided the police with another meeting to disrupt. Lucy Parsons was writing for a new anarchist paper, the *Rebel*, published in Boston. She commented about the police. "The animals thought they saw a chance to bleed a few more dollars from the capitalists. . . . They hung out their breath for an airing, got the bloom out of their noses (as well as they could), read up on the best method of taking the blur out of their eyes and steadying the step; this done, the animals put themselves much in evidence. They . . . brushed the dust from their uniforms, tried their clubs over lampposts and innocent people's heads, and finally declared there 'was going to be no red flag anarchy nonsense preached in Chicago.' "

Lucy had good reason to hate the police. "Kill the murderers of my husband!" she shouted sometimes. The *Rebel* proudly reported she'd said she was bringing up her son to assassinate his father's murderers. It was an almost impossible atmosphere in which to raise a child. Lucy was frequently on the road lecturing. Sometimes she was jailed, but more often just arrested and released. Sometimes she took Albert Jr. with her; the high school boy sat quietly with his mother in Justus Schwab's New York saloon and anarchist gathering place while she talked politics with her friends.

That November 11th there was another crisis. The Cemetery Association refused to permit the radicals to hold their demonstration at the cemetery. Some irate radicals wanted to exhume the bodies and remove them to some place they could meet each November 11th. Lucy adamantly opposed the move, saying the $2,000-$4,000 cost would be better spent elsewhere, and she felt her own personal pain would be too much to endure. Her simple request was, "Speaking personally, I say, spare me the opening afresh of the wound. I shrink from standing by that mound and seeing my dear one brought forth, hearing the sensational capitalistic press gloat over the whole scene, lay bare the horror. If my husband must be disturbed in his last rest, there need be no hurry. Let it be when I, too, am gone." The *Arbeiter-Zeitung* refused to publish her letter.[15]

Disaster seemed to stalk Lucy; in August, 1896, her house burned, and with it much of her literature. She was later able to sell several hundred damaged copies of *Anarchism* at 30¢ for hardback and 15¢ for paper and a few copies of *The Life of Albert R. Parsons* for 75¢. The hardback books had originally been $1.25, 60¢ for paper.

Over twelve hundred persons gathered to pay their respects to the Haymarket martyrs on November 11, 1896. Red flags decorated the stage and walls; streamers with the martyrs' last words on the scaffold hung among the flags. A chorus of young women dressed in white with black sashes sang the martyrs' favorite songs. The audience quietly awaited Johann Most's arrival.

During an intermission Graham Taylor of the Chicago Commons settlement house was introduced to Lucy Parsons. Then the audience began to demand that Lucy speak. Taylor was vividly impressed by this "tall, well built and poised" woman who commanded her audience's attention "by her serious manner and resonant voice."

"I am the widow of Albert R. Parsons and the mother of his son," Lucy began. "I charge the police and the court with murdering my husband. I live to bring up his son to take up the work which was stricken from his father's hand."

Before she could continue, a police captain arrested her and took her to the police station. One man jumped up yelling "Forwarts!" but his companions quickly silenced him. The chairman announced in German, "The next speaker will be Herr Most," and the meeting continued as if nothing had happened. Lucy was promptly released from police custody, but she had been prevented from speaking "as she had been whenever and wherever she had attempted to speak since the riot," recalled Taylor. The Chicago police were more afraid of Lucy Parsons than of Johann Most.

Shortly after her meeting with Taylor, Lucy came to a Free Floor Forum at Chicago Commons. About 100 persons came to the Free Floor Forum each Tuesday night to hear speakers on such controversial topics as "Socialism," "The Single Tax," "Municipal Ownership," "Child Labor," and "The Social Boiling Point." The speaker gave a 20 minute talk, followed by discussion from the floor. The only restriction was "that advocacy of violence would be out of order."

Speakers were always invited by suggestions of the people who attended. When Lucy Parsons came, the people demanded that she be invited back to give a lecture. Graham Taylor was slightly taken aback when the people voted unanimously that she speak the next Tuesday, and he knew that inviting Lucy Parsons to speak would be the "supreme test of the freedom of the floor." He talked with Lucy and told her that she would probably not be arrested at the privately conducted Free Floor Forum, as she always was at public meetings. He asked her to "state the underlying motive which justified, to herself at least, her attitude toward the social order." He recalled, "The suspicioning look as of one who was hunted faded from her face as she replied: 'You will not be disappointed in having spoken kindly to me.'"

The next Tuesday night she presented a paper describing her experiences from the time she came to Chicago until May 4, 1886, detailing the reasons why she came to believe "that nothing short of the end of the existing capitalistic industrial order would bring either justice or peace." The audience demanded that she continue and tell the story of the trial and executions. "It is a matter of history," she answered, concluding her remarks.

Lucy Parsons, Emma Goldman, Tommy Morgan, Clarence Darrow, Abraham Isaak, and many others had spoken at the Free Floor Forums by 1902 when they were discontinued, because "extreme radical spokesmen and their retainers from other parts of the city" had taken over the meetings.[16]

In 1896 the political scene in America seemed to be changing. Governor John P. Altgeld of Illinois captured the Democratic Party from Grover Cleveland. Altgeld was determined to end the career of the man who had sent federal troops to Chicago to defeat the Pullman workers. Because he had been born in Germany, Altgeld could not run for President himself. He endorsed Senator Richard Bland from Missouri for President; the platform was Altgeld's, and it concluded with a slap at Cleveland, denouncing "government by injunction as a new and highly dangerous form of oppression."

William Jennings Bryan's Cross of Gold speech, however, ruined Altgeld's plans and won Bryan the nomination.

Henry D. Lloyd attempted to get Eugene Debs to accept the presidential nomination of the People's Party. When Debs refused, the People's Party endorsed Bryan and went down in defeat with him, as did Altgeld, who did not win re-election as governor. The Republicans put up William McKinley, Ohio political boss Mark Hanna's choice for President. All they had to do on election day was have all their factory owner friends post signs saying, "If Bryan is elected, this plant will remain closed" and let the workers off two hours early to go vote for McKinley. This happened all across the country, and Altgeld knew he was "defeated" as soon as this evidence began coming in.

In the 1890's radical-intellectual anarchism began to consider the sex question and women's emancipation a first priority. *Women's Emancipator* and then *Lucifer* (1880-1905), published by Moses Harman, a tall, distinguished old man with flowing white hair and beard and eternally young, friendly eyes, in Valley Falls, Kansas, and later in Chicago; *Firebrand* (1895-1896) and *Free Society* (1895-1904), published by west coast anarchists who moved to Chicago, then to New York; *Discontent* (1898-1902), published by anarchist colonists on Tacoma Bay in Washington State; and *Clothed With the Sun,* a little sheet put out by Lois Waisbrooker in Home Colony, all advocated free love or variety in sex.

Emma Goldman spent a year on Blackwell Island in 1893-94 for inciting to riot. After her release, she went to Europe to study nursing and midwifery and returned to the U.S. in the fall of 1896 to become the anarchists' foremost advocate of free love. Goldman could study in Europe and travel in educated circles, opportunities which Lucy Parsons' dark skin precluded for her. Goldman became interested in the freedom of the individual; Parsons remained committed to the freedom of the working class from capitalism.

While the anarchist movement became more and more involved with women's emancipation, sexual freedom, and individual liberties, Lucy Parsons became involved in the Social Democracy, led by Eugene Debs and formed from the remains of the American Railway Union. Lucy Parsons and Emma Goldman first met at the June, 1897 convention in Chicago which dissolved the A.R.U. and initiated the Social Democracy. The Social Democracy planned to colonize Washington state and turn it into a Cooperative Commonwealth. Mother Jones was the only woman on the Executive Committee of the Social Democracy.

In addition to the colonization plan, the convention called for a shorter working day, public works projects for the unemployed, and public ownership of all utilities and monopolies. When Judge Woods, who had sentenced Debs to jail after the Pullman strike, was mentioned, Lucy Parsons called the judge a coward, and the entire crowd hissed him.

On the last day of the convention, Debs said in his closing speech, "We shall eliminate all 'rot' from the Constitution and make it as simple as possible. That government is best governed which is least governed, and that land which is perfectly governed has no government at all." The convention passed a resolution that no member of the organization could accept an elective or appointive office "without the consent of the Executive board, except in States already under control of this body."

Mother Jones stood and shouted her approval. Then Lucy Parsons, who heartily approved of Debs' call for no government, arose and asked Debs for another parting statement to the convention, to which he responded:

> Under the competitive system, American manhood is reduced to merchandise which is not quoted in the stock markets. . . . Manhood and womanhood are sunk to the lowest depths. The cheapest commodity in this whole country is human flesh and blood. . . .
>
> There is going to be a change. My mental vision does not deceive me. I can see the handwriting on the wall.

Lucy Parsons endorsed the Cooperative Commonwealth plan.

Her old antagonist Tommy Morgan and the Socialist Labor Party denounced Debs and the colony plan. Morgan was kept out of the convention; his credentials were "lost" in committee until it was over.[17]

Lucy Parsons had claimed to be an "anarchist" when the title was pinned on her by the bourgeois press and her state socialist enemies. She believed her husband had died for anarchism, and she was prepared to defend and die for anarchism. Although her beliefs were syndicalist rather than anarchist, she tried to cling to the "anarchist" movement as it changed shape.

Publicly, Lucy Parsons held marriage, monogamy, family, and motherhood as ideals. In private, she entered into more than one extra-legal relationship with a man. She may have been prevented from marrying by laws forbidding miscegenation; if this was the case, she demanded what capitalist society denied her—marriage. Perhaps her break up with Martin Lacher in 1891 soured her on "free love."

The women's question was a real problem for Lucy. She had three strikes against her from birth: poor, non-white, woman. She felt poverty the most acutely, and she put the fight against racism and sexism secondary to class struggle. She believed in monogamous marriage and the nuclear family as fundamental "natural" principles and argued that the problems of marriage resulted from the economic system, not from flaws in the institution itself.

The "women's question" was dealt with in her paper *Free-*

dom in 1892. In the surviving issues there are three articles on women and marriage—including one on rape and one on divorce. There are also guarded best wishes to Gretchen Spies and activist Robert Steiner on their marriage. *"Freedom* wishes the newly married couple all the happiness possible in the marriage relation under present social arrangements."

In the question of a rape for which the rapist had been lynched, the author said that the rapist should have been confined to a mental institution instead and the nature of his illness or crime kept secret. The woman victim, because the rape had been publicized, would be treated as a criminal and would be the further victim of stares and gossip. The paper committed itself to freedom of divorce and suggested that the married houseworker is frequently nothing but the servant "for which she does not get a servant's wages."

Freedom concentrated on industrial warfare, class conflict and police repression.

Radical feminism was a working class development which came out of the analysis of the role of women under capitalism. Lucy Parsons' feminism, which analyzed women's oppression as a function of capitalism, was founded on working class values.

Emma Goldman's feminism took on an abstract character of freedom for women in all things, in all times, and in all places; her feminism became separate from its working class origins. Goldman represented the feminism being advocated in the anarchist movement of the 1890's. The intellectual anarchists questioned Lucy Parsons about her attitudes on the women's question.

In response Lucy wrote "Cause of Sex Slavery" for the *Firebrand* in 1895. "I hold . . . that the economic is the first issue to be settled, that it is woman's economical dependence which makes her enslavement to man possible. . . . How many women do you think would submit to marriage slavery if it were not for wage slavery? . . . These are in brief my views upon the sex-question, and it is for this reason I have never advocated it as a distinct question." She had known for a long time that women's and children's low wages lowered the living standard of the entire working class. For her the women's question was part of the class question. She believed that women would be emancipated when wage slavery in the factories, fields, and mines of capitalism had ended.

She argued that prostitution and rape could occur within marriage, but she did not believe that the nuclear family structure was inherently oppressive to women. For her, the nuclear family could be the ideal social form in a free society. For many working class men and women the family *was* the last refuge from employer and state. She could think of her 15 happy years with Albert Parsons; they had each other whatever the Ku Klux Klan, the bosses, the state, or the Citizens' Association did to them.

Parsons' and Goldman's differing positions on the women's question were not a question of right and wrong. They were the result of different backgrounds and social milieus. Goldman discovered that many "anarchists" in the East shared Lucy Parsons' views. Goldman felt more at home with the West Coast group.

In 1896, Oscar Rotter wrote a controversial article for *Free Society*. He argued that only free love would end the private ownership of one person by another, generally the private ownership of the woman by the man. "Free sex companionship" would require "the complete emancipation of woman intellectually, socially, legally, economically, and sexually." He argued, moreover, that free love was the natural state of existence, that people are not naturally monogamous.

Lucy Parsons was outraged that an anarchist paper would deal with such questions; for her advancing the working class revolution came first at any cost. She struck at Rotter on a personal level. Mr. Rotter's name "by some strange coincidence, well demonstrates what society would come to if his system of variety was adopted!" she raged.

She wrote of "the virtue of womanhood" and the "purity of my sex." She was horrified that Rotter had not mentioned "the sweetest of all words under the sun: family life, child life."

For her the biggest question was how the free lovers would determine the father of children and who would take responsibility for them. She was afraid it would almost inevitably fall to the mother. Her attack on the "varietists" was bitter. "There could be no particular objection to these 'love relations' if those engaging in them were of the samples I have usually met who advocate this kind of nonsense, because they have nine times in ten been away passed middle age and the reproductive period."

Lucy felt a responsibility to her son, a seventeen year old high school student. "Might my tongue cleave to the roof of my mouth, and my brains become as jelly, before my son should hear such language fall from my lips." She felt that under ideal conditions people would not have "an ownership in the 'person' of the other, because they agree to live an exclusive life in sexual relations."

Veneral disease and pregnancy were the dangers which Lucy saw in free love. Emma Goldman, who had an inverted womb, was freed from the dangers of pregnancy. Few women in the 1890's were free to have sex without pregnancy.

Lucy Parsons was even willing to renounce the name "anarchist" if "anarchist" were identified with "varietist." "Mr. Rotter attempts to dig up the hideous 'Variety' grub and bind it to the beautiful unfolding blossom of labor's emancipation from wage-slavery and call them one and the same. Variety in sex relations and economic freedom have nothing in common. Nor has it anything in common with Anarchism, as I understand Anarchism; if it has then I am not an Anarchist." She argued that monogamy was the natural state of human beings just as vehemently as her opponents argued that variety was the natural state.

Henry Addis, one of the editors of *Firebrand* and of *Free Society,* pointed out that if variety was not natural then it should present no danger to society; under freedom it would simply disappear. But if it were natural, it could only be prevented by force. He concluded, "If Comrade Parsons would prevent variety by force, she is an advocate of government."

This Comrade Parsons had to consider carefully. She decided she would have to accept Addis' argument about force and government. But she had another idea. "The *Firebrand* has had a good deal from the men in favor of variety. . . . Now we would like . . . our sisters who are free to state their opinions."

Her appeal elicited a number of responses from women. Comrade B from Omaha laid out her unhappy experience; she and her husband had had sex before marriage; but under pressure from relatives they married. The marriage resulted in children they could not support. Her health failed, and her husband insisted that he continue to enjoy sexual freedom. Finally he left her, with no support for the children.

Lucy's fears were realized in this and other stories. Unemployment and poverty intervened in the lives of those who tried to establish their own microcosm of personal freedom.

Oscar Rotter prepared a well thought out rebuttal to Lucy's position. He declared himself an enemy of the monogamous family, because he could not conceive of dignified human life without complete freedom which each individual could exercise at any time. He felt the family was a unit for social control dominated by church and state, which allowed no possibility for woman's emancipation.

He continued, "Contrary to Mrs. Parsons' opinion the abolition of marriage . . . has an integral connection with the struggle for economic freedom. Marriage is a property institution, which had its origin in the capture, sale, or giving away of woman by her male relatives in barbaric and half civilized ages. With the abolition of private property in the natural resources and the instruments of production, woman will become economically free. Marriage will no longer be for her the necessary evil of an institution for her support in compensation for exclusive and eventually forced sexual favors."

Rotter argued that women were capable of determining their biological destiny, that they could choose when sex was for reproduction and when it was for pleasure only.

In October, 1897, the Chicago anarchists held a defense meeting for the *Firebrand* editors who were being prosecuted for allegedly sending obscenity through the mails. Walt Whitman's "A Woman Waits for Me" was the material in question. Lucy Parsons, Emma Goldman, and Moses Harman were the principal speakers. What Lucy Parsons had to say at that meeting aroused the ire of all the free love anarchists and alienated her forever from Emma Goldman. "There has been some dirty reading in the *Firebrand*," Lucy exclaimed. In the next issue of *Free Society* Abraham Isaak, one of the editors facing legal action, charged her with "blackguarding."

She defended herself in print and repeated what she had said at the meeting. "If it is necessary to advocate variety to be an Anarchist, then I am not an Anarchist. . . . I stated further that it made no difference to me what people did in their private lives . . . but when they set up their ideas as a reconstructive theory of society, it became public property and I had a right to disagree with them and to criticize them."

Isaak backed down from his original criticism, and the editorial board told him he had to take personal responsibility for his statement. He decided that the word "Comstockism" should replace "blackguarding"—after Anthony Comstock, the postmaster general who devised the regulations.[18]

The rift between Lucy Parsons and the people who were to lead the anarchist movement for the next two decades was irrevocable. It was Emma Goldman who captured the headlines, and the two women had no use for each other. Lucy Parsons had wanted to remain the unquestioned leader of the anarchist movement, but the leadership changed and with it the direction of the movement.

On November 11, 1897, ten years after the executions of Albert Parsons, August Spies, Adolph Fischer, and George Engel, Emma Goldman spoke at the commemoration in Chicago. Jay Fox, another rising star in the movement also spoke; as a 16 year old he had lost a finger on May 3, 1886, in the shooting outside McCormick Reaper works. Theodore Appel, a partisan of Johann Most, chaired the meeting. Lucy Parsons was present, wearing a faded black hat; she did not speak. Perhaps the comrades who were angered by the episode the month before forced her into an involuntary silence. Perhaps her arrest at the November 11th meeting the year before resulted in a decision that she remain silent.

After the November 11th meeting, Emma Goldman left for her first trip to the west coast. In Denver she visited Lizzie and William Holmes, who shared their memories of 1886 and 1887 with her; the three became good friends.[19]

By the end of the 1890's Lucy Parsons had turned away from advocating propaganda by the deed. On February 7, 1898, she wrote to Joseph Labadie asking him to help arrange a lecture tour in the East for her. "I wish to speak along trades union lines. I recognize the fact that the real stamina of the reform movement is in organized labor. I have prepared two lectures, showing the history, development and progress of Trades Unions, and the part they will play in solving the labor problems. Of course, my position is radical, but it will hardly frighten anyone, but the *very* timid."[20]

In 1898, the U.S. went to war with Spain in Cuba. Assistant Secretary of the Navy Theodore Roosevelt had carefully arranged for the American fleet in the Pacific to sail into Manila Harbor in the Philippines if the U.S. should declare war on Spain. He wanted to attack Spain on two fronts.

While news of the Spanish American War captured headlines daily, the Social Democracy met in Chicago on June 12 to admit that the colonization plan had failed. The organization became the Social Democratic Party and its program emphasized social ills in the industrial centers of the Midwest and East.

Lucy Parsons bitterly opposed the imperialist war with Spain. But her son, Albert Jr., now 18, enlisted against his mother's opposition.

Lucy held street demonstrations to discourage other young men from enlisting for the war in the Philippines. On July 16, 1899, she stood in the sweltering sun on State Street. A hundred persons expectantly waited for her lecture to begin. She announced that Cuba was free, but that the battle had shifted to the Philippines where "the sword which struck down the Spaniards [was] turned upon the people" of the Philippines.

"I appeal to you young men," she shouted, "to refuse to enlist and go to those far-off islands for the purpose of riveting the chains of a new slavery on the limbs of the Filipinos. . . . What will it avail you? Don't you have to fight enough battles against the trusts here, without traveling across the Pacific?"

Two weeks later Lucy Parsons committed her son to the Illinois Northern Hospital for the Insane. On July 27, 1899, she appeared in court to testify to her son's insanity. Lucy stated that up until three years ago her son had been a model youth— an extremely gentle, good natured young man who stayed up until all hours of the night reading and studying. After an operation he had become listless, lazy, and dreamy. She said that he had once been very neat, but that she could no longer get him to change his clothes.

Albert testified in his own behalf and brought several witnesses who testified to his sanity. Albert had become a clerk after he finished high school. He had defied his rebel mother by joining the army and by attending church services and becoming involved in the Spiritualist movement.

Lucy claimed that he had drawn a knife on her and threatened her life, beginning in January, 1899.

The court declared him insane and issued a warrant for his arrest. Lucy signed a bond and put up $100 to guarantee that she would pay for his clothing while he remained in the hospital.

The sheriff delivered him to the Illinois Northern Hospital for the Insane four days later—on July 31, 1899. The second half of his life had begun.

On August 3, the hospital doctor examined him and found absolutely nothing abnormal about either his physical or mental condition.

Once in the hospital, Albert deteriorated mentally and physically. He was accused of being an anarchist, which he denied. The guards and other inmates knew who his parents were. He refused to work on the ward; he was put in confinement and in restraints, and he repeatedly fought with guards and other patients.

Emma Goldman referred to Lucy's "horrible treatment" of the boy, "whom she drove into the army and then had him put in a lunatic asylum." Lucy was thought of badly in some quarters for her treatment of her son.

There is no evidence that Lucy ever saw her son alive again. She must have been aware of the hell to which she was sending him; Dorothea Dix's exposure of the conditions in mental hospitals were making headlines. When Albert died of tuberculosis on August 15, 1919, she arranged to have the body brought back to Chicago and cremated; she then kept the ashes in her home.[21]

There must have been a long history of conflict between Lucy and Albert Jr., most of it unknown due to Lucy's refusal to discuss her private life. What remains is that she committed him to the mental institution. She had put her political commitments first and had attempted to make Albert Jr. a part of her larger political vision. When he failed to measure up to her expectations, and began to actively fight her, she put him away. Her son would never carry on his father's work; few children could have filled the role Albert Parsons, the Haymarket Martyr, had played in the labor movement.

Like the court decision in favor of free speech for radicals in 1889 and the decision in the Martin Lacher vs. Lucy Parsons case in 1891, the court decision to commit Albert Jr. was based on property rights. He was a minor child (19) and therefore the legal property of his mother, who, in the court's view, had the legal right to commit him.

The Haymarket affair and Albert Parsons' execution was a heavy burden on the Parsons family. Albert Jr.'s traumatic childhood resulted in his commitment to a mental institution for half his life. Edgar Albert Parsons' wife, a young bride in 1886, felt tremendously disgraced by Albert R. Parsons' execution and kept the story concealed for many years. Only when her children found a trunk containing newspaper accounts of the execution among their grandfather, William Henry Parsons', possessions, did she finally admit that Albert Parsons was their great uncle with whom their father had grown up in Texas. Edgar Parsons received injury reports and the notification of the death of Albert Parsons Jr. from the Northern Illinois Hospital for the Insane. Edgar must have maintained some contact with Lucy over the years, and it was probably Edgar who notified her of the death of her son.[22]

In the 1890's the Western Federation of Miners arose, a militant organization which united miners against the brutal bosses on the industrial frontier. The W.F.M. was in part based upon structures left by the Knights of Labor in the West. In 1896 the W.F.M. affiliated with the A. F. of L., but let the affiliation lapse a year later. In 1896 Eugene Debs went to Leadville, Colorado, to participate in a W.F.M. strike there. He and Ed Boyce, the W.F.M.'s president, and Big Bill Haywood, a strapping one-eyed miner who became the union's secretary-treasurer in 1901, began to talk about a new industrial union, based on the groundwork laid by the defeated A.R.U.

In 1900 a number of prominent socialists left the Socialist Labor Party which was dominated by Daniel DeLeon, and joined the Social Democratic Party. Debs ran for president for the first time in 1900.

In 1901 the Social Democratic Party became the Socialist Party of America, a party destined to become a mass organization rather than a small socialist sect. Lucy Parsons was a member of this new party.

The revitalized socialist movement would soon be in a position to challenge the conservative leadership of the A. F. of L. How this was to be done was the problem. Some leaders believed that the radicals should set up their own union structure in opposition to the A. F. of L.

However, the socialist influence within the A. F. of L. was very strong; in 1900 nearly all A. F. of L. unions had socialist principles in their constitutions. In 1902, the socialist Max Hayes, who had been the party's vice presidential candidate in 1900, failed to unseat Samuel Gompers as head of the A. F. of L. by only 4897 to 4171. Hayes and his supporters argued that the Socialist Party should not make the mistake of Daniel DeLeon and the S.L.P. and attempt to set up a "dual union."

The socialists were strong in 1900, but the capitalists were even stronger. In 1901 the United States Steel Corporation became the first billion dollar industry when J. P. Morgan bought the Carnegie Steel Co.

In 1899 Chicago builders had formed the Building Contractors Council to defeat the Building Trades Council which the workers had built in 1888. A year long fight followed which destroyed the Building Trades Council and left the bosses in complete control of construction in Chicago.

At the turn of the century Lucy Parsons was writing the Chicago column for *Free Society*. She reported that the new century had not opened well for working people. Bradstreet's showed that the cost of living had gone up 25 to 33% while wages had advanced only 12 to 15%. Forty five thousand Chicago building trades workers were locked out, and the piano makers had been locked out for 16 weeks with no end in sight. Lucy reported that "McKinley's 'wave of prosperity' is hitting this city so hard just now that it is a very good place for the workingmen to keep away from." The next months she reported that the custom tailors were locked out for demanding an end to homework, and the united machinists were out demanding reduced hours and increased pay. Lucy had just been to Mount Olive to speak at the unveiling of the monument in honor of miners who had lost their lives at Virden and Pana.[23]

Comrade Johann Most was in Chicago lecturing and acting in a play called the "Weavers;" there was standing room only when Lucy went. Errico Malatesta, the Italian anarchist, spent an evening discussing politics with Lucy in her home one evening early in 1900. In April Peter Kropotkin visited Chicago and stayed at Hull House. On Memorial Day Lucy Parsons and Jay Fox addressed an "anarchist" picnic in the woods near Waldheim cemetery. Chicago, which had become a bustling metropolis with a population rapidly approaching two million, remained a center of radical activity.

In the summer of 1901 a young man visited Chicago. He said his name was Nieman, the German word for "Nobody," and he also gave the name Csolz. He wanted to learn more about anarchism, and he talked with Emma Goldman, Abraham Isaak, and other members of the *Free Society* group. Emma Goldman recognized him as the same good-looking blond young man with the dreamy, searching eyes, who had asked her for suggestions on reading material at a meeting in Cleveland.

But Emma was busy and didn't have time to talk with Csolz when he went with her on the "L" on her way to the train station. Nieman or Csolz struck Isaak peculiary, and Isaak printed a warning in *Free Society* that the young man was a police spy. Emma Goldman was convinced of Csolz's sincerity, and she forced Isaak to retract the charge.

On September 6, 1901, the young man was heard from again. He shot President McKinley at the Buffalo Exposition. The *Chicago Tribune* immediately announced that the U.S. Secret Service suspected connections with the "Haymarket Gang," and they sent a reporter off to see Lucy Parsons and Oscar Neebe.

Lucy was amicable when the reporter came to her home. She expressed hope for McKinley's recovery and her belief that he was as good as any President could be under capitalism. She had been afraid that something like the assassination of a president would occur. "Nothing could be worse for the cause of anarchism," she exclaimed. "What is the use to strike individuals? That is not true anarchy. Another ruler rises to take his place and no good is accomplished." She had never heard of the assailant, and she did not believe he was part of a conspiracy.

Lucy even praised McKinley, whom she believed had been forced into the Spanish American War against his will, and she feared the presidency of the military man Theodore Roosevelt, who had been elevated to the office of vice president by the political bosses to keep him out of national politics.

Oscar Neebe called the would-be-assassin "a crank or insane man." He pointed out that the assassination of a thousand presidents would not alter the fact that the country is ruled by capital. "Of course every man who does a crazy or foolish deed is an Anarchist in the eyes of the public." He said there were no anarchists in Chicago, only a variety of socialists.

The Chicago police and the papers left Lucy Parsons and Oscar Neebe alone after these unsatisfying interviews. They concentrated on finding Emma Goldman. The young man being held in Buffalo had said he was inspired by Emma Goldman. A massive woman-hunt with the purpose of implicating Goldman in a conspiracy to assassinate the president began.

In Chicago the police destroyed the *Free Society* press and arrested Abraham and Marie Isaak and their two children, Jay Fox, Hippolyte Havel, Henry Travaglio, Julia Mechanic, and other members of the *Free Society* publishing group. The Isaaks' neighbors claimed that a man had moved a trunk from Isaak's home shortly before McKinley was shot. When the delivery man was located he said he had also taken a trunk to Lucy Parsons' home in June. This trunk "mystery" was the only flimsy link between Parsons and the Isaaks, and the police dropped it. The link between the Isaak family and the assassination was even flimsier.

Officer Schuettler had a dual problem on his hands. He gloried in rounding up the hated anarchists, but the question arose, "How come they're loose? Haven't you been doing your job?" He had to attend to his public image first, and he stated that violent anarchism had been pretty well dead in Chicago for about six years and that the assassin had definitely not visited any of the anarchists in his district. It must have been those policemen on the West and Northwest sides who weren't doing their jobs.

Radicals were arrested across the country. Henry Bauer was arrested in Allegheny City. Republican papers charged that Randolph Hearst's vicious attacks on McKinley inspired Czolgosz (as he became known); Hearst responded by attacking the anarchists. Johann Most was arrested. The citizens of New York had not forgotten that an Italian-American anarchist, Gaetano Bresci, had returned to Italy the year before and assassinated King Humbert. A mob prepared to cross the river and sack the Italian community in Paterson, New Jersey, which was supporting Bresci's small daughter. The mob was stopped.

Citizens of Spring Valley, Illinois, prepared to administer loyalty oaths to the Italian anarchist coal miners who published

L'Aurora and who hailed Czolgosz as a hero. The miners outfoxed the enraged citizenry, and the paper remained in operation in Mine No. 2, where the miners had moved the press to save it from the mob.

On the west coast, a vigilante mob from Tacoma intended to destroy the anarchist colony across the bay at Home. The ferry boat's captain and a minister dissuaded the mob. However the authorities did take away the colony's post office, from which it mailed its paper.

Emma Goldman was visiting Carl Nold in St. Louis. She was determined to go to Chicago and join her imprisoned comrades; Nold tried to discourage her, reminding her of 1887.

The papers were filled with talk of new laws to suppress and deport anarchists. The nation was hysterical over the assassination, as it had been over the bombing in Haymarket Square 15 years before. On September 10 the *Tribune* reported the arrests of Carl Nold and Harry Gordon in Pittsburgh; on September 11, it reported that the dreaded Emma Goldman was in the clutches of the law. She had gone to Chicago to surrender herself, but the law had gotten her first.

For the imprisoned radicals in Chicago, McKinley's death on September 14, meant only the same sort of concern and sympathy that a worker's death would occasion. Jay Fox said, "For Mrs. McKinley I have the same sorrow which I have for my cellmate of yesterday, who heard of the death of his child and wept bitter tears." Goldman said, "Suppose the President is dead. Thousands die daily and are unwept. Why should any fuss be made about this man?"

For the capitalists of the country, the biggest concern was how the shooting and death of the president would affect the stock market. On the 8th the *Tribune* reported "Stocks Decline Sharply on False Rumor of the President's Death." As his condition worsened, finance page headlines read, "Market Breaks Under Bad News. Expectation of the President's Death Nearly Causes Wall Street Panic."

Emma Goldman got first-hand experience with the Chicago police. "Schuettler was most ferocious," she wrote. "His massive bulk towered above me, bellowing: 'If you don't confess, you'll go the way of those bastard Haymarket anarchists.' " An officer held a reflector close to her eyes after she fell asleep. She woke

up, shouting and pushing him away. "You're burning my eyes!"
"We'll burn more before we get through with you!"

Jane Addams of Hull House and Raymond Robbins from Chicago Commons took a strong stand against the arrests and secured the release of the Isaaks, who had been put through the sweat box, and the other members of Free Society. For their efforts, the two settlements got their windows broken.

Chief of Police O'Neill came to talk with Emma Goldman. He told her he thought she was innocent, and a remarkable change occurred. Gifts began appearing at the jail for her, then a fantastic turkey dinner. Finally, when the benefactor offered to put up $5000 towards her bail, the matron informed her it was "the ward heeler and he hates the Republicans worse than the devil." Not everyone in Chicago was mourning McKinley's passing.

The Chicago police refused to extradite Goldman to New York. O'Neill wanted to send two police captains to the penitentiary for perjury and bribery. These two had seized the cry "Anarchy!" and had tried to pose as saviours of society. A friend told Goldman, "It wasn't to O'Neill's interest to let those birds pose as heroes and get back into the department."

Finally, newspapers quietly noted on their back pages, "After a month's detention Emma Goldman was found not to have been in complicity with the assassin of President McKinley."

By 1901 Lucy Parsons had rejected propaganda by the deed and assassination as ways of advancing the interests of the working class. She believed that only a well organized and united working class could seize the means of production.

For Emma Goldman, the attitude of radicals who considered Leon Czolgosz a madman was devastating. Her own experience with Berkman and the attempt on Frick nine years before made her sympathetic to Czolgosz's motivation. But in 1901 even Berkman wrote from prison condemning Czolgosz and the assassination. Berkman argued that an act against a political figure was insignificant compared to an act against an economic figure. A president was only a puppet; a Rockefeller, a Carnegie, a Frick, a Morgan—they were the real oppressors of the people.

Goldman wanted to help Czolgosz, who was being railroaded to the electric chair, but her comrades considered it an act of political suicide. For her courageous defense of Czolgosz, her friends ostracized her. She retired from public life for a time and worked as a nurse under the name E. G. Smith.

In the public mind, McKinley's assassination was linked to the Haymarket bombing and Berkman's attempt on Frick as anarchist terrorism.

States passed anti-anarchist statutes. President Roosevelt, who had urged that the Haymarket defendants be shot without trial in 1886, urged Congress to suppress anarchism. The result was the Anarchist Exclusion Act, passed in 1903, which provided that "No person who disbelieves in or who is opposed to all organized governments, or who is a member of or affiliated with any organization entertaining or teaching such disbelief in or opposition to all governments . . . shall be permitted to enter the United States." The law provided for the deportation of alien radicals and was loosely interpreted by immigration authorities and courts.

John Turner, the English radical unionist, was the law's first victim. Turner was arrested in late 1903 and ordered deported; the case was appealed to the Supreme Court in 1904, where Clarence Darrow and Edgar Lee Masters argued for Turner. The ruling of the lower court was sustained, and the court's decision emphasized that Congress had arbitrary power to exclude any alien it so desired.

In 1903 Lucy Parsons raised the money to reprint *The Life of Albert R. Parsons* with a preface by Clarence Darrow. In September, 1904, she arrived in the East with copies of the book to sell.[24] She planned to lecture on "Trade Unions and the Open Shop," "The Struggle for Liberty," and "Anarchist and World-Wide Propaganda." Lucy Parsons, Emma Goldman, James F. Morton Jr., the young literary editor of the *Demonstrator* at Home Colony; and Harry Kelly, who had edited the *Rebel,* addressed two November 11th meetings in New York that year.

The following spring James F. Morton Jr. met with Lucy Parsons, Jay Fox, and other comrades, at Lucy's home in Chicago to discuss the possibility of starting a new movement paper to take the place of *Free Society,* which had folded in the wave of persecution which followed McKinley's assassination.[25]

In January 1905 Bill Haywood and Thomas E. Hagerty from the W.F.M. and Mother Jones were among the delegates who met secretly in Chicago to plan for the formation of a new industrial union. Max Hayes was invited, but he did not attend and rejected the plan to set up a dual union. Hayes spoke for many Socialist Party members who still believed they could take over the A. F. of L.

In April, 1905, the Chicago Teamsters struck. Black strike-breakers were brought in; the racial clashes which followed resulted in hundreds of injuries and a number of deaths. Lucy Parsons boycotted all the State St. stores that sold scab shipped goods.[26]

In Russia the guns of revolution had sounded. The workers' struggle seemed to be making progress around the world. With Chicago labor mobilized in support of the Teamsters and a "Continental Congress" of labor scheduled to open in Chicago in late June, Lucy Parsons and her friends decided it would be a good year to bring out a new English language paper in Chicago.

"Every Jail on the
Pacific Coast Knows Me"

Nearly 20 years after the Haymarket bombing, Big Bill Haywood called to order the founding convention of the Industrial Workers of the World. "Fellow workers," he said, ". . . We are here to confederate the workers of this country into a working class movement that shall have for its purpose the emancipation of the working class from the slave bondage of capitalism."

Lucy Parsons sat on the platform with Mother Jones and Eugene V. Debs listening to Haywood. Mother Jones was the first woman and Lucy Parsons the second to join the I.W.W.

Anarchists, syndicalists, socialists and trade unionists all came to the convention. Lucy Parsons did not consider herself a representative of any organization, but the representative of the most oppressed of humanity, child laborers and prostitutes— "my sisters whom I can see in the night when I go out in Chicago."

On the afternoon of the 29th Lucy Parsons addressed the convention, following such noted labor and socialist leaders as Eugene Debs, Daniel DeLeon, Thomas Hagerty, William D. Haywood, Charles Moyer, and A. M. Simons.[1] She felt a responsibility as a woman to speak to the particular problems of women.

"We, the women of this country, have no ballot even if we wished to use it. . . but we have our labor. . . . Wherever wages are to be reduced the capitalist class uses women to reduce them." She said that women would have to learn not to buy scab made and shipped goods. "When we look around for cheap bargains . . . it simply means the robbery of our sisters, for we know that the things cannot be made for such prices and give the women who made them all fair wages."

When the question of dues came up, Lucy spoke on behalf of the women textile workers of Rhode Island, who made only $3.60 a week. She wanted to be sure they could afford to join the I.W.W. "They are the class we want. This organization is for the purpose of helping all, and certainly it is the women in the textile mills that are the lowest paid. . . . Make it so that the women who get such poor pay should not be assessed as much as the men who get higher pay."

Lucy Parsons discussed the general strike; the syndicalist germ of thought which she had had in the 1880's had blossomed forth. "My conception of the strike of the future is not to strike and go out and starve, but to strike and remain in and take possession of the necessary property of production. If any one is to starve—I do not say it is necessary—let it be the capitalist class."

Lucy was past 50 in 1905; she had learned many hard lessons in the last 20 years, and she cautioned her listeners to be very sure of what they meant when they called themselves revolutionists. "Do you think the capitalists will allow you to vote away their property? You may, but I do not believe it. . . . It means a revolution that shall turn all these things over. . . to the wealth producers. . . . When your new economic organization shall declare as brothers and sisters that you are determined that you possess these things, then there is no army that is large enough to overcome you, for you yourselves constitute the army."

Lucy Parsons no longer stood on the lakefront and urged tramps to use dynamite against the capitalist class. She was older and wiser and knew that only a well organized working class could take control of the means of production through long and serious struggle.

The I.W.W. offered what Lucy Parsons wanted: a militant working class organization which fought at the economic level with strikes and direct action rather than engaging in political campaigns. However, this division between economic and political meant the I.W.W. and the Socialist Party never fully cooperated with each other, a fact which limited both.

The I.W.W. was thoroughly class conscious. In the Preamble adopted at the founding convention, the delegates agreed that

> The working class and the employing class have nothing in common. There can be no peace so long as hunger and want are found among millions of working people and the few, who make up the employing class, have all the good things of life.

> Between these two classes a struggle must go on until the workers of the world organize as a class, take possession of

the earth and the machinery of production, and abolish the wage system. . . .

The army of production must be organized, not only for the everyday struggle with capitalists, but also to carry on production when capitalism shall have been overthrown.

"Abolition of the wage system" and "An injury to one is an injury to all" became the fighting mottos of the I.W.W.

The I.W.W. picked up where the Knights of Labor had left off in rural, southern and western organizing. It adopted new techniques of class struggle, including sabotage, work stoppages, and slowdowns. The organization opposed contracts and urged workers to strike whenever it was to their advantage. "The old craft unions with their 'sacred' contracts are simply the crucifiers of labor," Lucy Parsons wrote. "Contracts are only good between equals; but as the laborer is never on an equal footing with capital, the contract is a fraud."

Throughout the summer, Parsons, Fox, and other "anarchists" held socials and picnics to raise the money to launch their new paper. They solicited funds from the radicals who came to Chicago for the I.W.W. convention.

By August it had become clear that James F. Morton Jr. would not stay on as editor of the *Demonstrator* at Home Colony, and the western group offered to combine resources with the Chicago group and make Jay Fox editor of the *Demonstrator*. Fox accepted the offer; without Lucy Parsons' knowledge, he sent the money they had collected to Home and then sent out a letter to comrades saying plans for the Chicago paper had been dropped.

Lucy Parsons felt she had been doublecrossed. She felt it imperative that the paper come out in a major industrial center rather than in the backwaters of Puget Sound. She decided to publish the Chicago paper anyway, and comrades were surprised when the *Liberator* appeared in September, 1905.

The two groups met at Lucy's home for the confrontation. Lucy was furious that Fox had sent the money to Home without even notifying her. Fox had to concede that the group was split right down the middle on the question. He had no clear majority, but he justified his decision by claiming that comrades with experience with English language papers favored the *Demonstrator*. He forgot to mention that Lucy's experience with such papers went back to 1878.

At the meeting at Lucy's house, the divided group agreed to ask contributors to determine the destination of their money. Lucy denounced the decision as "a piece of political trickery," but she agreed to comply. Fox claimed that he had $60, all but $2 being designated for the *Demonstrator*. However, Lucy published a number of letters in the *Liberator* from comrades who wanted their money to stay in Chicago.

Antagonism was deep. Lucy charged that Fox had been "personally abusive" to her and that Morton, Barnard, and Fox were boycotting the *Liberator*. Fox sent Parsons a letter from the "American Committee" which charged, "A few of our Jewish comrades and Lucy Parsons are unwilling to listen to the voice of reason and insist upon getting out a paper here even if the first issue be the last one." The letter was signed by W. T. Barnard, S. T. Hammersmark, Frank Kreamer, J. Goldman, T. Carlin, T. Apple, J. Lifshitz and J. Fox.[2] Lucy retorted that there weren't many "Americans" in the "American Committee."

Lucy heard from New York that "most of the comrades in New York and vicinity have responded with money" to the call for a Chicago paper. She began to suspect that Fox had more money than he claimed to have.

The American Committee said they could publish a paper in Washington state for half the cost in Chicago. The Post Office insisted that the *Liberator* be mailed as second class material until a subscribers list could be filed with the postal department, qualifying the paper for third class mailing privileges.[3] Mailing the paper second class required a 1¢ stamp on each paper, $10 more an issue than third class. The total weekly postage cost was $20, for a mailed circulation of 2000 papers. Bundles were sent out and comrades hawked the paper on streets in other cities. Bundle money was slow to come in, and it was hard to meet the $50 a week publishing cost. The Liberator group held socials and a necktie party, but it wasn't enough. In January Eugene Debs made the honor list with a $1 contribution.

Jay Fox suffered an eye injury in the fall of 1905 and was unable to move to Home at that time. The Social Science League, which supported the *Demonstrator*, joined the Liberator Group's New Year's Eve party and contributed $4.10 to the *Liberator*, a note of harmony for the new year. On January 21, Jay Fox addressed the Liberator Group on "The General Strike or the

Ballot, Which?"

A reconciliation of sorts had been reached, but the *Liberator* was never accepted by the old subscribers to *Free Society,* who had received complimentary copies. *Mother Earth,* which Emma Goldman brought out in March, 1906, was more in line with *Free Society.* The *Demonstrator,* too, was supported by Goldman, the Isaaks, and others who emphasized cultural revolution as well as class revolution.

The *Liberator's* message was of strikes and industrial conflict, oriented to the class struggle. The other papers dealt with all facets of life and social revolution—sex, women's emancipation, literature, art, theater—and found their readership in the avant garde of the literary and artistic world.

The *Liberator* decided to publish under the I.W.W. label rather than under the A.F. of L. Allied Printing Trades Council and thus make explicit its choice of industrial unionism over trade unionism. However, when I.W.W. member A. Klemensic, who wrote both for the *Liberator* and the *Demonstrator,* put the I.W.W. label at the top of an issue of the *Demonstrator,* Fox criticized him severely. Fox wanted to act as a critic to both the A. F. of L. and the I.W.W.

A contributor to the French paper *Les Temps Nouveau* in Paris wrote to Lucy Parsons, asking her to help "unmask the Gompers and Mitchell unions as the instrument of the capitalist man and as progress's enemy." He wanted to dispel the European belief that American Trade Unionism was the best organization in the U.S. for working class emancipation. He assured Lucy that her reply would have a strong influence in Europe. She wrote,

> The American Federation of Labor is doomed: first, because of its own inherent rottenness, and second, because it, in common with all other craft organizations, have outgrown their usefulness and must give way to the next step in Evolution, which is the Industrial union, which proposes to organize along industrial lines, the same as capital is organized. . . . I nevertheless recognize and am compelled to give credit to that organization for the great benefit it has been to the working classes of America.

She concluded by saying the I.W.W. was rising on the ruins of the A. F. of L.

Lucy pointed out that A. F. of L. members had handled scab-shipped goods during the Chicago teamsters strike and that of 22,000,000 wage workers in America, the A. F. of L. had organized only 2,000,000.

In the *Liberator*, Lucy attacked the election process. "The fact is, MONEY and NOT votes is what rules the people." She argued that abstention from voting would show "that we refused to endorse such frauds by voting for them. It would prick the bubble of suffrage by showing there are questions beyond the ballot. . . . The workers will force economic questions to the front which are now obscured in the halls of legislation. To vote is to give our influence to postpone the day of emancipation."

Lucy's class consciousness and her reading of history led her to write a series of articles called "Labor's Long Struggle with Capital" for the *Liberator*. It was a history of the working class; she criticized historians who dealt only with "the course of wars, the outcome of battles, political changes, the rise and fall of dynasties and other similar movements, leaving the lives of those whose labor has built the world in contemptuous silence."

The role of women, not simply the question of "free love," had become an important topic of discussion in the radical movement. Lucy Parsons wrote a weekly column for the *Liberator* on "Famous Women in History." Louise Michel of the Paris Commune, the singer Jenny Lind, and the nurse Florence Nightingale were three of her subjects. She wrote a eulogy of the suffragist Susan B. Anthony, who died in March, 1906. "It is unnecessary for us to agree with her. . .; we can at any rate admire the sterling qualities of the woman herself. If the economic question had been a factor in American life at the beginning of Miss Anthony's career, she might have devoted her life to that cause, for she was a progressive thinker."

Lucy supported the right of people to divorce and remarry and the right of women to birth control information and wrote, "No woman should be obliged to live with a man whom she does not love, in order to get bread, clothes, and shelter." In describing a young mother who killed herself and her seven children, Lucy wrote, "You were a victim of our false society which makes it a crime to impart information that would have made your young life a mother's joy with a few healthy children to caress you."

Lucy Parsons came to the defense of Moses Harman who had again been arrested for sending "obscenity" through the mails. *Lucifer* had been held up by the postal authorities for the fifth time in the past several months, and 75 year old editor Moses Harman was sentenced to a year on the rock pile.

He teaches "proper sexual relations," she wrote, "and that woman should at all times be free to dispose of her affections as she pleases." Harman taught that young people should have knowledge of reproduction and birth control. "That Mr. Harman cannot at all times teach his philosophy couched in language that shall meet the approval of the moral genius who presides over the postal department, seems, unfortunately, too true, hence his trouble. . . . The government is determined that . . . the young shall be kept in dense ignorance of the laws governing the reproductive sphere of life" Lucy Parsons' views on the sex question had liberalized since 1896.

In a lengthy article on the "evolutionary development" of woman, Lucy argued that woman was first subjugated by man when man's physical strength made him a better hunter. When man "began to acquire property which he wished to transmit along with his name to his offspring, then woman became his household drudge."

Lucy believed that the advent of the steam engine had ended the significance of man's physical superiority and that woman was equalling, even outdistancing man. When muscles were no longer important "in producing the world's wealth," woman was able "to leave the narrow confines of the kitchen where she had been kept for so long."

"Oh, the direful predictions that were made if woman dared leave home to work. Why, she would become coarse, manish, unsexed, etc., but all to no purpose, woman went; she saw and conquered!" Lucy's proclamation of victory was a few generations premature.

She added a note of warning. "Woman is allowing herself to be used to reduce the standard of life by working for lower wages than those demanded by man." She was afraid that women's work could become a disadvantage instead of an advantage to the working class.

Lucy was proud of her sisters who were entering every profession. She praised a middle class woman who left her family to become a traveling saleswoman. "Probably Mrs. Hamblin never intended to sink her whole individuality when she married; finding it impossible not to do so and remain with her husband, she simply left him. . . . The 'new woman' feels very different from her man-tagged sisters of past generations, who imagined they couldn't move without man's assistance. The sooner men learn to make companions and equals of their wives and not subordinates, the sooner the marriage relation will be one of harmony."

Lucy had praise for her revolutionary sisters in Russia; a peasant woman had just assassinated the murderous general Sakharoff. Lucy cheered, "General Sakharoff has met the fate all despots should meet. He has been assassinated by a woman." She recalled the women in the Paris Commune who had persuaded the French National Guard to fraternize with the people.

President Roosevelt was deathly afraid of "race suicide." He feared that anglo-saxon women were not bearing enough children to keep pace with immigration from southern and eastern Europe and the birthrate in immigrant communities.

Lucy Parsons took her dig at Roosevelt during her visit to New York slums in 1906. "If President Roosevelt were to happen into this part of the town, his dentistry would shine forth resplendently; he would see no signs of race suicide hereabout."

On December 13, 1905, a bomb killed former Idaho governor Frank Steuenberg; on the night of February 17, 1906, Idaho authorities kidnapped I.W.W. leaders Bill Haywood, Charles Moyer, and George Pettibone in Colorado and illegally took them to Idaho to stand trial for Steuenberg's murder. To Lucy Parsons it looked like a repetition of 1887. Emma Goldman wrote her one article for the *Liberator* on the kidnapping. Lucy Parsons plunged into defense work. Eugene Debs wrote "Arouse, Ye Slaves!" for the *Appeal to Reason*. "There have been twenty years of revolutionary education, agitation and organization since the Haymarket tragedy. . . . and if they attempt to murder Moyer, Haywood and their brothers, a million revolutionists at least will meet them with guns."

President Roosevelt called the *Appeal to Reason* a "vituperative organ of pornography, anarchy and bloodshed" and attempted to prejudice the case against Haywood by referring to a certain railroad magnate as "at least as undesirable a citizen as

Debs, or Moyer, or Haywood." Debs reminded Roosevelt that in 1896 he had suggested that Altgeld and Debs be lined up against a wall and shot.

There was no evidence against Haywood in the murder of Steuenberg, only the testimony of a paid perjuror, Harry Orchard.

In March, 1906, Lucy went East to talk about the Haywood case, to honor Louise Michel at Paris Commune celebrations, and to honor the recently deceased Johann Most at a mass memorial meeting in New York. She joined Emma Goldman, Max Baginsky, and Abraham Isaak on the platform in Grand Central Palace; Lucy Parsons and Johann Most had shared the platform at the November 11th meeting in Milwaukee only five months earlier.

Lucy intended to raise money for the failing *Liberator* in the East and to lecture on "Curse of Child Labor," "The Industrial Workers of the World: Their Aims and Objects," "The Colorado Outrage," and "Anarchism Defined."

While on a "slumming" expedition on the lower East Side to gather material for the "Lib," Lucy stopped to buy a paper. She was rudely jostled as she opened her hand-bag, and a man grabbed it. She tried to follow the robber, but his two buddies blocked her way. She was bewildered for a moment, a thousand miles from home, hungry, and without a penny. She had been on her way to lunch when the thief made off with her $20. Her New York friends were not at all comforting. "Why, didn't you know you were in New York?" they asked.

The *Liberator* came out a few times after Lucy left for New York, but did not resume publication when she returned to Chicago. The rival *Demonstrator* survived until 1908. The most successful anarchist paper in the pre World War I period was Emma Goldman's *Mother Earth,* which reflected the dissociation of anarchism from strictly class struggle movements. Parsons turned to the I.W.W. for a revolutionary framework in which to work.

In 1907 the verdict in Haywood's case was handed down—innocent! Clarence Darrow gave a brilliant, class defense of his client. "You men of the Mine Owners' Association. . . who are seeking to kill him, not because it is Haywood, but because he represents a class, don't be so blind, be so foolish as to believe you can strangle the Western Federation of Miners when you tie a rope around his neck."

Lucy Parsons hailed Haywood's acquittal as a tremendous victory for the working class. "But, lo and behold, the class conscious wage class which has come into existence since 1886, had not been reckoned with by the conspirators. . . . The workers realized in what great peril their brothers stood and to understand what a great consolidation of capitalistic interests they must take a stand against." She believed it was the first time in American history that the working class had "stood shoulder to shoulder" and realized that the bosses wanted to destroy organized labor, not Bill Haywood as a person. "The last twenty years of my life," she wrote, "have suddenly become a great pleasure to me, because I see in the Haywood verdict the tendency of advanced thought of these times, and I realize that their [the Haymarket martyrs] lives were not sacrificed in vain. They only lived twenty years too soon."[4]

In 1907 Elizabeth Gurley Flynn, then only 17 years old and still a high school student, made the trip from New York to Chicago for the I.W.W. convention. Flynn, who was to become one of the leading women radicals of the twentieth century recalled, "At this convention I was thrilled to meet Mrs. Lucy Parsons. I remember Mrs. Parsons speaking warmly to the young people, warning us of the seriousness of the struggles ahead that could lead to jail and death before victory was won." Flynn admired Lucy Parsons as a woman and as a revolutionary.[5]

The I.W.W. split at the 1907 convention, and the Western Federation of Miners left the organization. Daniel DeLeon and the S.L.P. stayed in uneasy alliance for another year. Eugene Debs had stopped paying dues to the I.W.W., but never dropped his formal affiliation.

In 1907 Emma Goldman and Max Baginsky went to Amsterdam for an international anarchist conference. Lucy Parsons hoped that the conference would give the anarchist movement new vitality; to her that meant restoring the working class movement called anarchism to the dimensions of 1886. She complained that anarchism had moved too far from the working class. "Anarchism, as taught in recent years, is too far away from the mental level of the masses, hence, they have not been attracted to us."

Lucy Parsons increasingly concentrated her efforts on making known the history of the Haymarket police riot and the circumstances surrounding the frameup and executions of her husband and comrades.

In early 1908 Lucy Parsons was on a train to points west: St. Louis, Kansas City, Omaha, Denver, Salt Lake City, Portland, Spokane, Seattle, Vancouver, Butte, Winnipeg, Minneapolis. The trip was such a success that in 1909 she decided to reprint the *Famous Speeches* of the Haymarket Martyrs to add to her selection, which included pamphlets by Emma Goldman and Alexander Berkman, the majority of Kropotkin's works, and her own "The Principles of Anarchism."

The speeches suited Lucy's purposes perfectly. She made a living selling them, they preserved the memories of the martyrs, and they gave her a reason to get around the country to speak, which she thoroughly enjoyed.

The community of traveling radicals exchanged literature with each other, helped each other with sales, and found each other places to stay on their journeys. In the pre-war years radicals were not the only traveling lecturers. Before television and radio, Americans depended upon newspapers for the daily news. Lectures were a form of entertainment as well as a forum for information. The traveling salesman, the traveling circus, and the traveling speaker were important features of American life, which all moved by the most rapid means of transportation known—the train.

On August 12, 1909, Lucy Parsons attempted to secure a permit for a lecture on religion in Washington Square, across from the Newberry Library in Chicago. Acting Chief Schuettler told her, "We had one of your meetings twenty-one years ago, but we do not want another one. You will probably talk about one minute on religion and two hours advocating anarchy and villifying society. The permit is refused." Her battle for free speech in Chicago continued.

Lucy angrily stomped out of Schuettler's office and hurried to the mayor's office, but the mayor was "not in." The papers reported, "Mrs. Parsons was considered the real brains of the anarchist gang and the police are taking no chances with her." Lucy Parsons still sent the Chicago police force into action when she announced that she would give a speech.

Lucy announced her lecture tours in *Mother Earth* and asked comrades to arrange meetings for her; sometimes her meetings were not as well arranged as she thought they should have been. In 1910 Lucy Parsons, now a middle-aged woman, stood before the few Detroit unionists who had gathered to hear her and berated the Central Labor Union for its inefficiency in promoting her lecture.

Lucy was on her way to New York city, where she would spend the winter of 1910-1911 lecturing and selling the *Speeches.* What she saw in the slums of New York reminded her that "There is no overcrowding up town, where the rich live."

The Central Federated Union of New York endorsed Lucy's efforts, and night after night she went to A. F. of L. locals speaking, selling the *Speeches,* and trying to radicalize the members. Lucy found New York labor "weak and dispirited." The leaders told her, "You have no Ellis Island problem in the West to solve as we have here."

If Lucy was disappointed by the despair in organized labor, she was elated by the activity in revolutionary circles which reflected the international scope of the movement. She attended a successful rally in honor of executed Japanese anarchists. Young radicals jumped up and demanded a march on the Japanese Embassy. "The result was a fine demonstration in the streets, with the red flag," wrote Lucy. "The only regret I have is owing to a misunderstanding and the slow exit of the large audience, I missed being with the 'mob' of marchers. I have been kicking myself about this ever since." Lucy loved being in the center of a street demonstration where she could feel the anger and the strength of the people's movement.

Harrison Grey Otis, the notorious union-busting owner of the *Los Angeles Times* had led a drive to keep Los Angeles an open shop town. In October, 1910, a small charge of dynamite set in a tunnel leading to the *Times* ignited ink and set a fire which spread throughout the building, killing 20 persons. In March, 1911, John J. and James B. McNamara, officers of the Structural Iron Workers, were indicted for the bombing. John J. McNamara was attending a union meeting in Indianapolis when he was arrested and secretly extradited to California.

The entire labor movement, including Samuel Gompers and the Executive Committee of the A. F. of L., united to defend the McNamara brothers. Clarence Darrow took the case.

However, Darrow and liberal writer Lincoln Steffens agreed to plea bargain with the prosecution. In exchange for a guilty plea from the McNamaras, the brothers would not receive the death penalty, there would be no more indictments, and there would be a labor-capital conference in Los Angeles to arbitrate grievances. None of the terms of the agreement were adhered to except the life sentence for James B. McNamara.

Job Harriman, the socialist candidate and frontrunner for mayor of Los Angeles had made the McNamara case a major campaign issue. Their guilty plea five days before the election meant defeat for Harriman, a fact which the prosecution had counted on. Darrow and Steffens were severely criticized in labor and radical circles for their handling of the case. The McNamara case marked the beginning of the decline of socialist influence in the A. F. of L.

The McNamara case was quickly followed in 1912 by the Socialist Party's passage of Article 2, Section 6, an amendment to its constitution and by the recall of Bill Haywood from the Executive Committee of the S.P. in 1913. "Any member of the party who opposes political action or advocates crime, sabotage or other methods of violence as a weapon of the working class to aid in its emancipation shall be expelled from the membership in the party," read the amendment. It marked a final break between the S.P. and the I.W.W.

In November, 1911, Lucy Parsons was back in New York City after two circuits of the continent in 18 months. She and William D. Haywood spoke to packed November 11th meetings.

Lucy had had tremendous success selling the *Speeches* in her two circuits from Los Angeles to Vancouver, B.C., back to New York City. She had sold 10,000 copies and was about to place an order with the printer for another 2000. Carl Nold thought her work was exemplary. "How long would it take to distribute 8000 *Speeches* if Parsons would stay in Chicago and rely on the comrades?" he asked.[6]

Lucy and Carl saw each other frequently over the years. Carl could count on a warm hug and kiss, a glass of wine, and a place to stay when he dropped in on Lucy in Chicago. They were companions in Milwaukee for a few days the summer of 1911, as they went about their radical activities. Carl wrote to a friend, "If a white man is seen in her company he is, of course, exposed to the dirty looks of the public, but this did not bother me, and we drank happily."[7]

In Vancouver Cassius and Sadie Cook organized highly successful meetings for Lucy and handled her literature. The Cooks also handled Emma Goldman's tours through Vancouver. Lucy spoke "with a booming mellowness of voice that carried and proved very impressive," recalled Cassius Cook.[8] Lucy's powerful voice had already served the radical movement for over 30 years.

In 1911 William Z. Foster, a veteran of the Spokane Free Speech Fight, went to Budapest, Hungary, as the I.W.W. representative to an international trade union meeting. When Foster returned to the U.S. for the 1911 I.W.W. convention, he had concluded that dual unionism was a mistake, and he tried to persuade the I.W.W. to liquidate its dual unions and send its militant members back into the A. F. of L. to "bore from within."

Foster failed to win over the I.W.W. as a whole, but Jack Johnstone, Jay Fox, Joe Manley, Sam Hammersmark, Tom Mooney, Elizabeth Gurley Flynn's ex-husband J. A. Jones, and Lucy Parsons joined Foster in forming the Syndicalist League of North America in February, 1912. That winter Foster traveled 6000 miles as a hobo, organizing local Syndicalist Leagues throughout the country.

In 1912 Foster brought Tom Mooney to Lucy's house to introduce them. Mooney bought copies of *Famous Speeches* and *The Life of Albert R. Parsons*. Later in the year he arranged for Lucy to speak at the Molders' convention in Milwaukee.

Lucy Parsons and the Syndicalist League of North America worked out of the same building at 1000 S. Paulina in Chicago, Lucy added Foster and Ford's pamphlet "Syndicalism" to her literature list, and she contributed to the *Agitator* and then the *Syndicalist* published by Jay Fox and William Z. Foster. She changed the title of her speech "Anarchism: Its Aims and Objects" to "Syndicalism: Its Aims and Objects."[9]

The Syndicalist League received the help of English syndicalist Tom Mann when he visited the U.S. in 1913; Lucy Parsons helped promote the Mann meetings in Seattle in October, 1913. Although the Syndicalist League never became a major organization, the people who led it became leaders of the A.F. of L. and of the Communist Party, U.S.A. This was the political nexus within which Lucy Parsons operated for the rest of her life.

Lucy Parsons' involvement in the Syndicalist League of North America did not prevent her from writing in glowing terms of the I.W.W. for the *Industrial Worker* on May 1, 1912. Lucy lent her support to both organizations as they both opposed capitalism.

Twenty five years had passed since the execution of Albert Parsons when Lucy published a twenty-fifth memorial edition of the *Speeches* and wrote "Eleventh of November, 1887" for the *Agitator* in 1912.

Between 1909 and 1917 the Wobblies, as I.W.W. members were nicknamed, led a series of free speech fights in the West. The free speech fighters rode the rails to the scene of each struggle and filled the jails in defense of free speech in Spokane, Missoula, San Diego, Fresno and elsewhere. They knew more I.W.W.'s would arrive on the next freight train to speak from the soap-box and face arrest. The Wobblies practiced the confrontation tactics over free speech which Lucy Parsons had used for more than two decades.

By 1915 the I.W.W. had organized successfully among miners and lumberjacks in the West and among pulp and paper workers in the South. They had launched a major organizing campaign among migrant workers in the plains states and California who reached their jobs by traveling as hobos in box cars. At the height of the I.W.W.'s power no one rode a box car across the plains without a red I.W.W. card.

In the East the I.W.W. led textile strikes in Lawrence, Massachusetts in 1912 and in Paterson, New Jersey in 1913. Their colorful style of organizing captured nationwide headlines.

The National Women's Trade Union League conducted its most militant activities in the same period. "The Uprising of the 20,000" in New York in 1909 precipitated years of struggle in the New York garment industry and made the International Ladies Garment Workers Union a significant organization. The strike victory in 1910 resulted in the "Protocol of Peace" which provided for a Board of Arbitration, a Board of Sanitary Control, and a closed shop. However, workers remained suspicious of the bosses and the lengthy arbitration procedures and often walked out to win their demands.

The Triangle Shirtwaist Fire of 1911 which killed 146 workers brought about a national outcry against unsafe working conditions which resulted in factory inspection and safety laws in what became known as the "Progressive Era."

The "Uprising of the 20,000" was shortly followed by the Hart, Schaffner, and Marx strike in Chicago in 1910, which laid the groundwork for the formation of the Amalgamated Clothing Workers Union in 1914.

The most brutal attack against workers occurred against striking miners at Ludlow Colorado on Easter, 1914. Gunmen from the Rockefeller controlled Colorado Fuel and Iron Company periodically fired into the miners' tent colony. The strikers dug trenches under the tents so the people would have some protection from bullets.

Company gunmen drenched the strikers' tents in oil and kerosene, set fire to them, and machine-gunned everyone who ran out. Thirteen children and a pregnant woman burned to death in one of the trenches; six other people were killed that night.

The Ludlow massacre and other class violence brought public support for workers and prompted Congress to establish a Committee on Industrial Relations to investigate the explosive labor conflicts of the past several years.

Economic crashes in 1907-1908 and again in 1914-1915 resulted in significant unemployment organizing and in Hunger Demonstrations across the country. Lucy Parsons now concentrated her work in unemployment organizing.

The police were usually notified of Lucy's whereabouts and of her arrival in town; she was often harrassed and arrested. On April 13, 1913, Lucy and her friend George Markstall, who lived with her, were arrested in Los Angeles for peddling literature without a license. They were held incommunicado for 24 hours. The jail matron stripped Lucy and forcibly removed the ring from her finger, despite the fact that the couple was only charged with a misdemeanor. The city objected not so much to the violation of the peddling ordinance as to the content of the pamphlets. A court date was set for April 24; the judge took the case under advisement until April 30 and dismissed the case and released the defendants on their own recognizance on May 9, 1913.[10]

From Los Angeles, Parsons and Markstall traveled up the coast to San Francisco. They arrived on the heels of Emma Goldman who had just lectured in the city on June 1. The *Labor Clarion,* the voice of organized labor in the Bay Area where Lucy's friend Tom Mooney had become active, welcomed her and urged its readers to attend her lectures. Lucy planned four major lectures: "The Labor Movement in America for the Past Fifty Years," "Woman's Progress," "The French Revolution, What it Accomplished," and "The True Story of the Haymarket Riot and the Great Eight Hour Strike of 1886."

Emma Goldman had given two lectures: "Syndicalism, the Strongest Weapon of the Working Class, a Discussion of Sabotage, Direct Action and the General Strike," and "Woman as a Sex Commodity." Although the *Labor Clarion* welcomed Lucy Parsons, it devoted a long editorial to an attack on Emma Goldman's lecture on syndicalism.

Lucy arrived in Seattle, Washington, in September, 1913, and found Seattle socialists tied up in a mass trial for speaking on the streets. Judge Humphries had locked up 99 socialists, including one child. On October 2, Lucy attended the trial. The Judge referred to the Chicago Martyrs as murderers and argued that those socialists who had signed a resolution against the court order prohibiting street speaking were in the same position as the Haymarket anarchists.

"The signers of this resolution of defiance to the court may be held liable, in case of murder, just as Parsons was," declared Humphries. "You know he came into court and said, 'I didn't do anything; I just wrote an editorial,' but they hanged him for it. Now you fellows------"

Judge Humphries was interrupted by a voice from the back of the room. Lucy stood on a chair and commanded the attention of the courtroom. "My husband was no murderer."

Humphries replied, "Widow or no widow, you had better keep quiet or you'll find yourself down in the county jail." Judge Humphries refused to allow the socialist lawyers to defend their comrades.

The following day Colonel Blethen, editor and publisher of the *Seattle Times* and Humphries' ally who had instigated the sacking and looting of the I.W.W. and Socialist Party halls by drunken sailors several weeks before, printed an accusation that

Lucy Parsons had made a dynamite threat against Humphries. The charge was never substantiated, and a few weeks later the Washington State Bar Association censored Humphries for his conduct of the socialist trial.[11]

Lucy worked with Sam Hammersmark and other comrades in Tacoma getting out the paper *Why?* in October. On November 11, 1913, she lectured at the Social Science League in Tacoma. She said that current anarchist theories are "negative, vague and non-constructive," which brought disagreement from the audience. Lucy took up a collection for four Mexicans who were in jail in Texas for attempting to return to Mexico and participate in the revolution.

Cassius Cook again arranged lectures for Lucy in Vancouver. He anticipated difficulty getting her across the border. The I.W.W. members who were helping Cook thought that if she could get across on Thursday morning before they announced any meetings, they would have two days to advertise a Sunday meeting. Meanwhile she could talk to unions or hold street meetings.

On November 22, Lucy attempted to board a steamship in Seattle bound for Vancouver; Canadian immigration authorities stopped her.[12]

Having failed to get into Canada, Lucy returned to San Francisco for the winter. Conditions in San Francisco were desperate. A large building on Market St. was converted into a shelter for the unemployed. Over two thousand men slept in this vermin-infested place nightly. The place stunk from lack of ventilation and sanitary facilities. Throughout the city, men, women, and children slept in these "flops." Fires burned in empty lots at night as the homeless tried to keep warm. Some people slept in boxes or amid the garbage under the boardwalks. In the daytime these people waited in souplines for a bowl of thin soup. Those who sought medical attention were turned away by the hospitals, because they couldn't pay. An estimated 65,000 persons were unemployed in San Francisco alone; the city estimated that 10,000 a day were getting food in souplines.

On the night of January 20, 1914, a crowd of unemployed persons gathered at Jefferson Hall to hear Lucy Parsons. The proprietor refused to let the crowd in, claiming that the hall rent had not been paid. Lucy led the crowd across the street and began to speak from the curb.

The police immediately arrested her. The crowd shouted in protest, but the officers shoved them out of the way and took their prisoner to the entrance of Jefferson Hall where they kept her until the paddy wagon arrived to take her to the Central Police Station. After they had arrested Lucy, whom they considered the most immediate threat to property rights in San Francisco, the police arrested four more persons, including William Thorne, the I.W.W. head of the Unemployment Committee.

One thousand persons moved west along Golden Gate Avenue, angry at having their meeting broken up and their leaders arrested. They planned to hold an open-air meeting, but the police prevented it. Angry demonstrators smashed plate glass windows in what the police termed a riot. The police charged Lucy Parsons with inciting to riot.

Lucy appeared in police court the next day with the rent receipts for the hall. The owner admitted he had called police after he saw "inflammatory circulars" for the meeting; the police urged him to cancel the rental, and they were there to back him up.

Police Court Judge Sullivan dismissed the charge against Lucy. But as she was leaving the courtroom, Detective McPartland re-arrested her, this time on the more serious charge of rioting.

A week later Judge Sullivan dismissed the rioting charge against Lucy because of insufficient evidence. He ruled that Parsons was not a party to a riot which took place while she was in police custody.

Sullivan dismissed all the riot-connected cases which came before him. Other police court judges handed out jail sentences and orders to get out of town.

Disturbances such as occurred the night of January 20 dramatized the need of the unemployed for work, shelter, and food.

Some of the unemployed were agricultural workers who spent winters in the city. Some had been working at the Durst Ranch the preceeding August when officers of the law broke up a meeting of 2,500 workers. To these people who had worked in 105 degree weather with only the acidy "lemonade" sold by Durst's cousin to drink, the lack of sanitary facilities was nothing new. Few had outlasted the dysentery which raged through the camp to collect the ten per cent of their wages which had been withheld until the end of the season.

The Hop Field Riot, as it was later termed, resulted in the deaths of two workers, the District Attorney, and a sheriff. It brought about a reign of terror against the I.W.W. in California. Feelings against labor were still high in the aftermath of the McNamara trial. The showcase trial of I.W.W. members Richard "Blackie" Ford and Herman Suhr which opened in Maryville, California, resulted in scare headlines about the I.W.W. Eventually the testimony at the trial resulted in an investigation into conditions at the Durst ranch and unwanted publicity for the growers.

When Lucy Parsons and I.W.W. members began working with the San Francisco unemployed and took over the Unemployment Committee, city and state officials were frightened.

California Governor Hiram Johnson appointed a commission to investigate the conditions among the unemployed. The Congressional Committee to Investigate Industrial Relations took lengthy testimony in San Francisco.

The Progressives understood that something had to be done, but they did not want radicals to provide the solutions. The state government withheld aid as long as possible, but under pressure from the I.W.W. and other "dangerous agitators," it finally inaugurated a public works project. The supervisors of the public works project refused to deal with the radical Unemployment Committee.

The refusal of the public works officials to recognize the new committee resulted in a march of 10,000 persons from Howard St. Square to Union Square Plaza across from the St. Francis Hotel. The unemployed women were in charge of the meeting. Lucy Parsons, Ida Adler of the Cloak Workers, Pearl Vogel of the Waittresses' Union and James Thompson of the I.W.W. addressed the meeting.

A militant committee from the demonstration walked into the St. Francis and asked for donations for the starving women. The frightened guests choked on their expensive dinners as the ragged, hungry women entered. They quickly dug into their pocketbooks for contributions.

San Francisco was shaken hard by the massive demonstrations

and militant organizing tactics. The unemployed refused to work for less than union wages, $3 for an eight hour day. The city's businessmen were afraid that their plans for a world's fair in San Francisco would go down the drain if the militant organizing persisted.

The San Francisco Labor Council was threatened by the success of the I.W.W. in unemployment organizing; its fondness for Lucy Parsons waned.[13]

Lucy was pleased with events in San Francisco. "We have been having some pretty stirring old times down here this winter," she wrote to Cassius and Sadie Cook. She planned to remain in San Francisco until April, then return to Chicago via Vancouver if Cook could promise to make expenses on the trip and arrange to get her across the border.[14]

On July 23, 1914, Lucy wrote to the Cooks from Cle Elum, Washington, a lumber town. She was on her way to Spokane and could receive a letter from them there. Cook wrote on July 31, 1914, the day before war broke out in Europe with news of mutual friends and a report on how many copies of *Famous Speeches* he had sold. "Hope that you get a cut on the front page," he said.[15]

Headlines were what Lucy sought; they would advance her cause and help her bring out more listeners at her next meeting. Each arrest, each night in jail contributed to her reputation —persecuted by the police, a friend of the poor and oppressed.

It was difficult to keep track of the traveling propagandist, moving from place to place on a shoestring budget and hoping to get expenses and maybe a little more as she went. Chicago was home, but for years Lucy Parsons was on the road more than in Chicago. Her second home became the lumber camp, the mining town, the I.W.W. hall, the A.F. of L. local union, and the liberal club meeting where she could talk with working people about social change.

By January, 1915, many factories had closed down or curtailed production, because the war had drastically cut the European market. Bread prices rose while grain speculators shipped wheat overseas. Even the government began to suspect irregularities in the wheat market; every Federal District Attorney's office was ordered to investigate the price of bread.

The front page *Tribune* cartoon on January 18 was a woeful

mother surrounded by her three hungry children. She had just finished knitting the words "Give Us This Day Our Daily Bread" into a large shawl. At her feet lay a newspaper which read "Vast Wheat Shipments to Europe Imperil American Food Supply."

Splashed across the front page were the headlines "1500 Idle Riot Around Hull House." The *Tribune* heartily endorsed the arrests of Lucy Parsons and 21 other persons who had marched in the streets demanding bread and called them "idle, anarchists, criminals."

That winter there had already been Hunger Demonstrations on the east and west coasts. Hungry people poured into Chicago by rail and onto West Madison St. skid row in hopes of finding work. Evicted families found shelter under bridges and in parks. Loop newsboys were mobbed by job hunters. At its 1914 convention the I.W.W. had responded to conditions by adopting a statement urging the hungry "to go to the granaries and warehouses and help yourselves" rather than gathering "around City Halls, Capitols, and empty squares."

In Chicago Lucy Parsons and the West Side Anarchists planned a Hunger Demonstration for January 17. Ralph Chaplin, I.W.W. poet and songwriter, complained that "those who planned it were not exactly hungry. They had newspaper headlines in mind and they got them." It had always been Lucy's style to command headlines; through headlines she could reach the thousands who never came to her meetings.

That Sunday Jane Addams was not at Hull House; she was downtown at a pacifists' meeting. Lucy Parsons was at Hull House that cold January day. Men and women of all nationalities were there; needle trades workers and a few white collar workers filled the hall. The garment industry of Chicago, scene of the bitter Hart, Schaffner, and Marx strike four years before, was concentrated only a few blocks away. The sky was heavy and gray, and a bitter wind chilled the poorly clad people who were glad to get inside and warm up. The factories were all but deserted.

Above the speakers' platform was a big black banner with the word "HUNGER" in white letters. Other cardboard signs scattered about the hall read "We Want WORK, not Charity," "Why Starve in the Midst of Plenty?" and "Hunger Knows

No Law."

Ralph Chaplin recalled, "The most radical speaker was Lucy Parsons. Mrs. Parsons was, as a rule, both frightening and beautiful in her intense earnestness. But at Bowen Hall she proved to be anything but a firebrand." Lucy was careful not to provoke arrest, knowing that many detectives had infiltrated the meeting. She knew that a violent speech might defeat the purpose of the meeting and result in public censure.

Aaron Baron, a Russian emigre, spoke, "I am a baker and I am expected to starve, because I cannot get work baking the bread you people need and cannot buy!" The response to Baron's speech was so enthusiastic that a member of the Hull House staff felt obliged to attempt to restore order.

She received her answer from the Russian Revolutionary Chorus in a burst of singing led by Fannie Baron. Then Lucy Parsons urged the meeting onto the street, and the crowd voted to parade north on Halsted St., through the fringe of industrial development to the heart of Chicago's financial district where the fancy clubs and hotels were located.

Policemen lined Halsted St. They parked a police ambulance directly in the line of march. The marchers had barely turned onto Halsted St. when the police began swinging their billy clubs in an attempt to cut off the head of the demonstration. Detectives wearing brass knuckles sent men and women sprawling. Although the newspapers reported no gunshot wounds, the officers fired their revolvers, and Chaplin reported, "Ragged figures slumped under the impact of slug shots. The distorted faces of plainclothes policemen hung over their victims with dripping slug shots. Blood spurted over hands, clothing, and paving stones."

The crowd retaliated. A young girl stuck a hatpin into a policeman, and a husky demonstrator knocked over a detective with a single blow of his bare fist. Lucy Parsons drove off Lt. Make Mills when he attempted to seize the HUNGER banner. The banner went down near the police ambulance, but it came up triumphant on the other side, leaving some policemen mauled. Five and six abreast the marchers fought their way eight blocks to Madison St., where the police broke up the demonstration.

Irwin St. John Tucker (Friar Tuck), a young Episcopalian

minister and prominent socialist, arrived just as the police were smashing a banner which read "Give Us This Day Our Daily Bread." He rushed in to help carry the banner and was arrested with Lucy Parsons, five young Russian women, and 15 other men. They were held at the Des Plaines St. Station where Black Jack Bonfield had waited the night of May 4, 1886.

Chicago liberals voiced a strong protest over police brutality at the Hunger Demonstration. Graham Taylor wrote, "That it was not more disastrous in its results was due to the good natured peacefulness of the crowd rather than the self control of the police. The rights of free assemblage and free speech should be provided for by the city government." Edward Nockels, secretary of the Chicago Federation of Labor and a member of the mayor's commission on unemployment, charged that the alleged riot was a police riot. "The whole affair was a concerted, prearranged attack upon a lot of helpless women and inoffensive men. The real I.W.W. of Chicago are the police." Sophonisba Breckenridge, Dean of Women at the University of Chicago, took Lucy Parsons' side. Jane Addams denounced police brutality and arranged bail for Lucy Parsons and the other women.

Deputy Chief Schuettler had no interest in preventing a clash which he could attribute to radicals, and he denounced Jane Addams. "If Miss Addams thinks it is all right for an avowed and dangerous anarchist like Lucy Parsons to parade with a black flag and a band of bad characters, I suggest that she go ahead and preach the doctrine outright."

Jane Addams' defense of Lucy Parsons in 1915 was no more popular than her defense of Emma Goldman had been in 1901. Lucy Parsons was the ideal person for the police to fix upon to justify their intervention in the march, because they could link her to the Haymarket bombing.

In her own defense, Lucy Parsons said, "What I wanted to do was to take some of the rags and poverty of the city and bring them on the street where everyone could see them." She advised the crowd, "As long as you accept charity, capitalists will not give you work."

The police claimed that Parsons had said some violent things. "Lucy was the strong one," said Officer Eastman. "She said it would be like that Paris stuff—lopping off heads and everything." Schuettler announced, "If any crowd of persons, headed by Lucy Parsons and without a permit, attempts to parade in the streets of Chicago, I will order them arrested. I have lists of the anarchists of this city, and I know what records are in other cities. I know Lucy Parsons' record, and I know what she says when she makes a speech." Police Chief Gleason said he wouldn't issue Lucy Parsons a permit even if she applied for one.

Friar Tuck succeeded in getting the *Tribune* to retract its misrepresentation of Lucy's speech and to print an apology to her. "A first," remarked Tucker, "and especially amazing, because Lucy Parsons was a Negro."

Friar Tuck liked Lucy Parsons very much; he recalled how she always contrasted human life with capital or money, how she described the dead capital sucking the lifeblood of labor. "She wasn't a hell-raiser; she was only trying to raise the obvious issues about human life. She was not a riot-inciter, though she was accused of it. She was of a religious nature."

Jane Addams and Sophonisba Breckenridge helped secure jury trials for the demonstrators; Jane Addams arranged for attorneys; and Addams, Breckenridge, and Rachel Yarros, also of Hull House, testified in behalf of Lucy Parsons and the other defendants on January 28. Breckenridge testified, "Mrs. Parsons said nothing that would start a riot. She merely explained that labor is different from other commodities: that if it isn't sold one day, it cannot be held in stock and sold the next."

The defense argued that the Supreme Court had invalidated the city ordinance which gave the Chief of Police the right to license street parades and won the case. However, the Chief of Police then secured a counter ruling from the Corporation Counsel which said he did have discretionary powers to issue parade permits.

The two rulings set the stage for another confrontation. The unemployed had issued a statement several days after the police riot: "It is useless to talk about 'permits from the police to parade.' The police will not issue permits to hungry men. If the police of this city think they can repress the hungry with club, blackjack and bullet they are wrong. Hunger knows but one law—the law of self-preservation. Violence breeds violence."

Ellen Gates Starr of Hull House told reporters that the unemployed would not ask for a permit from police for their next demonstration. "They have a court decision to justify them now, and I don't see why an opinion from the corporation counsel should stop them from parading."

Aaron Baron chaired the January 31 meeting at Hull House. He shouted to round after round of applause, "Are you animals, or bums, or men? If you are animals, get out of here and go to the Humane society. If you are bums, then start out for the back doors and whine and beg for a handout or a penny. But if you are men, act!"

Some jeered and some cheered as the Hull House women tried to prevent a demonstration. "Don't go," implored Jane Addams. "Be content with the splendid victory you already have won in the courts!"

Lucy Parsons stood at the door shouting to the people, "Come on! March! March! They're waiting for us outside. If you want jobs, then make the warehouses of the rich so insecure that through fear they will give you work."

By the time half the crowd had followed Lucy Parsons into the streets, Jane Addams could make herself heard above the uproar. She charged that a small group of radicals had taken over the unemployment meetings.

Despite Jane Addams' admonitions, 600 people marched through the rain and slush determined to test their court victory for the free use of the streets. Mounted police lined the parade route and ordered demonstrators to keep to the right side of Halsted St. The marchers turned east on Madison St., where their demonstration had been broken up two weeks earlier, and began to sing the Marseillaise. Seven policemen tried to stop the parade on Michigan Ave., and a skirmish took place. The marchers continued their circuit and returned to Hull House wet and tired, but victorious. They passed a resolution. "Whereas, the unemployed of Chicago have through this day's parade regained . . . the liberty to the public streets —and whereas the right to the public streets is only incidental to our program, . . . Therefore, be it resolved that we, the unemployed of Chicago, . . . shall continue to use the public streets . . . and fight for bread and work."

Lucy Parsons had not trusted the courts, but she trusted the people's victory in the streets. Because of Lucy Parsons and the West Side Anarchists' success in bringing people out for a militant demonstration, the Chicago Federation of Labor, the Socialist Party, and Hull House called a mass demonstration for February 12, Lincoln's birthday. They had to take militant action as well or risk the leadership of the unemployment movement falling to Lucy Parsons or Bill Haywood and the I.W.W.

Although Addams and Breckenridge obtained lawyers for the "rioters," they moved quickly to insure that they would not be caught off guard on their own territory again. Jane Addams and Lucy Parsons agreed to work together, and Lucy was appointed to the arrangements committee for the February 12 demonstration with John Fitzpatrick, head of the Chicago Federation of Labor, Irwin St. John Tucker, and others.

Within two weeks after Lucy Parsons led the march in Chicago, the federal government was considering strategies to decentralize the unemployed and hungry. Government planners suggested that seasonal workers should be paid in the area where they worked rather than returning to the employment offices in the cities where they were hired, which automatically brought the unemployed together at the end of a season.[16]

Boris Yelensky, an activist in the anarchist movement, was at the 1915 Hunger Demonstrations. Fannie and Aaron Baron and Yelensky returned to Russia together in 1917 to fight in the Russian revolution. The Barons died at the hands of the Cheka, but Yelensky escaped from Soviet Russia.[17]

Lucy was active in the contemporary unemployment struggle, but she never tired in her effort to reverse the record on the Haymarket case. On September 8, 1915, she wrote the introduction to her new edition of Altgeld's pardon. "Governor Altgeld was hounded, abused, ostracized, and boycotted by the 'mob in purple and fine linen,' " she wrote. "Ten years after his death, the people, the plain common people, assembled in beautiful Lincoln Park, and with uncovered heads, witnessed the unveiling of the grand statue, and the beautiful group, representing the working class. He was a man before he was a politician. He was one of those rare characters who could remain true to his high ideals in spite of politics."

Lucy pointed out that Altgeld had died defending the rights of the oppressed people in South Africa; she emphasized that

Altgeld was a judge before he was governor and "consequently, he could examine the Anarchists' case with a calm, clear, discriminating mind." She was unlike the Lucy who once considered all judges the instruments of capitalist oppression and who had taken issue with Judge Altgeld at the 1889 Economic Conference. Lucy Parsons had accepted the general liberal view of Altgeld as a friend of the working class.

When the war broke out in Europe only two socialist parties, those in the United States and in Italy, termed it an imperialist war and refused to endorse the war efforts of their respective governments. German and French social democrats eagerly killed each other. In Russia the Bolshevik faction did not support the war.

In 1912 Lucy Parsons had written optimistically about the anti-military spirit among European workers, but three years later her disillusionment with European social democrats was complete. "The political representatives of science (backed by more than four million voters) helped their imperial master lay a war levy of a billion marks or more for the prosecution of a war on workers of other countries. German scientific socialism has stifled the revolutionary tendency once so promising."

In the summer of 1916 Lucy Parsons went to the Mesabi Range in Minnesota to agitate among the striking iron miners. Her old friend Arthur Boose, who became known as "the old war horse of the I.W.W.," found her a room. The situation in the Range was explosive; strikers, their supporters, and I.W.W. organizer Carlo Tresca, Elizabeth Gurley Flynn's lover, were in jail charged with murder. The defendants plea bargained and secured the release of five of them and short jail terms for the other three; they incurred Haywood's wrath for the deal, which was less expensive and probably better than any outcome of a trial would have been, and Flynn, Tresca, and Joe Ettor left the I.W.W.[18]

In 1916 President Wilson was re-elected as the president who "kept us out of war." But preparedness was the key word of the day, and preparedness meant patriotism and preparation for war.

At a Preparedness Day parade in San Francisco on July 16, 1916, a bomb exploded killing ten persons. Tom Mooney, who had organized the streetcar workers of San Francisco the year before, was blamed for the bombing. Mooney's friend Alexander Berkman, who was editing the *Blast* in San Francisco and who had spent 14 years in prison for his attack on Frick, was a potential victim of the anti-radical feeling, and Emma Goldman, who was lecturing in the city at the time, was in danger of being indicted.

The authorities concentrated on Tom and Rena Mooney, Warren K. Billings, and several other labor leaders.

Berkman acted quickly and organized a national defense campaign for Mooney. An international protest against Mooney's death sentence resulted in a commutation to life in prison. The Mooney case was only the beginning of a wave of organized political repression which swept the country.

When William D. Haywood, Lucy Parsons, Emma Goldman, Theodore Appel, and Ben Reitman addressed the November 11th meeting in Chicago in 1916, Goldman was a little more than three years from deportation, Haywood was only a year from arrest and imprisonment, and Theodore Appel's *Alarm* had just been suppressed by federal authorities.

The war fever grew; in April, 1917, the United States went to war.

Although the worst of the anti-red raids were yet to come, many radicals were already in jail. A young man in the Justice Department, J. Edgar Hoover, was about to begin his rise to power and fame for persecution of radicals.

With the nation at war, George Creel's Committee on Public Information controlled the news and attempted to stamp everyone's consciousness with anti-German and anti-red attitudes. In June 1917, Congress passed the Espionage Act and in May, 1918, the Sedition Act. The Espionage Act provided for up to $10,000 fines and 20 years in prison for anyone who interfered with the draft or encouraged disloyalty. The Sedition Act provided the same penalties for insubordination, obstruction of the sale of government bonds, and for willfully uttering, printing, writing, or publishing "any disloyal, profane, scurrilous, or abusive language" about the American form of government, the flag, military uniforms, or the Constitution or who advocated "any curtailment of production . . . of anything necessary or essential to the prosecution of the war." Any socialist or anarchist fell under the provisions of these acts, and the war hysteria made it immaterial whether the "offense" occurred before or after the law was passed.

Lucy Parsons was not arrested for anti-war activities. Cassius Cook, however, was arrested for his work as secretary of the League of Humanity. He was jailed and a $40,000 real estate bail set. Sadie and Cassius pleaded with Lucy Parsons to put up her house. Aware that if the bond were seized, she would have no roof over her aging head, Lucy Parsons put up her house to cover the last $7,000 of the bond.[19]

Cook was released and went to consult with Clarence Darrow. Darrow had lined up in favor of the war, a position he was later to regret, and he offered no support to his anti-war friends.

In the anti-radical hysteria, Frank Little, chairman of the General Executive Board of the I.W.W., superb organizer, and militant opponent of the war, was lynched by copper trust interests in Butte, Montana, on August 1, 1917. The week before he had tried to persuade the I.W.W. leadership to actively oppose the war; the afternoon before his murder he made an anti-war speech.

Within months Bill Haywood and other leading I.W.W. members were behind bars. Haywood and 100 Wobblies were tried in 1918 for conspiring with the dead Frank Little to commit 10,000 crimes. All the men were convicted and sentenced to prison.

The entire executive committee of the Socialist Party, including Irwin St. John Tucker, was indicted under the Espionage Act. The government let the statute of limitations on the indictment run out and never brought them to trial.

Eugene V. Debs was convicted for an anti-war speech made in Canton, Ohio, and was sent to the federal penitentiary at Atlanta.

The Post Office denied hundreds of radical publications access to the mails; many of the editors were jailed or deported. Among the suppressed publications were *International Socialist Review, New Review, National Rip-Saw, Alarm, Blast, Revolt, Mother Earth, Masses,* and *Liberator.*

States passed "criminal syndicalism" acts outlawing the I.W.W. Mass trials of I.W.W. members took place in Wichita,

Kansas, and in Sacramento, California, in 1920.

On November 7, 1917, the Bolsheviks seized power in Russia; a major foreign power was no longer in the hands of the bourgeoisie. Emma Goldman and Alexander Berkman lauded the accomplishments of Lenin and Trotsky. Lucy Parsons and her friends William Z. Foster, Sam Hammersmark, and Jack Johnstone became firm supporters of the soviet revolution.

The Anarchist Exclusion Act was invoked. Emma Goldman and Alexander Berkman were deported to Russia on December 21, 1919.

Despite the concerted government attack on civil liberties, the repression of radicals, and a post-war conservative trend, the events of 1919 demonstrated that labor militancy was very much alive. The Seattle General Strike, the nationwide steel strike led by William Z. Foster, the coal strike, and the Boston policemen's strike intensified fears of revolution. Longshoremen in Seattle refused to ship arms to counterrevolutionary forces in Russia. A bomb exploded on Wall St., and the war profiteers were frightened.

There had been serious divisions in the Socialist Party of America for a number of years. The right wing, led by Victor Berger and Morris Hillquit, had expelled the left wing, which included the entire state organizations in Ohio, Michigan, and Massachusetts, the Brooklyn, Bronx, and Queens locals in New York, and the party's foreign language federations, before the 1919 party convention in Chicago. Several groups resulted calling themselves Communist. In December, 1921, the two groups joined to form the Workers' Party of America, which became the Communist Party, U.S.A.

Although the left wing parties declared allegiance to the Third International, founded by the Bolsheviks in 1919, the new parties did not have an entirely ideological basis. Many people found themselves expelled from the Socialist Party, because they had joined left wing branches which were expelled as a whole. Joining one of the new communist parties was the only route left open to them.

The Palmer Raids on January 2, 1920, against I.W.W. headquarters across the country and the mass trials, convictions, and deportation of I.W.W. members had virtually smashed the organization. Its leadership was in jail or in exile.

Attorney General A. Mitchell Palmer explained his fear of red revolution, "Like a prairie fire the blaze of revolution was sweeping over every American institution of law and order. . . . It was eating its way into the homes of the American workman, its sharp tongues of revolutionary heat were licking the altars of the churches, leaping into the belfry of the school bell, crawling into the sacred corners of American homes, seeking to replace marriage vows with libertine laws, burning up the foundations of society."

The ruling class organized to fight back with the "American Plan," a master scheme to bust unions, intimidate radicals, and regain the open shop. The race suicide arguments of jingoist Theodore Roosevelt were translated into racist anti-immigration laws in 1921.

Women's suffrage was won in 1920, but it was a hollow victory. The modest gain of the vote was achieved by the super-patriots of the women's movement who had aided and abetted the trouncing on civil rights during the war years.

On May 5, 1920, two Italian anarchists, Nicola Sacco and Bartolomeo Vanzetti were arrested for distributing radical propaganda, then charged with a payroll robbery and murder in South Braintree, Massachusetts. Although Sacco had positive proof that he was elsewhere at the time of the robbery, the state convicted Sacco and Vanzetti of murder and robbery and sentenced them to death, because they were immigrants and radicals.

Lucy Defends the
Victims of Capitalism

The climate was bad for radical activities. Lucy Parsons was despairing over the reaction which had set in since the war. She wrote to Cassius and Sadie Cook, who had written to her about their cooperative industry which had failed.

> The great rushing, restless, headless mob called "the public," or the people, care nothing, absolutely nothing for the pleadings and philosophizing of the radical who wishes to change the economic conditions. . . . Take conditions since the war. There is a careless indifference, a supreme contempt for all progressive ideas, that is simply amazing!
>
> Dear friends, don't make the mistake that so many thousands have made, chasing radical phantoms. . . . Lay a solid foundation for your *personal* comfort when the shadows of life's journey are slanting toward the setting sun.[1]

Lucy Parsons and George Markstall were reaching a lonely, impoverished old age. "Marks" was unemployed most of the time. Albert Jr. had died in the state hospital in 1919. Finally Lucy had to appeal to the officers of Typographical Union 16 to which her husband Albert had belonged for money to pay off the mortgage on her house.[2]

Lucy couldn't believe the disintegration of the movement after the 40 years she had struggled for social change. She had saved up nothing for her personal comfort; she had given everything to the people's struggle, and now she saw her dreams crashing down around her.

The reverberations from 1886 had never ceased. In 1921 *Daily News* editor Melville Stone published his memoirs, *Fifty Years a Journalist.* He claimed that George Schilling was a member of the revolutionary group and that Schilling had reported everything to Stone. A copy of Stone's article in *Collier's Magazine* was mailed to Schilling with the penned note in the margin: "Traitor. You have 30 days to live. Go kill yourself. You die in March."

The major Chicago papers refused to print Schilling's answer to Stone; he had to depend on the *Federated Press* and other labor papers. Schilling's message to Stone was, "If my life is taken by some misguided individual who takes your unsupported statement for granted, honestly believing that I am a traitor to the cause of labor, my blood will be on your hands rather than on his."

Stone had claimed that August Spies and George Schilling had told a *Daily News* reporter the details of a plan to dynamite the city by placing bombs in the manholes of sewers. Schilling did report on the eight hour movement, and Stone distorted his recollections and equated the eight hour movement with revolution.

Schilling urgently asked Lucy Parsons to defend him. Lucy replied, "He [Stone] not only lies about Mr. Schilling whom he accuses of being a part of the revolutionary anarchist groups, but he also lies about Mr. Parsons and myself when he says . . . he (Stone) was to have the privilege of surrendering my husband to the court. . . . It is true that Mr. Stone sent for me and offered me a substantial monetary consideration if such a privilege were granted him. . . . No one ever went near Mr. Stone afterwards."

Schilling tried to contact Samuel Fielden, the last surviving Haymarket defendant, only to learn from Fielden's son that Sam Fielden died February 7, 1921, the day Schilling dated his letter.[3] Schilling was not murdered.

Russian communism was becoming more and more attractive to Lucy Parsons. She could be happy in her old age if she knew that somewhere in the world the workers' revolution had come. Her old friend William Z. Foster and many of her comrades from the Syndicalist League had joined the Communist Party, U.S.A. Many "anarchists" who had been oriented to the class struggle came into Communist Party circles. Those with individualistic and libertarian views like Emma Goldman and Alexander Berkman, who became disillusioned with Soviet Russia, did not.

In 1922 Bill Haywood, who had insisted that all indicted Wobblies surrender to authorities in 1918, jumped bail and fled to the Soviet Union while out of prison on appeal. Mary Marcy, the former editor of *International Socialist Review,* had put up her house for part of Haywood's bail. She was in ill health, depressed over Haywood's action, and committed suicide.

Jay Fox announced his "conversion to Bolshevism" in 1925. Harry Kelly, editor of *Road to Freedom* attacked Fox "the apostate." "Jay Fox advocated anarchism for nearly thirty years, but when the test came he spiked his guns and fled to the enemy. What strikes me as significant in Fox's conversion to Dictatorship, Militarism and the Wage System is his fathomless ignorance of Anarchist theory."

Cassius and Sadie Cook broke off all communication with William Z. Foster, Jay Fox, and Sam Hammersmark, but they maintained their devoted friendship to Lucy Parsons, who shared the three's enthusiasm for communism.[4]

Sam Dolgoff, a well known anarchist-syndicalist writer, recalled that Lucy still came to anarchist Free Society Forums in the twenties. The anarchist comrades did not take her pro-Soviet remarks seriously and still considered her one of their own.

In 1925 Communist Party members entered a coalition to found the International Labor Defense. The I.L.D. took over defense work in Tom Mooney's case and in Sacco and Vanzetti's case. The Communist Party and the I.L.D. adopted the history of the Haymarket Affair and the Eight Hour Movement as its history and Lucy Parsons as a personification of revolutionary virtue. Lucy Parsons cooperated with them and lent her voice to the chorus proclaiming the Communist Party the legitimate successor to prior radical movements.

William Z. Foster introduced Lucy Parsons to James P. Cannon, secretary of I.L.D.,[5] and she went to work for the new organization, which included I.W.W. members for the first several years.

Lucy Parsons attended the second annual convention of the I.L.D. in 1927 in New York as the guest of honor. The convention was held on the 40th anniversary of the Haymarket executions.

Lucy Parsons was elected a vice-chairperson of the convention and a member of the National Committee of the I.L.D., which included such notable women radicals as Elizabeth Gurley Flynn, Rose Karsner, Juliet Stuart Poyntz, and Ella Reeve Bloor.[6]

In 1926 a year long textile strike at Passaic, New Jersey, led by Albert Weisbord, demonstrated that the unorganized were ready to be organized. The strike, however, did not fit into the plans of William Z. Foster's Trade Union Educational League, and was lost when the Communist Party ordered Weisbord out of Passaic and turned the strike over to the A.F. of L.[7]

The National Textile Workers' Union formed out of events at Passaic and at New Bedford, Massachusetts, and led by Weisbord took on the textile bosses at the Loray Mill in Gastonia, North Carolina, to fight pay cuts and speed up.

Vigilantes destroyed union headquarters and soaked the strikers' food in kerosene on April 18, 1929. Following mass evictions of the strikers from company owned houses on May 6, the union set up a tent colony. The first week of June company agents attempted to poison the tent colony's water supply and poisoned strike leader Ella May Wiggins' spring in nearby Bessemer City. By the night of June 7, strike leader Vera Buch had a commitment from workers inside the mill that they would come out if a picket line met them at the mill. After the union meeting the night of the 7th, which company agents attempted to disrupt, Buch led the picket line toward the mill. The picket line was brutally attacked by police and broken up. Then a carload of drunken officers invaded the strikers' tent colony. The Gastonia Chief of Police was killed in the shooting which followed; vigilante committees made mass arrests; the union organizers and strikers were charged with murder. Vera Buch was among the indicted.

In the approaching Gastonia trial, Lucy Parsons saw parallels to 1886. The mill owners were not interested in who had killed the Chief; they were interested in stopping the union drive. "This is no holiday, comrades," wrote Lucy in the *Labor Defender*. "The howl of the awakening imperialistic South at the audacity of the dauntless National Textile Workers Union and the International Labor Defense is resounding. The fate of the comrades, the horrible chain gang. The electric chair looms in the not far distance. Only the workers can save them!"

The working class had not saved Sacco and Vanzetti, who were executed in 1927 despite the confession of a gang member to the crime in 1925, and Lucy feared for the lives of the Gastonia defendants. After a mistrial, indictments against the three women and six of the men were dropped; seven men were tried and sentenced to prison.[8]

Lucy Parsons' last 15 years, as she approached age 90, were spent working closely with the Communist Party. She spoke at Paris Commune Celebrations, May Day celebrations, and November 11th meetings. Joseph Giganti, secretary of I.L.D. in Chicago arranged for her to speak at three separate Paris Commune commemorations in the 1920's. The I.L.D. office carried her publications.[9]

Lucy was always available as a speaker. She was always warm and friendly and eager to talk. Joseph Giganti found her a little on the odd side in her archaic dress, carrying her bundles of pamphlets wherever she went, but he grew quite fond of her. She welcomed the Communist Party's acceptance.

Lucy Parsons hailed May Day in the April 29, 1930, *Daily Worker,* and she was one of the Communist Party's May Day speakers at Ashland Auditorium in Chicago. In the *Daily Worker* she wrote, "On this day the workers of every land and every clime will abandon the factories, mines and other hell holes of capitalism and march by the thousands under the banner of the Communist International and will declare their intention to abolish the curse of capitalism, poverty, and misery."

Lucy attacked the American Federation of Labor as a sell-out organization. "There came to the front the A.F. of L. which has retarded and deadened the labor movement. In a population of 38 million of workers it has gathered some 2 millions of the mechanics and ignored the other 36 millions—virtually told them to go to hell! Now the Communists have risen as a challenge to this bunch of lazy racketeer A.F.L. officials, with their morally bankrupt organization. The Communists are here to stay."

Lucy had been in the parade 44 years ago; she was in it on May 1, 1930. Her speech at the 1930 May Day celebration was printed in *Hearings Before a Special Committee to Investigate Communist Activities in the U.S.* Her old antagonist, Make Mills, whom she had successfully fought off in the 1915 Hunger Demonstration, now headed the Chicago Red Squad and introduced her speech as evidence of communist activity.

Thousands of people heard Lucy's speech, and the *Daily Worker* asserted that 25,000 marched in the streets. The great depression had begun; the stock market had crashed six months before, and working people were feeling the impact of unemployment. A change had to come, and people flocked to Communist Party rallies.

Radicals had already begun quiet organizing in basic industry, building the base for the massive organizing of the unorganized which would take place in the 1930's under the auspices of the Committee for Industrial Organization.[10]

By 1930 Lucy Parsons had outlived many of her old anarchist comrades. Lizzie Holmes died in Santa Fe, New Mexico in 1926 at age 76, and William Holmes died there two years later at 78. Carl Nold and Joseph Labadie were living in Detroit, very old men. In 1930 Carl re-established contact with Lucy.

Carl Nold was helping anarchist librarian Agnes Inglis develop the anarchist collection in Ann Arbor, of which Joseph Labadie donated the core. Carl had heard that Lucy was working with the Communist Party, and he wanted to hear about it. "While I don't belong to the Communist Party," Lucy explained, "I have been working with them to some extent, as they are the *only* bunch who are making a vigorous protest against the present horrible conditions! I think the coming winter will be a horrible one for the wage class."[11]

When Lucy wrote to Carl in late May of 1932, she was recovering from a severe attack of pleurisy which she had suffered three months before. For the first time in her life, she had had to call a doctor. Carl had asked her for an evaluation of Emma Goldman's *Living My Life,* Goldman's autobiography written in exile.

Lucy replied that the book could have been improved by taking up half the space and by a preface containing an historical sketch of the movement instead of "beginning and ending with Emma, Emma . . . Really, I don't think it will be very interesting to anybody outside the bunch that she was associating with at the time. This great big busy world cares but little about Emma Goldman's scraps with the cops 25 years ago, at least not enough to pay $7.50 good dollars to learn it." Lucy did not think the history of individuals important; she thought the history of movements important. For this reason she never wrote about herself. Lucy did not know that Emma had struggled hard with her publisher to reduce the price of the book to $5 so that more people could afford it.

The two women's disagreements on sex surfaced, unresolved

since that defense meeting for the *Firebrand* in 1897. "Then, too, I think had she left out sex stuff the book would have appealed to a more thoughtful element, again may be mistaken. Just why she should have thought it interesting or instructive, or educating to list 15 of her 'lovers' is beyond me to understand. Certainly it is a poor specimen of a woman who can't get a number of you men to accommodate her sexually." Emma's former lover Ben Reitman was shocked by what he read about himself in the book. "Her accounts about herself and Ben Reitman are simply disgusting! to anyone who have anything but a debased, depraved mind," wrote Lucy. "I heard Reitman state in a public meeting that he was so shocked that he went to bed for three days after reading the book. Anything that is nasty enough to put Reitman to bed is pretty rotten."

Dr. Ben L. Reitman was the "Hobo Doctor" (also called the "Clap Doctor") who was employed by the city of Chicago to treat venereal disease in pimps, prostitutes, and hobos. Reitman and Emma Goldman had had a turbulent affair between 1908 and 1918. He was a close friend of Lucy Parsons in her later years and often drove her and George Markstall to the Haymarket Monument at Waldheim Cemetery.

Lucy did not share Emma's ideological position on sexual freedom, and she had never considered women's emancipation as important as class struggle.

Lucy took a hard Communist Party line against Goldman's and Berkman's perceptions of Soviet Russia. "I think Russia treated her and Berkman very tolerantly and cleverly; anyone could see that they were doing everything in their power to provoke arrest." Lucy defended the annihilation of the Kronstadt sailors. "As to the Kronstadt affair, that was war; nothing new about it, and the side that got licked are sour about that, too, nothing new about it either. I wonder what the Anarchists would have done, had they won out? Surrounded as they were by those hostile armies and enemies on every side?"[12]

For Lucy Parsons the end justified the means. The workers had seized power in Russia. She did not question the imprisonment and execution of anarchists in Russia, the exile of Makhno and destruction of his revolutionary peasant army by the Bolsheviks, or the execution of Fanya Baron and the disappearance of Aaron Baron while a prisoner of the Cheka. She did not ask whether there was freedom or workers' democracy under the new regime.

Lucy Parsons had been a part of the Socialist Party, the I.W.W., the Syndicalist League, and the Communist movement. Emma Goldman charged that Lucy Parsons "goes with every gang proclaiming itself revolutionary, the I.W.W., now the communists."[13] To Emma Goldman, Lucy Parsons was an opportunist.

However, viewing Lucy Parsons' career from the standpoint of the kind of work she did, it is remarkably consistent. Her first concern was for the foreign born, the hungry, and the unemployed. She always looked at her work from a working class perspective and analyzed society in terms of class struggle. It did not make so much difference to her under whose auspices she worked as it did that she struggled with the working class.

In 1933 Carl Nold arranged a reunion for the old comrades in Chicago. He stayed with Lucy Parsons for eight days, and they visited the World's Fair.

In January, 1934, Lucy wrote to Carl about the depressing radical scene in Chicago. "I have nothing worthwhile to write about. We radicals get together in our little groups, talk to each other, and go home. The Roosevelt wind has blown the radical movement to Hell!" She had just returned from Detroit, and things looked better there. "I found the Lucy Parsons' Branch of the I.L.D. to be composed of a fine lot of intelligent women."

Lucy Parsons and Carl Nold had both reached the conclusion that anarchism had no future in the United States. "Your letter," wrote Lucy, "was quite a surprise and illuminating to learn that you had arrived at the same conclusions that I had some years ago. That is, that Anarchism has not produced any organizing ability in the present generation. . . . Anarchism is a dead issue in American life today. Radicalism has been blotted off the map of Europe. The Vienna horror-slaughter is too shocking to realize."[14]

Lucy saw in Hitler's rise to power a tremendous threat to world radicalism; she sometimes wondered if the boundless energy she had expended in the radical movement had made a difference. She wrote to George Schilling, "Well, dear old friend, how are you standing the racket in the evening of your life? Have things grown better or worse since you and I, 50 years ago, began to watch the human procession. . . . Have they become more humane, more Christlike or are they a bunch of cold, brutal, heartless, cruel, money-mad maniacs? . . . . I had better stop or you will think I am crazy."[15]

Lucy Parsons wanted action, but action was difficult to find for an aging woman who was losing her sight. She wrote to Carl, "Radicalism is at a low ebb today. Despotism is on horseback, riding at high speed. The worker is helpless . . .; he just floats along on the tides of ill times. I went to work for I.L.D., because I wanted to do a little something to help defend the victims of capitalism who got into trouble, and not always be talking, talking and doing nothing." The I.L.D. hadn't given her enough work, and she wondered what she would do when she had finished "the little work that is now being doled out."

Even Emma Goldman's return to the United States on February 1, 1934, for a ninety day lecture tour, could not revive the anarchist movement. The Communist Party completely boycotted Goldman's meetings. She was no longer "the most dangerous woman in America," the woman who was accused of inspiring McKinley's assassination. In fact, her tour manager charged high prices for her lectures, thus keeping out the poor. Only in Chicago, Detroit, and Pittsburgh, where Goldman's comrades arranged the meetings, did she have large and enthusiastic crowds.

J. Edgar Hoover had detailed agents to follow Goldman, but the agents only reported that she advocated Jeffersonian democracy and civil liberties. Newspapers called her a "communist," because "communism" had taken the place of "anarchism" in the nightmares of the propertied class; a Hearst paper transformed Emma Goldman into "the leading Communist in the United States."

In the early 1930's Lucy still traveled and lectured. She spent her days walking the six or seven miles to the Chicago Loop from her home, selling pamphlets, and talking with people. If there was a demonstration or a picket line, Lucy was there. She stopped at radical meeting places like Hobo College on West Madison St. She was never in too big a hurry to stop and talk with a young comrade. In 1933 she passed her 80th birthday.

In the afternoon Lucy might be seen walking north along Halsted St. on her way home. Although there was a street-car line, she couldn't afford to ride. Friends slipped her carfare when they had change to spare. Marks walked with her sometimes, his tanned and weather beaten face showing his admiration for her. They respected each other and stuck together.

Young people came to the Dill Pickle Club, a radical avant garde gathering place in Tooker Alley near Bughouse Square, to see Lucy Parsons. "Step High and Stoop Low and Leave Your Dignity Outside" read the sign over the awkward entrance.

Other young radicals met Lucy at the Congress Plaza when the Communist Party set up a display of rotting food which the government passed out as relief. Mario Manzardo recalled talking with Lucy at a demonstration near Haymarket Square when mounted police charged. "Just like it's always been!" Lucy exclaimed as Manzardo went over a high fence and she made off in another direction.[16]

Lucy worked in the defense of Angelo Herndon and the Scottsboro Boys. Herndon, a black man, had led a march of 10,000 blacks in Atlanta, Georgia, protesting depression conditions, which hit blacks hardest. The Scottsboro Boys, the youngest of whom was 13, were charged with the rape of a white woman. The Communist Party, International Labor Defense, and the American Civil Liberties Union worked to regain their freedom and call attention to the oppression of blacks.

Lucy continued to work with I.L.D. for the release of Tom Mooney. She dug deep into her empty purse for $1 which she contributed to his defense. Mooney wrote to her, deeply moved,

Your contribution to my defense touched me as few things have. It carried something from your heart to mine. That old, black, dark spot in the American struggle of the workers loomed before me, and the only reason that such a terrible fate did not befall five innocent trade unionists 30 years later was because . . . the workers are . . . better organized.[17]

Tom Mooney wanted to put his own case into the context of the history of labor frame-up cases, and he asked Lucy to send him material on the Haymarket case. His own copies of *The Life of Albert R. Parsons* and *Famous Speeches* had been confiscated by police when he was arrested in 1916; he had been in prison 20 years. Mooney also wrote to William Z. Foster, Jay Fox, and Clarence Darrow as he placed his case historically and prepared his appeal for a writ of *habeas corpus.*

Lucy sent her old friend Mooney a copy of *The Life of Albert R. Parsons* and copies of the *Alarm* which she still had. "Well, dear Comrade," she wrote, "I have been very active in your cause to liberate you, have spoken in many meetings both here and in the east. I am not discouraged in the belief that justice will be done you and I can clasp your hand a free comrade, vindicated."[18]

In their last few years Lucy Parsons and Nina Spies, the widow of August Spies, resolved their differences. Ralph Chaplin, who had become a bitter enemy of communism, recalled a meeting in the Wobbly Hall on Fullerton Ave. at which the two aged women tried to reach a reconciliation.

The two had quarreled each year over who was to ride in the first car at the May Day parade; the question had been resolved by alternating years. In their last years the two women often spoke from the same platform and even went to the Dill Pickle Club together. Nina Spies was a member of the I.W.W. and devoted her time to the Hobo College. She made her shack available to all homeless persons, who shared her roof with her many dogs and cats.

There is a story, perhaps apocryphal, of the two women standing together at the Haymarket monument which meant so much to both of them. As they stood gazing at the monument, Lucy turned to Nina and asked, "Nina, when I croak will you deliver my funeral address?"

"Yes," replied Nina, "but if I go first you must speak at my funeral."

It was Nina who went first, on April 9, 1936. The I.W.W. conducted the memorial meeting which opened with the song "The Red Flag." Fred Thompson, long time editor of *The Industrial Worker,* first met Lucy at Nina's funeral.[19] Ben Reitman spoke. Lucy Parsons delivered a tremendous oration. "You and I, Comrade Nina, have passed along these fifty years together. Now the great curtain of mystery and death has fallen and you are beyond. It is only a matter of days or months or hours before I must render my account with nature. If there be another world, we will join hands and march on together, but

I know nothing of that. Comrade Nina, fare thee well."

As far as anyone knew, Nina Spies had left no money. After the memorial meeting, the I.W.W. took up a collection to pay expenses. It was later revealed that Nina had left $3,000 for the care of her eight dogs. Lucy Parsons was furious that the money had not been left to the movement or to maintaining the Haymarket monument.[20]

Lucy Parsons had become a legend in her own time and a folk hero of Communist Party youth. In 1936 she had lived 50 years beyond the Haymarket police riot. Chicagoans had a mixed sense of pride in this dark woman who had defied police in every city north of the Mason and Dixon line. The *Daily News* did a 50th anniversary piece on Lucy Parsons. "She led many street parades behind the red flag, being regarded by radical groups everywhere as a living symbol of revolt against the existing order. She was arrested many times as a disturber of the peace. She shouted defiance of the police from one end of the country to the other." The *Sunday Worker* published a feature article about Lucy Parsons.

Lucy spoke in Chicago on the 50th anniversary of the execution of her husband, November 11, 1937. Radical groups of all persuasions paid honor to the men who had died for labor that day fifty years before. Lucy wrote a 50th anniversary article for *One Big Union Monthly,* the journal of the I.W.W. She told the story of the trial and executions, concluding, "Oh, Misery, I have drunk thy cup of sorrow to its dregs, but I am still a rebel."

In 1937 International Publishers, the Communist Party press, published *Labor Agitator; The Story of Albert R. Parsons* by Alan Calmer. Lucy praised the author in an introductory note for having "dug beneath the mountain of lies" and having "given the bare, cold facts . . . proving that they were . . . simply lynched!—to satisfy a howling mob of greedy capitalists." She spoke of other labor leaders whom the capitalists had tried to crush, of Eugene Debs who was jailed "because he dared to raise his voice against the war craze of the capitalists," and of Big Bill Haywood "who had to flee the country of his birth and die in the land of promise—Soviet Russia," and of Tom Mooney "pining away his valuable life behind prison bars because the rich utility barons demand it." She compared the Memorial Day massacre of May 30, 1937 at Republic Steel in Chicago with what the bosses had done fifty years before.

Lucy Parsons had lived to see hundreds of thousands of workers organized into the C.I.O. in auto, steel, meat packing, and other industries. She felt that the Communist Party had led a movement for industrial unionism which compared with the size of the mass movement for the eight hour day which the "anarchists" had led in 1886.

The Communist Party's publication of the new biography of Albert Parsons brought Lucy closer to the party; it was Alexander Trachtenberg, the head of International Publishers, who persuaded Lucy Parsons to join the Communist Party in 1939.

Lucy Parsons had become estranged from the Pioneer Aid and Support Association, because of her involvement with the Communist Party. Irving Abrams, the last surviving member of the Pioneers, found Lucy Parsons a very difficult woman. "You see, she was already out preaching the communist philosophy and was so in the communist movement that anybody that wasn't a communist was a yellow traitor." Like Goldman, Abrams viewed Lucy Parsons as an opportunist. "Her sudden extreme adherence to the communist movement was because the communist movement, then in its heyday, seemed about to bring the revolution, and here was a field for Lucy to work."[21]

The most intimate picture of Lucy Parsons' later years came from Eugene Jasinski, a young member of the Communist Party and her neighbor. Eugene Jasinski's mother and Lucy Parsons had worked together with miners in southern Illinois at the turn of the century. They were then members of the Socialist Party.

The Jasinski family frequently invited Lucy to coffee or to dinner and drove out into the country with her on weekends; together they spent many pleasant hours in the Forest Preserve west of Chicago or under the old apple tree behind Mrs. Jasinski's house amid the catalpas, acacias, balsam trees, lilacs and flowers. Lucy would quote poetry or recite verses that she had written, and she sang for them in her melodic voice.

Lucy had converted one of the bedrooms into a library and study, where she kept 1500 books on "sex, socialism, and anarchy," according to Frank Beck's description in *Hobohemia*.

Eugene Jasinski recalled that she had the classics, Voltaire, Rousseau, Marx, Engels, works of French socialists, Tolstoy, and the complete works of Victor Hugo and Jack London.

Lucy and George had a rough time surviving the depression years; finally Lucy secured a blind pension. She preferred that her friends didn't know what deprivation she faced, and she kept the house clean and neat. Friends would send her money sometimes. Mrs. Jasinski would mail Lucy cash and would send Eugene over with stew and others of Lucy's favorite dishes. "I don't know how they survived!" he exclaimed. "I'd go out in the kitchen, and I'd sneak and take a quick look in the pantry, and it was like Mother Hubbard's cupboard. Pretty damn bare!"[22]

The Lucy Parsons that Irving Abrams knew was the same Lucy Parsons who sang lovely melodies and recited poetry to Eugene Jasinski and his mother, who brought tears to Stella Nowicki's eyes as she clasped the ancient lady's hand and looked into her wrinkled face, knowing that this woman had brought panic to property owners and stirred great hopes in the starving and homeless for more than half a century.[23]

During their organizing campaign at International Harvester, the Farm Equipment Workers announced that they would bring Lucy Parsons down the Chicago River on a barge to speak to the workers so that she wouldn't be arrested for trespassing on company property. Although Lucy never appeared on the barge, one of her last public appearances was to speak to strikers at International Harvester on February 23, 1941. International Harvester was the successor to the McCormick Reaper Works where the police brutality which prompted the Haymarket protest meeting occurred in 1886. Lucy Parsons emphasized the continuity of police and employer brutality from 1886 to 1941. On her last May Day—1941—Lucy Parsons rode as guest of honor on the Farm Equipment Workers float in the May Day Parade.

On March 7, 1942, the wood stove in the simple dwelling at 3130 N. Troy caught fire; Lucy Parsons, virtually blind, was trapped and burned to death. George Markstall had been out getting groceries. When he saw the smoke, he rushed into the house and tried to save her. When firemen arrived, Lucy was already dead, and George was overcome with burns and smoke inhalation. He was taken to Belmont Hospital where he died the following day.

The house was badly damaged, its exterior blistered. Many of the books were smoke and water damaged, but much of Lucy's extensive library was left intact by the fire.

Lucy had not feared death; she knew she would soon "check out for the Great Unknown." But she had wanted to be sure her affairs were attended to, by her specifications. She wanted to be sure the monument to the Haymarket Martyrs would be properly cared for, and she wanted to be buried at the monument.

A few years before her death she went to the Pioneer Aid and Support Association and said she wanted to will her house to the Association on condition that they keep the property and rent it, using the proceeds to maintain the monument. The Pioneers told her to leave it with no strings attached or forget it. She was granted permission to be buried at the monument.

She came back several times to argue about the property. Irving Abrams recalled, "We simply told her: 'Lucy, you want to leave it to the Pioneers, good! If you don't, it's all right, too. We are not going into real estate business.' And with that she left."

On May 6, 1938, she filled out her will. Despite the decision of the Pioneers, she left the house to George Markstall for his use. "But he is not to sell, mortgage, transfer or sell it . . . . At his death it is to go to the Pioneer Aid and Support Association to be used for the maintenance of the graves of my late husband Albert R. Parsons and his comrades. . . ." The will required the Pioneers to use the income only for the monument.[24]

In 1934, Lucy had made arrangements with Ben Reitman to conduct her funeral. She had notified the Pioneers that she had arranged and paid for the undertaker already.[25]

Lucy Parsons' death brought the anarchist and communist movements into conflict. She had left two groups which expected to conduct the funeral: the Pioneers, represented by Irving Abrams, and Ben Reitman, who would ask Communists to speak at the funeral. Abrams narrated the "final conflict."

We arranged for the funeral. I get a call from Benthal, who was then one of the shining lights in the Communist movement. He says, "Ben Reitman called me to speak at the funeral."

I said, "Ben Reitman called you!?! Ben Reitman hasn't anything to say . . . whether you'll be allowed to speak is a question that the committee will decide."

So I called up Ben Reitman and said, "Ben, who the hell gave *you* authority to invite people?"

"Well," he said, "I'm running the show."

"Ben, if you're running the show, that's fine, we're not running shows. Lucy will not be buried at the monument. We're through."

They compromised, and both Reitman and J. O. Benthal spoke at the funeral.

Three hundred persons came to pay tribute to Lucy Parsons and George Markstall. Win Stracke, founder of the Old Town School of Folk Music, sang.

The problems did not end with the confrontation between rival groups on the left. Permission for Lucy to be buried at the monument had been granted. But George was dead, too; and her son Albert's ashes had been kept in the house. There was nothing to do with the ashes except to bury them with Lucy under her marker at Waldheim.

Tributes to Lucy Parsons poured out. The labor movement had lost two of its leaders that week: Lucy Parsons and Tom Mooney.[26] The *Daily Worker* and the Communist Party set the standard for the historiography of Lucy Parsons. She was the wife of martyr Albert Parsons. She devoted her life to lecture and write on the historic labor case. She worked closely for many years with the International Labor Defense, and she wrote a biography of Albert Parsons which included a short history of the American labor movement.

At the age of 83 [89] this remarkable woman, who was proud of her Mexican and Negro ancestry, was a link between the labor movement of the present and the great historic events of the 1880's. . . .

The gallows which took the life of her husband and three other victims could not cow her spirit. For more than 50 years after the judicial murder of her husband, Lucy Parsons was an active figure in every progressive movement. . . .

She was one of America's truly great women, fearless, and devoted to the working class.

Lucy might have been surprised to hear she was proud of her Negro ancestry, a heritage which she had denied for years. But in the end, she may have identified with her black brothers and sisters through the Communist Party's work for black liberation.

This became the traditional Communist Party view of Lucy Parsons. Elizabeth Gurley Flynn did better than most C.P. historians when she wrote of Lucy Parsons' own qualities and work as a woman and revolutionary. "Lucy Parsons spoke in a beautiful melodious voice, with eloquence and passion. She had her roots in the people, which gave her strength. She never lost faith in the power, courage, intelligence and ultimate triumph of the people. Years ago she accustomed trade union men to listen respectfully to a woman speaking for labor. . . . She helped to build up a strong tradition of labor defense. . . ."

Flynn realized that Lucy Parsons had made her own task as a woman easier by making men listen to her. She talked about Lucy Parsons' role in the foundation of the I.W.W. and the pleasure which Lucy took from the growing C.I.O. "What a great satisfaction to her it must have been to realize the number of splendid young women, many of her color, who are enrolled in it today. What a joy to see trades unions millions strong! She did not live in the past. She lived for the future. She will live in the future, in the hearts of the workers."

Lucy's old friends Cassius and Sadie Cook missed her deeply. They were living in California, but Cassius had been to see her only a month before her death. He had found her hale and hearty with plenty of spirit, despite her blindness. Sadie affectionately wrote to a friend, "I have learned so much from past experiences, and now we have no Emma or other great leaders with which to carry on. . . . There is no one I can see that takes dear old Lucy Parsons' place, or Emma's place, or a hundred and one others." Ben Reitman said that Lucy had ". . . great ideas to which she was faithful all her life." Ben Reitman and the Cooks did not join other anarchists in condemning Lucy Parsons.[27]

The questions of Lucy's house and her library were not settled. It took more than a year to dispose of the property. Her will turned out to be invalid as it was illegal to leave a bequest to a private monument. A friend of Irving Abrams at Chicago Title and Trust guaranteed the title, and the lot was sold in the fall of 1943 for $800.[28]

Irving Abrams had gone to the house the day after the fire to take possession of Lucy's extensive library. When he arrived, he found only the most badly damaged books left. The rest were gone. The policeman on duty told Abrams the F.B.I. had taken the library away.

Abrams called the F.B.I., which denied taking anything. He asserts, "With the connivance of the police, someone stole the library."

Ben Reitman tried to locate the papers and books. He and Lucy had agreed that part of the material would go to the University of Chicago and part to the State Historical Society of Wisconsin.

Make Mills, the head of the Chicago Red Squad, told Reitman he had turned down the papers when the police department in Lucy's district offered them to him and suggested they go to the F.B.I. Reitman wrote to the F.B.I. director of Chicago, "Mrs. Parsons promised me some of her letters, papers, and photographs. The Lucy Parsons collection of books and papers had absolutely nothing to do with the present war. . . . I hope you can see your way clear to turn the papers, books, and pamphlets over to her executors and permit us to distribute them to the libraries."

No agency of the law even admitted it had Lucy Parsons' books and papers. The Chicago Police, the Chicago Red Squad, and the Federal Bureau of Investigation feared even a dead Lucy Parsons.[29]

Chapter Notes

NOTES—Chapter 1

1. This section comes from *Waco Day*, May 6, 1886; clipping in Waco-McLennan County Library; *Knights of Labor*, Nov. 6, 1887; *The Life of Albert R. Parsons*, ed. Lucy Parsons; Albert Parsons' autobiography in *The Autobiographies of the Haymarket Martyrs*, ed. Philip Foner; *Dictionary of American Biography; Chicago Herald*, Sept. 18, 1886 from Des Plaines St. Officers' scrapbook, Chicago Historical Society; clippings in the Albert R. Parsons Papers, State Historical Society of Wisconsin; and Mrs. Lucie C. Price's extensive research on the careers of William and Albert Parsons in Texas.

2. William Parsons' official rank was Colonel, but he was called General. Albert Parsons apprenticed as a printer under the secessionist Willard Richardson of Galveston. Richardson was a follower of John C. Calhoun and had fought for the annexation of Texas by the U.S. and for the continuation of slavery in Texas. Although Albert Parsons claimed to have been only 13 in 1861 when he joined the Confederates, the 1850 Montgomery County, Alabama Census lists him with his father Samuel and gives his age as 5. In 1860 he was listed with Willard Richardson and his age was given as 15. See also *Condensed History of Parsons Texas Cavalry Brigade* by W.H. Parsons, 1883. *Waco Day* and *Waco Bar and Incidents of Waco History* by William M. Sleeper and Allan D. Sanford, pp 36-38 describe the incarceration of District Court Judge Oliver for lunacy. Albert Parsons raised a band of blacks to free the judge, but backed down when confronted by a large, well-armed group of whites.

3. Announcement for the book in Earl Vandale Collection. See William Parsons to Gov. Clark, Apr. 30, 1861, Edward Clark Papers, for further documentation of William Parsons' involvement in the secessionist movement. University of Texas Archives, Austin.

4. Even Lucy's middle name is a question. Standard labor histories, e.g. *Labor's Untold Story* and Philip Foner's works, give Lucy's middle name as Eldine. However, the birth certificate of her daughter and her own death certificate (Lulu Parsons, April 20, 1881 and Lucy Ella Parsons Markstall, March 7, 1942, County Clerk, Cook Co., Illinois) give Ella. Lucy usually signed her name "Lucy E. Parsons." Although the Parsons family denied publicly that Lucy was black, Katharine Parsons Russell suggested (1976) that the family privately considered Lucy Parsons black. Photos of Lucy are proof of her black ancestry.

It is possible that Lucy, as well as Oliver Gathings, was a slave of the wealthy Gathings brothers (James G. and Philip) who owned 62 slaves in 1860. Philip Gathings had a daughter named Lucy born in 1849; it is possible that a slave child born four years later would have been named after the master's child. The most precise birthdate available for Lucy Parsons is March, 1853. In 1860 James J. and Philip Gathings each owned two little girls who were about Lucy Parsons' age. However, the slave schedules provide only age, sex and color (negro or mulatto)—no given names. Slave schedules for Hill County, 1860.

Waco-McLennan County Library. *A History of Hill County, Texas, 1838-1965* by Ellis Bailey.

Henry and Marie del Gather (whom Lucy claimed were her uncle and mother, respectively) and John Waller (the civilized Creek Indian who was supposedly her father) are probably fictitious. Albert's story that he met Lucy at her uncle's ranch in 1869 while traveling for the *Houston Daily Telegraph* (pub. by his brother) is probably untrue. Lucy gave the maiden name Carter on her son's birth certificate in 1879 and the name Hull on her daughter's in 1881. Although she usually gave her birthplace as Buffalo Creek, Texas, she gave Virginia on both children's birth certificates. Lucy provided Gonzales as her maiden name to the *Dictionary of American Biography* for its account of Albert Parsons. On Lucy's death certificate her parents are listed as Pedro Diaz and Marie Gonzales. Lucy identified herself as Native American and Chicana in an effort to cover up her black heritage.

There are other stories of Lucy Parsons' origins, but her relationship to Oliver Gathings was the most frequently publicized and repeated—with the exception of her own stories, which conflict with each other. The *Waco Day's* assertion that "hundreds of colored as well as white people here remember her" suggests that Lucy was well-known in Waco.

5. *Travis County, Texas Marriage Records, 1840-1882* by Lucie C. Price, (Austin, 1973). Mrs. Price could find no evidence of a marriage license in Austin where Lucy and Albert claimed to have been married. Neither could she find evidence of a notary public named Owsley, whom Lucy claimed married them. In his autobiography Albert said he and Lucy were married the fall of 1871; William Parsons said fall of 1871 in his account in *The Life of Albert R. Parsons;* Lucy fixed upon June 10, 1871, as the exact date when she provided information to the *Dictionary of American Biography.*

6. The description of Ku Klux Klan activities in Waco comes from records of the Bureau of Refugees, Freedmen, and Abandoned Lands, v. 168. National Archives. The Freedmen's Bureau, as it became known, was established by Congress on March 3, 1865, under the War Department. The Bureau became the Radical Republicans' policy implementing machinery; at first they envisioned using the Bureau to divide Southern land and redistribute it to blacks. But the Bureau became primarily involved with handling relief, setting up displaced persons camps, handling complaints of violations of civil rights of freedpeople, and handling job placement of blacks—an indenture system which differed little from slavery. A quarter to a third of the black refugees died in some of the camps.

7. *Austin Statesman,* July 20, 1873 for account of convention. There is some discrepancy in dates of the Parsons' arrival in Chicago; the fact that Albert Parsons participated in this convention makes Lucy's January, 1874, date the most likely.

NOTES—Chapter 2

1. *Chicago City Directories* and the *Socialist. A History of Chicago,* v. 3, by Bessie Louise Pierce and *The Tenements of Chicago* by Edith Abbott for information on slum tenements.

2. The First International was founded in London in 1864. Its headquarters were moved to New York in 1872 in an effort by Marx to crush Bakunin's influence in the organization.

3. George Schilling's introduction to *The Life of Albert R. Parsons.* This section comes from *The Life;* Albert Parsons' autobiography in *The Autobiographies of the Haymarket Martyrs,* ed. Philip Foner; and "Socialism and Anarchism in Chicago" by Floyd Dell in *Chicago: Its History and Its Builders,* ed. J. Seymour Currey.

4. *Eugene V. Debs* by Ray Ginger and *The Autobiography of Mother Jones.* The account of the railroad strikes comes from *1877, Year of Violence* by Robert V. Bruce, *Strike!* by Jeremy Brecher, *Chicago Tribune* and the *Socialist.* The *Tribune* used precisely the violent language which appears in the text. In fact, in the account of Albert Parsons' encounter with the Citizens' Association, the *Tribune* attributed more violent language to the members of the Citizens' Association than did Parsons in his autobiography.

5. *The Socialist Labor Party of America, Proceedings of the 1877 National Convention,* microfilm, State Historical Society of Wisconsin.

6. Articles by Lucy Parsons in the *Socialist:* "A Parody," Dec. 7, 1878; "An Illustration," Dec. 7, 1878. "The True Reformer," Dec. 28, 1878; "Relics from the Late Carnage," Jan. 25, 1879; "Workingwomen," Feb. 1, 1879; and "America's Aristocrats," Feb. 15, 1879.

7. *Trade Union Organization Among Women in Chicago* by Emily Barrows, p. 42. Dissertation at the University of Chicago.

8. "Extracts from History of Socialist Party of United States," ms. by Thomas Morgan, Thomas J. Morgan Papers, Illinois Historical Survey, University of Illinois, Urbana.

9. Birth certificate. County Clerk, Cook Co., Illinois. The baby was delivered at home by a midwife.

10. *The Socialist Labor Party of America, Proceedings of the 1880 National Convention,* microfilm, State Historical Society of Wisconsin.

11. Justus Schwab was a leader of the New York radical movement and ran a bar at 51 First St.

12. "Speiss" refers to August Spies.

13. Philip Van Patten to George Schilling, Sept. 24, 1880. See also Van Patten to Schilling, Aug. 2, 1880, in which Van Patten denounced Frank Hirth, George A. Schilling Collection, Illinois State Historical Library.

14. Elizabeth Morgan to Philip Van Patten, Oct. 29, 1880, *The Socialist Labor Party of America,* microfilm, State Historical Society of Wisconsin.

15. Birth certificate, County Clerk, Cook Co., Illinois. Albert Parsons' occupation is listed as clothier on this certificate.

NOTES—Chapter 3

1. The known extant issue of the *An-archist* is at the Newberry Library. *Bulletin of the Social Labor Movement* is at the Detroit Public Library. This section comes from *The History of the Haymarket Affair* by Henry David, *The History of the American Labor Movement* by John R. Commons and Associates, and *The History of Socialism* by Morris Hillquit.

2. "The Parsons Family," Knights of Labor, Oct. 8, 1887.

3. Autobiography of Michael Schwab in Foner, ed., pp. 122-123.

4. The International Workingmen's Association was distinct from the International Working People's Association. The I.W.A.'s strength was in Colorado and in California. See *The Story of a Labor Agitator* by Joseph R. Buchanan.

5. *Chicago City Directories,* 1883-1885. Lizzie May Swank also wrote under the name May Huntley and as Lizzie Holmes after she remarried. She was sometimes known as Lizzie Swank-Holmes.

6. "Extracts from History of Socialist Party of United States," ms. by Thomas Morgan. Thomas J. Morgan Papers, Illinois Historical Survey, University of Illinois, Urbana.

7. Philip Van Patten to George Schilling, Apr. 11, 1893. Labadie Collection at the University of Michigan Library.

8. *Denver Labor Enquirer,* undated clipping, Albert R. Parsons Papers, State Historical Society of Wisconsin. Much of this section comes from *Denver Labor Enquirer, Alarm, Truth* (published by Burnette Haskell of the I.W.A. in San Francisco), and clippings in the Parsons Papers.

9. *Arbeiter-Zeitung.* See *New Yorker Volkszeitung,* Sept. 28, 1884, for Grottkau's side of dispute. *Milwaukee Sentinel,* May 6-8, 1886.

10. *The Historical, Philosophical and Economical Bases of Anarchy* by William Holmes. Albert Parsons in *Knights of Labor,* Dec. 11, 1886.

11. Lucy Parsons in *Advance and Labor Leaf,* Mar. 12, 1887.

12. The proposed treaty provided for the extradition of Russian radical exiles and Jews to Russia where they could expect no mercy; American radicals fought the treaty for years.

13. *Chicago Times,* Jan. 1889. Bonfield's brother was Corporation Counsel under Mayor Heath, and he got John Bonfield his first job with the Chicago Police Department.

14. *Autobiography of Mother Jones,* pp. 19-20.

15. *Chicago Tribune.* The boy who was lynched had killed a white boy in self defense. When he was convicted, the judge had stated that if the defendant were white, he would have been released without a moment's hesitation.

16. Judge Prendergast later incurred the wrath of the Citizens' Association by ruling that "tramps" (people without homes) could vote in the districts in which they lived. William M. Salter was a well-known philosopher and theologian and the lecturer for the Ethical Culture Society of Chicago. He was the author of a number of books and became the lecturer on Nietzsche at the University of Chicago (1909-1913). Dr. Randall was connected with the publication of the *Chicago Express.*

NOTES—Chapter 4
1. *The Haymarket Affair and the Trial of the Chicago Anarchists, 1886,* by John S. Kebabian, ed., p. 26. The book is a description of Prosecutor Grinnell's private collection which the H.P. Kraus Co. is trying to sell for $75,000. The collection is not open to researchers. The letter from Lizzie Holmes to Lucy Parsons was confiscated by police.

2. After May 4 William Holmes lost all the pupils in his elocution and shorthand school. See Cato (William Holmes), "Our Women Martyrs" in *Denver Labor Enquirer*, May 15, 1886 and William Holmes, "The Eleventh of November, 1887!" in *Firebrand*, Nov. 15, 1896, etc.

3. Cemeteries could accept bodies for burial on a physician's death certificate without registering the death with the County Clerk. Victims may have been buried by their families in this way; people who died of complications at a later date (or outside Cook County) may not have turned up in the search of the Cook County records.

4. Address of Oscar Neebe in *Famous Speeches*, ed. Lucy E. Parsons, pp. 28-29. Neebe was questioned and released.

5. "Socialism and Anarchism in Chicago," by Floyd Dell in Currey, ed., p. 400. *The History of the Haymarket Affair* by Henry David, p. 193. Material on the Haymarket case comes from Dell and David, Chicago papers, *Famous Speeches, Autobiographies, The Life of Albert R. Parsons, The Great Trial of the Chicago Anarchists* by Dyer D. Lum, *Labor Agitator, the Story of Albert R. Parsons* by Alan Calmer, *Anarchy and Anarchists* by Michael Schaack, *Anarchism* by A. R. Parsons, the trial record at the Chicago Historical Society, etc.

6. Autobiography of Louis Lingg in Foner, ed. Lingg's father had jumped into a frozen river at the request of his boss to rescue some logs which had broken loose. Other workers had refused to jump in. The man never recovered from the icy plunge; he could not go back to his old job, and the boss first reduced his pay, then fired him. He died from the effects several years later.

7. Dusey was a stockyards worker. Gerhard Lizzius had moved from Indianapolis to Chicago to become city editor of the *Arbeiter-Zeitung*. John Henry was a printer and former *Tribune* employee. Albert Currlin became editor of the *Arbeiter-Zeitung* after Spies' arrest.

8. W.P. Black, 1842-1916, was decorated with the Congressional Medal of Honor for heroism in the Civil War. The son of a Presbyterian minister, he had begun to prepare himself for the ministry before he enlisted. Black ran for Congress in 1882 and for judge on the United Labor Party ticket in 1887. He had been a charter member of the Chicago Bar Association. He lost his lucrative practice as a result of the Haymarket trial and thereafter made only a modest living as a lawyer. Both he and Hortensia Black were greatly influenced by the ideals and characters of the defendants. See "William Perkins Black: Haymarket Lawyer" by Herman Kogan in *Chicago History,* Summer, 1976.

9. *Chicago Express,* May 15, July 10, Aug. 10, Aug. 28, 1886. The fact that the *Express* favored both the Knights of Labor and the eight hour movement suggests the extent to which Chicago Knights members were involved in both. Chicago Historical Society.

10. *Reminiscences of the Anarchist Case* by Sigmund Zeisler, pp. 19-20. Black gives essentially the same account in *The Life of Albert R. Parsons,* pp. 170-172. Black wrote that the question of Albert Parsons' return "was first brought to our attention by Mrs. Parsons." In referring to his letter to Albert Parsons, Black wrote, "I expressed the personal belief that we could satisfactorily establish his innocence, and therefore could secure his acquittal."

11. One of the persons who testified to Gilmer's *good* character was Joshiah B. Grinnell, first cousin of the prosecutor. (J. B. Grinnell donated the land for Grinnell College where the author went to school.) Dr. Mary Herma Aiken of Grinnell to *Commonweal*, May 4, 1889. Dr. Aiken organized a small section of the I.W.P.A. in Grinnell, Iowa.

12. "Truth About the Anarchists" by Joseph Gruenhut in *Knights of Labor*, Nov. 19, 1887. Gruenhut stated that he and Dr. Schmidt were to have spoken at the Haymarket. "But it turned out that all trades-union agitators were engaged in closed meetings and Spies, Parsons and Fielden were hurriedly pressed into service to speak at the Haymarket," Gruenhut explained.

13. *Knights of Labor*, Nov. 6, 1886.

14. *Chicago Herald*, Sept. 18, 1886, Des Plaines St. Policemen's Scrapbook, Chicago Historical Society. Oliver Gathings was interviewed in Texas and insisted that Lucy Parsons was his wife. Hortensia Black later insisted, "'Mrs. Lucy Parsons is not a negress as reported. Her mother was a Mexican and her father a Creek Indian." *New York World*, Sept. 26, 1887. *Knights of Labor* also carried the Mexican mother and Indian father version of Lucy's birth.

NOTES—Chapter 5
1. The account of Lucy's defense campaign comes from clippings in the Albert R. Parsons Papers at the State Historical Society of Wisconsin and from Chicago newspapers.

2. Lizzie Holmes to Albert Parsons, Dec. 23, 1886, Albert R. Parsons Papers, State Historical Society of Wisconsin.

3. "We Are All Anarchists" by Lucy E. Parsons in *Advance and Labor Leaf*, March 12, 1887.

4. Lucy Parsons' account in *Advance and Labor Leaf*, April 2, 1887. Clippings in Albert R. Parsons Papers, State Historical Society of Wisconsin. *Arbeiter-Zeitung*. Bail was reduced to $100.

5. William H. Parsons' letter to *Chicago Daily News*, Feb. 12, 1887. William Parsons' manuscript has been lost.

6. *Alarm*, July 7, 1888.

7. *Progress and Poverty* was first published in 1879. George advocated a "single tax" on land which would return the increase in land values to the public and eliminate rent.

8. A.R. Parsons to Comrade Peterson, June 29, 1887. Ernst Schmidt to George Schilling, July 19, 1887. George A. Schilling Collection, Illinois State Historical Library. Schmidt argued against buying the underwear out of defense committee money, saying the committee had been criticized for using defense money to pay for Meta Neebe's funeral in March, 1887. It is not clear whether or not Parsons got his underwear.

9. Secret testimony taken by Knights of Labor District Assembly 89 of Denver on July 15, 1887. State Historical Society of Wisconsin.

NOTES—Chapter 6

1. Leonard Swett, a friend and law associate of Abraham Lincoln, replaced William A. Foster. Benjamin F. Butler, Roger A. Pryor and J. Randolph Tucker, all lawyers with national reputations, joined the defense for the argument before the U.S. Supreme Court.

2. William Holmes in the *Alarm*.

3. George Schilling to Joseph Labadie, nd, Labadie Collection at the University of Michigan Library.

4. George Francis Train had been a renowned orator, financier, organizer of the Credit Mobilier, and a participant in the 1870 Marseilles Commune. For years he had refused to speak to anyone but children; the Haymarket trial brought him back to activity.

5. Henry Demarest Lloyd was a wealthy journalist, who had been financial editor of the *Chicago Tribune* from 1873-1885.

6. See Preface to the Second Printing of *History of the Haymarket Affair*, pp. 8-9. According to John F. Kendrick, Neebe had told him of an unknown death watch who had been with Lingg the morning of Nov. 10. After Neebe was released from prison he attempted to find the man, and he learned enough from jailers to convince him that the man had murdered Lingg to influence the governor against pardoning the men. George Schilling to Joseph Labadie, nd, said he was convinced Lingg committed suicide. Agnes Inglis to Irving Abrams, Nov. 28, 1947, said that Voltairine de Cleyre's son told her that he had learned from his mother that Dyer D. Lum provided Lingg with the material to kill himself. Labadie Collection at the University of Michigan Library.

7. William Holmes, who had made a defense campaign tour to Colorado and the west coast the fall of 1886, lost his office job with the Chicago Northwestern Railway Co. for being absent without leave on Nov. 11 and 12 and for appearing as a pallbearer on Nov. 13. His discharge was published in Chicago papers, and he was virtually blacklisted. After helping Lucy Parsons publish *Anarchism*, he finally got a job with an iron and steel manufacturer. Dr. Randall became "General" Jacob Coxey's lieutenant and organizer of the Chicago contingent in the 1894 unemployed march on Washington. See *Coxey's Army* by Donald L. McMurry, p. 232 for clash between Lucy Parsons and Randall.

8. Note in the front of the English edition of the book at Newberry Library. On Dec. 30, 1887, the *Arbeiter-Zeitung* reported that Lucy had taken legal action to release 3,238 copies of the book from the sheriff. The sheriff had confiscated the books along with the other possessions of the printer, because the printer had not paid rent.

NOTES—Chapter 7

1. Charter of Pioneer Aid and Support Association, Chicago Historical Society. The official yearly report of the Association in the *Arbeiter-Zeitung*, Feb. 15, 1889 listed $12,569.86 income and $4,404.75 expenses. During the existence of the Defense Committee Lucy had been loaned $593 to publish *Anarchism*. Nina Van Zandt Spies, the heiress who had married Spies while he was in prison, had also been loaned money for publishing a volume on Spies, and Mrs. Engel had been loaned money for a store. The Association wanted to recover the money

by holding back small amounts of support money. This didn't work, and the other families were given similar amounts with the amount paid to Lucy taken as a standard. The Sept. 24, 1890 *Vorbote* (weekly edition of *Arbeiter-Zeitung*) reported a fight between Adolph Spies and Louis Zeller. Zeller was beaten for his opposition to giving money to Lucy Parsons and Nina Spies. W.P. and Hortensia Black had attempted to prevent Spies' marriage to Nina Van Zandt, and she was not well accepted by the radicals. Letters in George A. Schilling Collection, Illinois State Historical Library.

2. *Arbeiter-Zeitung,* June 22 and 23, 1888.

3. *Commonweal,* Aug. 11, 1888. Letter from Henry T. Charles, Newark, N.J.

4. Robert Steiner to a friend, Jan. 8, 1891. Joseph Ishill Collection. By permission of the Houghton Library, Harvard University.

5. *Chicago Labor Enquirer, The Story of a Labor Agitator,* George A. Schilling in *Knights of Labor,* Oct. 27, 1888, and other clippings in the Thomas J. Morgan Papers, Illinois Historical Survey, University of Illinois, Urbana. Buchanan started the *Chicago Labor Enquirer* in Feb., 1887. William Holmes became assistant editor.

6. John C. Ambler Scrapbooks (the scrapbooks may have been prepared for the Citizens' Association), v. 90, clipping. Chicago Historical Society.

7. *Alarm* and *Commonweal* and clippings in the Albert R. Parsons Collection, State Historical Society of Wisconsin. Sarah Ames addressed the crowd at Cooper Union with Lucy. Ames had spoken at the Boston Anarchists Club on May 20, 1888, a few weeks after Lucy spoke there for the Paris Commune commemoration. She moved to the East shortly after the Haymarket affair.

8. *Chicago Times* and *Chicago Tribune* for police exposure. Clippings from Albert R. Parsons Papers, State Historical Society of Wisconsin and from Thomas J. Morgan Collection, Illinois Historical Survey, University of Illinois, Urbana. William Holmes to Thomas Morgan, Jan. 30, 1889, Morgan Collection. In the letter Holmes indicated that he had some assurance that Morgan would cooperate with the "anarchists" and that the two factions could work together. However, Morgan's behavior at the last meeting had convinced him otherwise. William Holmes in *Alarm* Jan. 26, 1889 and Feb. 2, 1889 for comments on Lucy Parsons and the police. Detective Nordrum had infiltrated radical groups in 1886 and was exposed as a police agent on July 5, 1887. *Anarchy and Anarchists* by Michael Schaack, pp. 219-220. Lowenstein had worked closely with Schaack in 1886-87 persecuting radicals.

9. George Schilling to Joseph Labadie, nd, Labadie Collection at the University of Michigan Library.

10. Labadie Collection at the University of Michigan Library.

11. Death certificate, County Clerk, Cook Co., Illinois. Although the children were born "Negro" and "nigger," they were both registered "white" on the death certificates. *Chicago Knights of Labor,* Oct. 19, 1889.

12. Chicago newspapers. *Nowhere at Home,* ed. Richard and Anna Maria Drinnon, p. 94. Emma Goldman to Alexander Berkman, Nov. 23, 1928.

NOTES—Chapter 8

1. *Arbeiter-Zeitung,* Nov. 8-29, 1890. Dyer D. Lum to Voltairine de Cleyre, nd, said that he expected Lucy to be sentenced to 90 days. Joseph Ishill Collection. By permission of the Houghton Library, Harvard University. See Schilling, Lum and Labadie letters about struggle within Knights of Labor, Labadie Collection at the University of Michigan Library.

2. *Attentat* is a general French term meaning attempt. Here it is used to refer to an act of violence by the radical left.

3. William Holmes to Joseph Labadie, Apr. 7, 1889, Labadie Collection at the University of Michigan Library. Dyer D. Lum to Voltairine de Cleyre, Oct. 18, 1892 and Feb. 4, 1892. Joseph Ishill Collection. By permission of the Houghton Library, Harvard University. The only extant issues of *Freedom* are April, June and August, 1892, held by the Houghton Library. George Schilling was president of the Alarm Publishing Co., 1887-1888.

4. Lum to de Cleyre, Jan. 13, 1892. A number of Lum's letters to de Cleyre describe his addiction. Joseph Ishill Collection. By permission of the Houghton Library, Harvard University.

5. Lum to de Cleyre, nd, followed by Mar. 6, 1893 letter. Joseph Ishill Collection. By permission of the Houghton Library, Harvard University.

6. William Parsons to George Schilling, Oct. 28, 1892, George A. Schilling Collection, Illinois State Historical Library.

7. The information from the *Spring Valley Gazette* was provided courtesy of Judge William J. Wimbiscus. George A. Schilling to Lucy Parsons, Dec. 1, 1893. George A. Schilling Collection, Illinois State Historical Library. By permission of Kathleen S. Spaulding. In a battle between Italians and blacks at Spring Valley in 1895, one person was killed.

8. Agnes Inglis to Barnard Van Horne, May 31, 1948. Labadie Collection at the University of Michigan Library.

9. And neither has the author. *Chicago Inter-Ocean,* Oct. 21, 1893, reported that Kropotkin and Johann Most were present. On Oct. 23 the *Inter-Ocean* reported that Police Chief Brennan had stated that Kropotkin wasn't there. C.L. James said 30 delegates were present, representing Canada and most of Europe, two boxes of clippings on Haymarket, Newberry Library. Other material in this section comes from these clippings.

10. *Graham Taylor, Pioneer for Social Justice 1851-1938* by Louise C. Wade, pp. 73-74.

11. In 1894 H.D. Lloyd published *Wealth Against Commonwealth,* the attack on Standard Oil which became the pioneer and classic "muckraking" book.

12. Thomas Bogard autobiographical ms., by permission of Washington State Historical Society, Tacoma, Washington. A scissor-bill is a worker who thinks like a boss. The classic I.W.W. definition is "a worker from the ears down and a capitalist from the ears up."

13. "Anarchists and Their Occupations" by Lizzie M. Holmes, May 20, 1900; "The Facts in the Case" by Lucy E. Parsons and "A Creedless Anarchist" by William Holmes, June 10, 1900, in *Free Society.*

14. William Holmes to Joseph Labadie, Sept. 7, 1893 on Lizzie's health. "Strictly Confidential. To Our Friends and Comrades," Feb. 20, 1898, letter from William and Lizzie Holmes announcing their intention to start the paper. William became editor and Lizzie associate editor. William Holmes had been editor and general manager of the *Industrial Advocate*, pub. by L.W. Rogers of the A.R.U. Labadie Collection at the University of Michigan Library.

15. "The Waldheim Agitation," by Lucy Parsons, *Firebrand*, Dec. 15, 1895. It is not known why the *Arbeiter-Zeitung* refused to print her letter.

16. *Pioneering on Social Frontiers* by Graham Taylor, pp. 131-134 and *Graham Taylor* by Louise C. Wade.

17. *Chicago Tribune. Living My Life* by Emma Goldman, p. 220. Goldman said that Lucy Parsons "took an active part in the proceedings." The Socialistic Labor Party became the Socialist Labor Party ca. 1891.

18. "Cause of Sex Slavery" by Lucy Parsons in *Firebrand*, Jan. 27, 1895. The controversial articles appeared in *Firebrand* from Aug.-Nov., 1896. *Free Society* in 1897 and 1898 carried the announcements and conflict over the *Firebrand* defense meeting.

19. *Living My Life*, pp. 222-224. In reference to Albert Parsons, Goldman wrote, "He not only repudiated both [state and slavery], but married a young mulatto." Goldman's failure to mention Lucy Parsons by name is notable; Lucy must have been the center of lively discussion, as Goldman was outraged by Lucy's comments at the *Firebrand* meeting. Goldman also mentioned that "For their insistance on sex equality, they [the Isaaks] were severely censored by many anarchists in the East and abroad." Lucy Parsons was not alone in her opposition to variety in sex.

20. Lucy Parsons to Joseph Labadie, Feb. 7, 1898, Labadie Collection at the University of Michigan Library.

21. *Nowhere at Home*, p. 170. Emma Goldman to Alexander Berkman, Jan., 1932. Transit and Burial Permit, issued Aug. 18, 1919. County Clerk, Cook Co., Illinois. George Markstall accompanied the body from Elgin to Chicago. Albert Jr. was cremated at Graceland Cemetery, and it was common knowledge that Lucy kept his ashes in her home. Max Metzkow to Agnes Inglis, Oct. 26, 1943, Labadie Collection at the University of Michigan Library recalled seeing Albert with his mother in Justus Schwab's saloon in New York City when Albert was about 15 and hearing that he was institutionalized shortly thereafter. "Extracts from History of Socialist Party of United States." Thomas J. Morgan Papers, University of Illinois, Urbana. Morgan mentions that "the girl died and the son went insane." Carl Nold to Max Metzkow, Apr. 14, 1931, Houghton Library, Harvard University mentioned that Lucy Parsons' son was said to have died 20 years ago in a Chicago insane asylum.

22. *Chicago Daily News*, July 27, 1899. Conversations with William D. Parsons and Katharine Parsons Russell. It is the opinion of Mr. Parsons that the above describes Albert Parsons Jr.'s experience in the hospital.

23. A miner's strike began at Mount Olive, Illinois, July 4, 1897. The Chicago-Virden Coal Co. and the Pana Coal Co. discharged white miners and brought in black strikebreakers. The Chicago-Virden Co. hired armed guards from St. Louis, and the Pana Coal Co. kept blacks in a heavily guarded stockade near the mine. When the Chicago-Virden Co. brought a second trainload of black strikebreakers, armed miners stopped the train. Seven miners and four guards from the private detective company were killed. Governor Tanner condemned the coal company and sent troops to Virden and Pana the next day to keep out scabs. The frightened blacks were unloaded in Springfield. They had been unaware of the situation until they were already on the train; the company turned the workers' anger into racism. The miners were buried at Mount Olive, where a shrine was built in their honor.

24. *Free Society,* Aug. 23 and 30, 1903 announced Darrow's preface and an article by Samuel Fielden, but neither appeared in the book. Lucy became involved in controversy with other comrades who refused to raise money for the publication of the book unless she included biographical sketches of all eight defendants; the sketches were included.

25. *Aliens and Dissenters* by William Preston, *Living My Life, Rebel in Paradise* by Richard Drinnon. *Discontent* ceased publication in 1902 and was followed by the *Demonstrator* in 1903.

26. *The Founding Convention of the I.W.W. Proceedings,* Speech of Lucy E. Parsons, p. 168. As far as is known Lucy Parsons made no statement about the use of black strikebreakers in the teamsters' strike or the racism generated by their use. Lucy Parsons was by no means the only radical who held the race question subsidiary to the class question. Eugene V. Debs opposed a resolution passed at the 1903 Socialist Party convention to make a special fight for black rights. He denied that poor blacks were worse off than poor whites. *Eugene V. Debs* by Ray Ginger, p. 277.

NOTES—Chapter 9

1. Algie M. Simons was the scholastic editor of the *International Socialist Review* until Charles H. Kerr fired him in 1908 saying the magazine was for workers, not college professors. Mary Marcy became editor, and the *I.S.R.* soon became a lively magazine which everyone on the left read. Hagerty was a former Catholic priest who had become a socialist and activist in the W.F.M. He had toured the West with Debs in 1902 and was one of the people who persuaded Debs to join in the founding of the I.W.W. He dropped out, of sight, but Ralph Chaplin later located him on 69th St. in Chicago practicing as an oculist under the name Dr. Ricardo Moreno. *Wobbly* by Ralph Chaplin, pp. 162-163. Charles Moyer had been a skilled worker in Lead, S.D. before he became president of W.F.M.

2. W. T. Barnard was a poet. Sam Hammersmark was a long-time associate of Lucy Parsons. He moved to Tacoma, Wash., but returned to Chicago where he later ran the Communist Party bookstore. Annie and Jake Livshis (probably the correct spelling) were friends of Emma Goldman. They nursed Voltairine de Cleyre until her death of throat cancer in 1912. The other signers are unidentified as are Lucy Parsons' side: Tobias Kleinman, Wiesmanbeer, and Goebel.

3. *Utopias on Puget Sound*, 1885-1915 by Charles P. LeWarne offers a discussion of the newspaper controversy. Turning over subscription lists to radical periodicals gives the government a persecution list.

4. Much of this section comes from the *Demonstrator*.

5. *The Rebel Girl* by Elizabeth Gurley Flynn, p. 79.

6. Carl Nold to Max Metzkow, April 11, 1911, Joseph Ishill Collection. By permission of the Houghton Library, Harvard University.

7. Carl Nold to Max Metzkow, Aug. 21, 1911, Joseph Ishill Collection. By permission of the Houghton Library, Harvard University.

8. Cassius Cook to Dr. Pryns Hopkins, June 15, 1942. Labadie Collection at the University of Michigan Library.

9. The *Agitator* was published in Home Colony, then moved to Chicago where it became the *Syndicalist*. Fox returned to Chicago for a time, but lived in Home Colony almost continuously after 1910. "A Call to Direct Actionists" by William Z. Foster in *The Toiler*, pp. 22-23. *The Rebel Girl*, p. 175.

10. Los Angeles newspapers, *International Socialist Review, Industrial Worker,* and court dockets for the case from Los Angeles County Courthouse. Markstall was sometimes referred to as Lucy's husband, but it is not known whether they were formally married. Carl Nold in letters to Max Metzkow often referred to "Parsons," a man, evidently meaning Markstall.

11. Seattle newspapers and *Revolution in Seattle* by Harvey O'Connor.

12. *San Francisco Chronicle,* Nov. 23, 1913. Lucy Parsons to C.V. Cook, Dec. 12, 1913, Labadie Collection at the University of Michigan Library.

13. *Labor Clarion, New Review,* San Francisco papers and court dockets for the case from the Archives of San Francisco. The *Labor Clarion* did not mention Lucy's name in connection with the "riot," but blamed the unemployment organizing and "riot" on the I.W.W.

14. Lucy Parsons to Cassius and Sadie Cook, Feb. 27, 1914. Labadie Collection at the University of Michigan Library.

15. Cassius Cook to Lucy Parsons, July 31, 1914. Labadie Collection at the University of Michigan Library.

16. Clippings and ms. account in the Irwin St. John Tucker Papers, the Manuscript Collection, University of Illinois at Chicago Circle. Conversations with Irwin St. John Tucker. *Wobbly* by Ralph Chaplin.

17. Correspondence with Boris Yelensky, 1973-74.

18. Lucy on war, *Agitator,* 1912 and *Instead of a Magazine* pub. Herman Kuehn, Sept. 1915. Labadie Collection at the University of Michigan Library. Joseph Ettor and Arturo Giovannitti were leaders of the Lawrence textile strike of 1912. Tresca was assassinated in New York in 1943, possibly by agents of Mussolini, Thomas Bogard autobiographical ms., Washington State Historical Society, Tacoma, Washington.

19. Cassius Cook to Agnes Inglis, Mar. 26, 1943 and Jan. 22, 1949. Labadie Collection at the University of Michigan Library. Cook was never prosecuted.

NOTES—Chapter 10

1. Lucy Parsons to Cassius and Sadie Cook, Aug. 16, 1921. Labadie Collection at the University of Michigan Library.

2. Conversation with Henry Rosemont, I.L.H.S. member and retired printer.

3. Lucy Parsons to Editor, Federated Press, Feb. 27, 1922. George A. Schilling Collection, University of Chicago Library. Michael Schwab had died June 28, 1898 and Oscar Neebe on Apr. 22, 1916. Neebe had been active in the S.L.P. (See Carl Nold to Max Metzkow, Aug. 21, 1911. Joseph Ishill Collection, Houghton Library, Harvard University.) George Schilling had been sympathetic to "anarchism" for many years. In a letter to George Schumm, Jan. 9, 1920, he said that although he'd been very active in the Single Tax Movement for years, he still leaned towards the anarchists. Labadie Collection.

4. Cassius and Sadie Cook to Agnes Inglis, June 22, 1949. Labadie Collection at the University of Michigan Library. *Road to Freedom,* Apr., 1925. Fox's statement appeared in *Workers Monthly.*

5. Interview with James P. Cannon, March, 1974. Cannon left the Communist Party in 1929 a Trotskyist and eventually became the founder of the Socialist Workers Party.

6. Rose Karsner and her husband David, a biographer of Debs, had been active in the Socialist Party. Juliet Stuart Poyntz had been active in the education department of I.L.G.W.U., was a former professor at Columbia U., and became active in Communist Party work. She disappeared in New York City in 1940, a mystery which has never been solved. Ella Reeve Bloor ("Mother" Bloor) worked in the Chicago packinghouses to gather data for Upton Sinclair's *The Jungle.* She was the state organizer in Connecticut for the Socialist Party and later joined the Communist Party. She was the representative of the Minneapolis Trades and Labor Council to the Red International of Labor Unions in Moscow in 1921.

7. *The Passaic Strike of 1926* by Morton Siegel. PhD Thesis at Columbia University, 1952.

8. Conversations with Vera Buch Weisbord and Albert Weisbord. Ms. of the autobiography of Vera Buch Weisbord (to be pub. by Indiana U. Pr.). Ella May Wiggins was singled out and shot through the heart on Sept. 14, 1929, while on her way to a union rally. Her murderers were never brought to trial, although their identities were known. The charges against the nine were *nolle prossed* and never pressed. The charges against the remaining defendants were reduced from first degree murder and conspiracy to second degree murder and assault. Albert Weisbord had been expelled from the N.T.W.U. the summer of 1929. Union activities in the Gastonia area were suspended in early 1930. See also "Gastonia 1929, Strike at the Loray Mill," ed. Carolyn Ashbaugh and Dan McCurry, *Southern Exposure,* winter 1974.

9. Conversations with Joseph Giganti.

10. The Committee for Industrial Organization became the Congress of Industrial Organizations after the expulsion of the C.I.O. unions from the A.F. of L. in 1936.

11. Lucy Parsons to Carl Nold, Sept. 25, 1930. Labadie Collection at the University of Michigan Library.

12. Lucy Parsons to Carl Nold, May 30, 1932. Labadie Collection at the University of Michigan Library. Emma Goldman to Ellen, June 21, nd, Labadie Collection at the University of Michigan Library on price of book. George Markstall to Ben Reitman, July 28, 1941, Ben L. Reitman Papers, the Manuscript Collection, University of Illinois at Chicago Circle. Markstall mentions going out to Waldheim and says he and Lucy are glad money is being raised for a monument to Emma Goldman, who died on May 14, 1940.

13. *Nowhere at Home,* p. 170. Emma Goldman to Alexander Berkman, Jan., 1932.

14. Lucy Parsons to Carl Nold, Feb. 27, 1934. The quotation ff. note 15 also comes from this letter. Labadie Collection at the University of Michigan Library. Carl Nold to Max Metzkow, Aug. 8, 1933 mentions staying with Lucy during World's Fair, Houghton Library, Harvard University.

15. Lucy Parsons to George Schilling, Sept. 19, 1935. George A. Schilling Collection, Illinois State Historical Library.

16. Conversations with Mario Manzardo. See *Rank and File* by Alice and Staughton Lynd for oral history of Manzardo.

17. Tom Mooney to Lucy Parsons, June 4, 1936. Quoted by permission of the Bancroft Library.

18. Lucy Parsons to Tom Mooney, July 11, 1936. Quoted by permission of the Bancroft Library.

19. Conversations with Fred Thompson, who was in charge of funeral arrangements. Thompson spent time in San Quentin in the 1920's for his I.W.W. activities. He wrote *The I.W.W.—Its First Fifty Years.*

20. Agnes Inglis to Li Pei Kan, Dec. 19, 1948; April 4, 1949; and Feb. 28, 1950. Labadie Collection at the University of Michigan Library.

21. Conversations with Irving Abrams.

22. Conversations with Eugene Jasinski.

23. Conversations with Stella Nowicki. See *Rank and File* and the film *Union Maids* by Julia Reichart, James Klein, and Miles Mogulescu.

24. Conversations with Irving Abrams. A copy of the will is in the Labadie Collection at the University of Michigan Library.

25. Lucy Parsons to Ben Reitman, May 8, 1934. Ben L. Reitman Papers, the Manuscript Collection, University of Illinois at Chicago Circle.

26. Tom Mooney was released from prison in 1939.

27. Sadie Cook to Agnes Inglis, Dec. 31, 1949. Labadie Collection at the University of Michigan Library. Ben Reitman to Charles H. Dennis, Mar. 12, 1942. Ben L. Reitman Papers, the Manuscript Collection, University of Illinois at Chicago Circle.

28. Minutes of the Pioneer Aid and Support Association for Sept. 12 and Oct. 10, 1943. Labadie Collection at the University of Michigan Library.

29. Conversations with Irving Abrams. Ben Reitman to Mr. Johnson, Director F.B.I., Chicago, Aug. 15, 1942. Ben L. Reitman Papers, the Manuscript Collection, University of Illinois at Chicago Circle.

Selected Reading List

Addams, Jane. *Twenty Years at Hull House,* (New York: Macmillan, 1945).

Adelman, William. *Haymarket Revisited,* (Chicago: Illinois Labor History Society, 1976).

Adelman, William. *Touring Pullman,* (Chicago: Illinois Labor History Society, 1972).

Boyer, Richard O. and Herbert M. Morais. *Labor's Untold Story,* (New York: United Electrical, Radio & Machine Workers of America, 1974).

Brecher, Jeremy. *Strike!,* (San Francisco: Straight Arrow Books, 1972).

Bruce, Robert V. *1877. Year of Violence,* (Cambridge: Harvard U. Pr., 1970).

Buchanan, Joseph R. *The Story of a Labor Agitator,* (New York: The Outlook Co., 1903).

Cahn, William. *A Pictorial History of American Labor,* (New York: Crown Pub. Inc., 1972).

Calmer, Alan. *Labor Agitator*: *The Story of Albert R. Parsons,* (New York: International Pub., 1937).

Carwardine, William H. *The Pullman Strike,* (Chicago: Charles H. Kerr, 1973).

Chaplin, Ralph. *Wobbly*: *The Rough-and-Tumble Story of an American Radical,* (Chicago: University of Chicago Pr., 1948).

Darrow, Clarence. *The Story of My Life,* (New York: Charles Scribners' Sons, 1932).

David, Henry. *The History of the Haymarket Affair,* (New York: Collier Books, 1963).

Debs, Eugene Victor. *Walls and Bars,* (Chicago: Charles H. Kerr, 1973).

Drinnon, Richard. *Rebel in Paradise. A Biography of Emma Goldman,* (Chicago: University of Chicago Pr., 1961).

Drinnon, Richard and Anna Maria. *Nowhere at Home; Letters from Exile of Emma Goldman and Alexander Berkman,* (New York: Schocken Books, 1975).

Dubofsky, Melvyn. *We Shall be All. A History of the Industrial Workers of the World,* (Chicago: Quadrangle Books, 1969).

Fast, Howard, *The American,* (New York: Duell, Sloan and Pearce, 1946).

Flynn, Elizabeth Gurley. *The Rebel Girl,* (New York: International Pub., 1973).

Foner, Philip, ed. *The Autobiographies of the Haymarket Martyrs,* (New York: Humanities Pr., 1969).

Foner, Philip. *History of the Labor Movement in the United States,* (New York: International Pub., 1947), 4v.

Ginger, Ray. *Altgeld's America,* (New York: Funk and Wagnall's, 1958).

Ginger, Ray. *Eugene V. Debs,* (New York: Collier Books, 1966).

Goldman, Emma. *Living My Life,* (New York: Dover Pub. Inc., 1970), 2v.

Haywood, William D. *Bill Haywood's Book,* (New York: International Pub., 1958).

Hofstadter, Richard and William Miller and Daniel Aaron. *The American Republic,* (Englewood Cliffs, N.J.: Prentice-Hall Inc., 1970), 2v.

Jones, Mary Harris. *The Autobiography of Mother Jones,* (Chicago: Charles H. Kerr, 3rd ed., 1976).

Kedward, Roderick. *The Anarchists. The Men Who Shocked an Era,* (New York: American Heritage Pr., 1971).

Kipnis, Ira. *American Socialist Movement,* 1897-1912, (New York: Columbia U. Pr., 1952).

Kornbluh, Joyce L., ed. *Rebel Voices. An I.W.W. Anthology,* (Ann Arbor: University of Michigan Pr., 1964).

Lum, Dyer D. *A Concise History of the Great Trial of the Chicago Anarchists in 1886,* (Chicago: Socialist Pub. Co., 1887).

O'Neal, James and G.A. Werner. *American Communism,* (New York: E.P. Dutton, 1947).

Parsons, Albert R. *Anarchism: Its Philosophy and Scientific Basis as Defined by Some of Its Apostles,* (Chicago: Mrs. A.R. Parsons, 1887).

Parsons, Lucy E., ed. *Altgeld's Reasons for Pardoning Fielden, Schwab and Neebe,* (Chicago: Lucy E. Parsons, 1915).

Parsons, Lucy E., ed. *The Famous Speeches,* (Chicago: Lucy E. Parsons, 1909, 1910, 1912, etc.).

Parsons, Lucy E., ed. *The Life of Albert R. Parsons,* (Chicago: Mrs. Lucy E. Parsons, 1889 and 1903).

Parsons, Lucy E. *The Principles of Anarchism: A Lecture by Lucy E. Parsons,* (Chicago: Lucy E. Parsons, nd).

Pierce, Bessie Louise. *A History of Chicago.* (New York: Knopf, 1937), 3v.

Preston, William. *Aliens and Dissenters,* (Cambridge: Harvard U. Pr., 1963).

Rayback, Joseph R. *A History of American Labor,* (New York: Macmillan, 1968).

Shannon, David A. *The Socialist Party of America,* (New York: Macmillan, 1955).

Sister of the Road: The Autobiography of Box-car Bertha as Told to Dr. Ben L. Reitman, (New York: Harper and Row, 1973).

Taylor, Graham. *Pioneering on Social Frontiers,* (Chicago: University of Chicago Pr., 1930).

Tuttle, William. *Race Riot. Chicago in the Red Summer of 1919,* (New York: Atheneum, 1970).

Wade, Louise. *Graham Taylor, Pioneer for Social Justice,* 1851-1938, (Chicago: University of Chicago Pr., 1964).

Weinberg, Arthur. *Attorney for the Damned,* (New York: Simon and Schuster, 1957).

Index